Further praise for SpeakOut

'The SpeakOut is a terrific new model for engaging a wider public than the usual suspects. The facilitated drop-in format is relevant in fields far beyond planning and design, combining the face-to-face intimacy of a small-group public meeting with the flexibility of a web-based engagement process. Practitioners will also appreciate the exemplary detail provided by the handbook, taking the guesswork out of replicating this important model.'

**Ann Forsyth, Professor of City and Regional Planning,
Cornell University, USA**

'This is a wonderful tool for training the next generation of planners and designers in good participatory process... There are few books that integrate the tools and process, then walk you through how to "make sense of the outcomes", as this one does... No voice will be left out if you follow this book.'

**Sheri Blake, Professor,
Department of City Planning, University of Manitoba,
and Director, Detroit Collaborative Design Center
... amplifying the diminished voice.**

'This book offers civic innovators one more valuable tool... This highly interactive, open-structured, even playful mode of dialogue and deliberation complements the more formal, parliamentary-style models and will help to draw out quieter citizens, organize diffuse ideas and give free expression to youthful voices.'

**John Gastil, Professor, Department of Communication,
University of Washington,
author of *Political Communication & Deliberation*
and co-editor of *The Deliberative Democracy Handbook***

'It's time to deepen the public conversation! *SpeakOut* gives us an intimate look at how we can do that.'

**Dr Patricia A. Wilson, Professor of Planning and Civic Engagement,
University of Texas, USA**

'SpeakOut! Because the community's input is too important to be tokenized; because people are too busy to be invited to community workshops without vibrant, engaging and informative participation. And "because people of goodwill need help to get it right".'

Arthur Orsini, Director of Child & Youth Engagement Programs, Urbanthinkers, Vancouver, Canada

'This is a very practical book. It's a welcome and refreshing addition to the tools around to help planning practitioners to hear a more diverse range of community views.'

Julian Hill, Victorian Department of Planning and Community Development, Melbourne

'Sarkissian et al understand how people learn – with short, interesting stories which inform clear guidelines for future practice... *SpeakOut* is a practical guide ... that ensures people's voices are captured in a way that is respectful, creative and productive.'

Janette Hartz-Karp, Curtin University Sustainability Policy (CUSP) Institute, Curtin University, Western Australia

'This book provides practical instructions on organizing SpeakOuts, a productive way of engaging diverse communities, with helpful tips and informative case studies. A particular delight of the book is that case studies are provided by local organizers themselves, thus demonstrating reflective learning and the ease of becoming a leader in a SpeakOut.'

Dr Carolyn Whitzman, Senior Lecturer, Urban Planning, University of Melbourne

'Listening to Wendy Sarkissian talking about SpeakOut is so inspiring you just want to get started right away – with this book Wendy and her co-authors share with us their deep knowledge and life-long experience with innovative spirits and sparkling commitment!'

Henrik Nolmark, Managing Director of Urban Laboratory, Gothenburg, Sweden

SpeakOut

This book is dedicated to Karl Langheinrich, long-time organizer and supporter of SpeakOuts and dedicated 'gofer', and to SpeakOut participants everywhere.

Numerous SpeakOut activities over the past two decades in several countries have involved far too many individuals to name individually. We thank colleagues and clients who embraced this creative process, community people, students and agency employees who trained as supportive facilitators, community activists and innovators, passers-by on the day who took time to participate, older people, children, teenagers, parents, homeless people ... volunteers. And consultants.

We needed the insights and patience of all of these people to develop this community engagement method and we acknowledge their contributions with deep gratitude.

SpeakOut

The Step-by-Step Guide to SpeakOuts and Community Workshops

Wendy Sarkissian and Wiwik Bunjamin-Mau
with Andrea Cook, Kelvin Walsh and Steph Vajda

Ipas Resource Center

publishing for a sustainable future

London • Sterling, VA

First published by Earthscan in the UK and USA in 2009

This book is part of Earthscan's Tools for Community Planning suite.
See www.communityplanning.net for further information.

ISBN: 978-1-84407-704-5

Typeset by Safehouse Creative
Cover design by Rob Watts

For a full list of publications please contact:

Earthscan
Dunstan House
14a St Cross St
London, EC1N 8XA, UK
Tel: +44 (0)20 7841 1930
Fax: +44 (0)20 7242 1474
Email: earthinfo@earthscan.co.uk
Web: **www.earthscan.co.uk**

22883 Quicksilver Drive, Sterling, VA 20166-2012, USA

Earthscan publishes in association with the International Institute for Environment and Development

A catalogue record for this book is available from the British Library

Library of Congress Cataloging-in-Publication Data
Sarkissian, Wendy.
  SpeakOut : the step-by-step guide to speakouts and community workshops / Wendy Sarkissian and Wiwik Bunjamin-Mau ; with Andrea Cook, Kelvin Walsh and Steph Vajda.
    p. cm.
  Includes bibliographical references and index.
  ISBN 978-1-84407-704-5 (pbk.)
  1. Community organization. 2. Community development. 3. Social planning. 4. Small groups. I. Bunjamin-Mau, Wiwik. II. Title.
  HM766.S37 2009
  361.2'5–dc22
                                                          2008046230

At Earthscan we strive to minimize our environmental impacts and carbon footprint through reducing waste, recycling and offsetting our CO_2 emissions, including those created through publication of this book. For more details of our environmental policy, see www.earthscan.co.uk.

This book was printed in the UK by CPI Antony Rowe.
The paper used is FSC certified and the inks are vegetable based.

FSC
Mixed Sources
Product group from well-managed
forests and other controlled sources
Cert no. SGS-COC-2953
www.fsc.org
© 1996 Forest Stewardship Council

Contents

List of Figures

List of Acronyms and Abbreviations

ABCD   asset-based community development
AI   Appreciative Inquiry
ANC   Action for Neighbourhood Change
BRG   Bonnyrigg Residents' Group
CBD   central business district
CRG   Community Reference Group
DSSAB   District Social Services Administration Board
FCN   False Creek North
LGAQ   Local Government Association of Queensland
OST   Open Space Technology
PGC   Pacific Gateway Center
POE   post-occupancy evaluation
PPP   Public Private Partnership
SCARP   School of Community and Regional Planning
TCC   Townsville City Council
VWYH   Vote with Your Hands

Appreciations

Wendy Sarkissian

This book is the result of an international collaboration, with researchers and authors in Australia, Canada and the United States contributing innovations, insights, editorial assistance and chapters. I speak for all of us to thank many people and to acknowledge the staff of Earthscan for their assistance in its production.

Wendy makes a deep bow of gratitude to her friend, the wonderful and indefatigable Wiwik Bunjamin-Mau, who embraced the SpeakOut model and brought it to life with fresh ideas and inspiration in the Hawai'ian context. Deepest thanks to her Beloved, Karl, for being the best SpeakOut gofer in the Southern Hemisphere and for logistical, computer, editorial and writing help.

Wendy thanks Andrea Cook for years of delightful professional association, for co-inventing the method in 1990 and for inventing many imaginative interactive SpeakOut activities. She blesses Kelvin Walsh for a long and rich professional association and friendship, for being the best client anyone could ever hope for and for writing the original *Workshop Checklist*. She thanks Karen Umemoto for friendship and a generous Foreword, the Institute for Sustainability and Technology Policy (particularly Susan Davidson and Peter Newman, now of Curtin University) for support in previous community engagement publications, Steph Vajda for many wonderful professional associations and SpeakOuts and for writing two chapters for this book.

Linda Wirf and Nancy Hofer generously edited and contributed to several parts of this book and their help is gratefully acknowledged.

A special debt is owed to Christine Wenman for writing one of the chapters and for editing the book on short notice and to Frank Wilson in Thunder Bay, Canada, for writing a chapter and enthusiastically experimenting with the SpeakOut model in a remote community.

Yollana Shore is beloved for the reminder that all life is nourishing, editorial assistance and help with writing several chapters of this book.

Many communities, clients and colleagues deserve my thanks, including: the Bonnyrigg community in Sydney (especially Liz Coupe), the Bonnyrigg Living Communities Program (especially Bernie Coates and Deb Follers) and Bob Agres and Puanani Burgess for Hawai'ian SpeakOuts, training and support.

Students in the post-occupancy evaluation course at the University of British Columbia, School of Community and Regional Planning, brought the SpeakOut alive in Vancouver in a research context in 2007. Blessings and thanks to their warm hearts, sharp minds and bright faces (especially to Christine Wenman, Dianna Hurford, Brendan Hurford, Nancy Hofer and Renee Coull) and to the False Creek North community, the Roundhouse Community Centre, Leonie Sandercock, Larry Beasley and Penny Gurstein for making that possible.

The ongoing loving support of Noel Mau and Wendy Truer is acknowledged with gratitude that extends far beyond grateful appreciation of late-night airport pick-ups and the best moo shu pork in Honolulu. Wendy Truer must know how much her blessings infuse every word of this book.

Wiwik Bunjamin-Mau

My dear friend, Wendy Sarkissian, for graciously inviting me to co-author this book and for being an inspiration and much more; Andrea Cook and Kelvin Walsh, for welcoming me so warmly into this project; Steph, for his support in this project. For Noel, my husband and best friend: I'm eternally grateful for his unconditional love and support that allow me to continue to blossom throughout this process; my baby boy, Sydney, for constantly melting my heart with his cute smile when I needed encouragement.

Thanks to those that believed in me and helped make the *Talk Any Kine* SpeakOut a special project, including Hawai'i Arts Alliance, Kim Coffee-Isaak, Erik Takeshita, Louise Li, Susanna Sipes, Kahele Porter, Empower Oahu, Bob Agres, Layla Schuster, Taian Miao and many more.

Last but not least, thanks to my professors, Dolores Foley, Luciano Minerbi, Karen Umemoto, who didn't give up on me and provided support and encouragement when I most needed it. You have taught me the importance of listening to all voices.

Andrea Cook

Andrea struggled to pick any one handful of people to acknowledge among the (literally) thousands who have helped and supported her during the past 19 years of conducting SpeakOuts. Andrea thanks all the co-authors of this book in particular as well as the unsung heroes of SpeakOut ... from clients who have engaged in this creative process to community people who trained as supporting facilitators to passers-by on the day who have taken time to participate. We needed *all* of them to develop this methodology and acknowledge their contributions with deep gratitude.

Kelvin Walsh

Kelvin would like to acknowledge his colleagues, Andrea Cook and Wendy Sarkissian, for their work together using the SpeakOut model for the past 19 years, many clients who undertook innovative workshop and SpeakOut models and the City of Maribyrnong for their support of the SpeakOut model in several projects in the municipality in recent years. A special thanks to the community facilitators who worked in Maribyrnong from 2004 to 2008.

Steph Vajda

Steph would mostly like to thank Wendy Sarkissian for training and mentoring in the SpeakOut process and support throughout the many they have organized together. Thanks also to Andrea Cook for her support and training in developing the Footscray SpeakOut. I would like to acknowledge Yollana Shore, Abbie Trott, Sam La Rocca, Jim Gleeson and all other colleagues with whom I have collaborated to develop SpeakOuts around Australia. Last but not least, thanks to the clients with whom I have worked for their trust in an engagement process that doesn't always make complete sense until it is actually happening!

Foreword

In the most hopeful light

In the most hopeful light, planning greases the wheels of participatory democracy. It can engage the disenfranchised, inspire the disenchanted and encourage the public to participate in future-building. Planners can create safe spaces for the quiet thinkers as well as for the boisterous crowds to share their opinions, formulate workable solutions and dream a dream together. Planners can facilitate the rich dialogue that pulls ideas from deep in the gut and arrange ideas on the table for everyone to piece together, much like weaving a basket or stitching a quilt. When everyone can make their contribution known, when everyone can consider others' opinions and when collaborative solutions are discovered through mutual exchange, beautiful things can come about. And this is the hope behind this book and the motivation of the authors who wrote it.

I met Wendy Sarkissian on a visit she made to the University of Hawai'i nearly a decade ago. She made a presentation to our Department of Urban and Regional Planning at the University of Hawai'i on the SpeakOut. None of us knew what a SpeakOut was then. But the presentation made a lot of sense. Instead of the town hall spectacle or stuffy public hearing, here was a participatory format primed to engage regular folk in planning their futures. Rather than asking people to line up in front of a microphone and speak for a given number of minutes, you had multiple booths that highlighted different topics with listeners and writers making note of your every idea, pulling out the insights from the storage of wisdom within. Those notes were then hung alongside others' notes for all to read and react to.

And then you would go to the next booth. And so on. So that whether the planner was seeking ideas for the preservation of open space, for the development of affordable housing, for the location of the transit line, everyday people could chime in to have a say on a range of complex issues surrounding a particular planning project. Thoughtful planners would facilitate the weaving by helping to construct viable alternatives based on everyone's considerations. It is not the squeaky wheel that gets the oil in a SpeakOut, but just the opposite. The SpeakOut *de facto* discourages any one individual from hogging the spotlight and encourages everyone who has the time to speak their mind.

Soon after her presentation, I tried the SpeakOut with a group of talented youths who wanted to improve the conditions in their public housing neighbourhood in urban Honolulu. The youths created eight different booths, four for the younger kids and four for older kids and adults. Each had interactive planning activities. The 'mapping change' booth consisted of an aerial photograph of the neighbourhood. The youths drew the changes they wanted to see on the laminated map, explaining the desired change and why it was important to them. In another booth, we had interviewers to solicit ideas for identifying and addressing the neighbourhood issues such as crime, bus services and pest control problems. Note-takers carefully recorded their ideas. In another, kids wrote down the gifts they bring to the community on paper stars that were strung like Christmas lights criss-crossing the booth, a version of a human assets inventory.

You get the idea. You create inspiring spaces in the form of workstations or booths organized by a topic or set of questions. It's facilitated so that people can express themselves and interact with the ideas of others who may have stopped at the booth earlier. Booths can also have educational displays that provide background information on the topic of choice. People can hang around the booth and chat with others while thinking about what they want to say. You can go to as many booths as you like. You can stay for as long as you can. And you can say whatever you want (within norms of etiquette, of course). It worked wonders. We had about 300 youths leisurely share their ideas in a six-hour event, while having fun doing it.

Sometimes you attend successful planning events and wonder how the facilitators pulled it off (in this case, it was the youths themselves along with our planning students). How did they make the event feel so welcoming? How did they attract such a large crowd? How did they solicit so many ideas? How did they make people feel good about contributing? How did they synthesize the information into a succinct plan? How did they encourage ordinary people to come up with extraordinary ideas? How did they generate creative synergy? How is it that they engaged people in planning and made it educational, interactive and fun?

The SpeakOut isn't for everyone or for all occasions, but it is one of the most conducive formats I have seen to solicit broad citizen input, especially from those whose opinions are often overlooked. What I appreciate about this manual is that it includes every subtle detail one could ever think of. It's based on years of experience on the part of Wendy Sarkissian along with Wiwik Bunjamin-Mau, Andrea Cook and Kelvin Walsh. In addition to the SpeakOut, the manual also covers one of the most widely used planning tools, which is workshop facilitation.

In reading the SpeakOut and workshop facilitation how-to's, I was happy to find that it was written with the forethought of a social psychologist. The authors anticipate the problems and questions that would cross a facilitator's mind in the midst of the event or meeting and they provide advice as to how one may deal with common social dynamics. The instructions include such pointers as observing body language, gauging eye contact, checking the subtleties of language usage and other cues that are important to catch if one is to be a successful facilitator. These pointers are collected through years of experience. Rarely do we get this with easy-to-use, step-by-step how-to manuals.

We've seen the SpeakOut format take root locally, as planners are adapting it to different places, populations and circumstances. One group used the SpeakOut to solicit ideas for addressing the issue of rural homelessness. Author Wiwik Bunjamin-Mau took the lead in organizing a SpeakOut in Chinatown to address issues of urban revitalization and the arts. Another solicited input on rural town planning. There is something about the SpeakOut and workshop formats as described that easily accommodates the rhythm and diversity of a community. Perhaps it is the ease and intimacy of interaction that they encourage. Or perhaps it is the philosophical foundation upon which they are based. Regardless, this manual offers useful tools that planners can use to grease the wheels of participatory planning and, ultimately, to work towards a more inclusive and deliberative democracy.

Karen Umemoto, PhD, Professor, Department of Urban and Regional Planning, University of Hawai'i, Honolulu

Preface: Visualizing your SpeakOut

The imagining

On this winter Sunday afternoon, residents of the Village are eager to express their views about proposals for two sites in their community, one of which is quite close to the centre of the Village.

They drop in to the SpeakOut during the afternoon and spend as much time as they need discussing the pros and cons of options for each of the two sites and having their views recorded.

When they arrive, they are asked to register and given a lunch voucher and two voting papers (ballots), one for each of the sites under consideration.

They mingle with their neighbours, enjoy a BBQ lunch and talk to representatives of the Village Association, who also are providing tea and coffee for participants.

When they first arrive, they may be apprehensive, as there has not been a great deal of trust built up between the industry operator and developer and the Village community. People may feel cynical about this exercise and suspicious of the developer's intentions. As they read the material that has

been prepared and look at the alternative plans and the models that will be displayed, they begin to get a clear idea of what is involved for both sites and what the options are for each one. They ask questions of the helpers who are clearly identified with bright badges and they see their comments clearly recorded.

They may choose to look over the model of the proposals and the aerial photographs and speak to the Managing Director of the company (the developer) and their specialist planning consultant.

Finally, they vote on their preferred options in separate voting processes for each site.

Residents linger, talking with their neighbours in the warm hall and discussing their opinions about the two sites. They leave feeling that they have had a fair chance to make their views heard, that maybe this is the beginning of more balanced and respectful approaches to community engagement in the Village and that community members have expressed their views strongly about matters that concern them.

INTRODUCTION

My mouth must have been noticeably agape, for he continued,
'Don't you worry. I will get a large jar of instant coffee.
And you could bring plastic spoons and cups. I'll get a litre of milk.
And voilà, catering done.'

Introduction

Introduction

This is a manual designed to help people organize, plan and manage community planning workshops and make sense of the outcomes. Specifically, we introduce and explain a unique type of community engagement process called a SpeakOut.

Origins and aims of the SpeakOut

The SpeakOut, described in detail in Chapter 3, was developed to incorporate the features of a staffed exhibition and a workshop, emphasizing trained facilitation. Two Canadian-born community planners, Wendy Sarkissian and Andrea Cook, sought a way to engage Australians in an informal, drop-in manner that would still generate reliable information about community views and perceptions.

What this book aims to do

This book is the practical outcome of 19 years of reflective practice refining the SpeakOut model in three countries. It represents a distillation and updating of material published in previous manuals and checklists. We have attempted to provide it in as user-friendly a format as possible. This book is for people who wish to design and manage community planning processes. It is designed for professional planners, urban designers, architects, policy makers, social workers, community engagement practitioners, qualitative researchers, community activists, community-based organizations, non-governmental organizations, public space proponents and community members themselves. This book can also be used in undergraduate and postgraduate courses in planning, architecture, geography, landscape architecture, environmental and political science, as well as many others.

Contents of this book

The book consists of 13 chapters, illustrated by tailor-made illustrations and photographs from professional practice:

- **Chapter 1 Introduction**: introduces the book and describes the book's origin, aims and target readership.
- **Chapter 2 Why Manuals Are Important**: explains the importance of manuals to address the prevalent ineffectiveness and inadequacy in community engagement processes. It includes lessons from past SpeakOuts.
- **Chapter 3 Introducing the SpeakOut**: introduces the SpeakOut model by examining the need for this approach and offering a clear, step-by-step explanation of its features.
- **Chapter 4 Five Successful SpeakOut Stories**: presents recent SpeakOut case studies in three countries, focusing largely on methods in very different contexts. The five cases are:

  1 Bonnyrigg, Sydney, 2005
  2 *Talk Any Kine,* Honolulu, 2006
  3 Thunder Bay, Ontario, Canada, 2007
  4 Townsville, Queensland, 2007
  5 False Creek North, Vancouver, 2007.

- **Chapter 5 Designing a SpeakOut:** details the essential components for preparing, designing and managing a SpeakOut, including the organizing structure of the 'Outer Circuit' and 'Inner Circuit'.
- **Chapter 6 Interactive Exercises at SpeakOuts:** offers a rich menu of innovative interactive activities piloted and refined at SpeakOuts over two decades.
- **Chapter 7 SpeakOuts for Children:** introduces SpeakOuts for children and describes an innovative SpeakOut conducted in 2007 in Queensland.
- **Chapter 8 Vote with Your Hands:** describes an exercise called *Vote with Your Hands*, a common and popular feature of SpeakOuts.
- **Chapter 9 Designing and Managing Community Workshops:** explores requirements for a community workshop, building on Chapter 6.
- **Chapter 10 Staffing, Facilitation and Recording:** outlines essential requirements to ensure effective staffing, facilitation and recording.
- **Chapter 11 Analysis of Materials Generated by a SpeakOut or a Workshop:** the amount of work put into a SpeakOut by committed staff and participants does not automatically morph into a completed report. This important chapter briefly summarizes the steps for analysing materials to create a reliable record.
- **Chapter 12 Other Considerations:** addresses other requirements for achieving a successful SpeakOut, including communication (technology, signs and badges), audio and visual recording, drawcards, models and aerial photographs, child and infant care, food, entertainment, interpreters, involvement of senior people, 'greening' and insurance.
- **Chapter 13 Evaluation:** briefly summarizes some useful approaches for assessing and evaluating SpeakOut exercises.

The book concludes with Notes for all chapters and a comprehensive Bibliography. It also contains a detailed Glossary and two Appendices: a checklist for SpeakOuts and templates for some typical interactive activities (the Footscray Stall Prompts).

Why Manuals Are Important

Introduction: The necessity for community engagement

This manual has been written by people with a keen commitment to an engaged citizenry and growing despair about the state of the Earth and ordinary people's opportunities to contribute to decisions that can make a difference. It's a companion volume to *Kitchen Table Sustainability* (Sarkissian et al, 2008).

This is not the first manual we have written to assist people organizing community engagement processes. Kelvin Walsh and Wendy Sarkissian initially embarked on an ambitious process to prepare what finally became five books (co-authored with Andrea Cook and others) in a suite of books published by Murdoch University in Australia from 1994 to 2003 (*Community Participation in Practice*). We have been inspired by the books by Nick Wates (see Wates, 2000 and 2008) and have used his work widely in the processes described in this book.

How the original Workshop Checklist came about

Wendy's husband, Karl, to whom this book is dedicated, is really responsible for this book and a book that preceded it, *Community Participation in Practice:*

Workshop Checklist (Sarkissian et al, 2000) (1st edn, 1994). Following the events recounted in Karl's story below, Wendy and Kelvin decided that they had enough of meetings like the one Karl describes. The *Workshop Checklist* was born on that day in 1993.

But first, let's hear Karl's story.

Karl's story: a packet of biscuits and a litre of milk ...

This is my personal story about how the original *Workshop Checklist* came to be. It is about the little (and important) things that some people choose to ignore when they are organizing community workshops and SpeakOuts.

The tale begins in early 1993, when Wendy and Kelvin received an invitation to conduct the community engagement component of a scoping study about the future of a disused industrial site on the outskirts of a State capital. There was a change of State Government and with it began an assault on the unions and the rail network, both seen as money-wasting anachronisms deserving annihilation.

This was my first-time experience working with planners and other professionals, my previous experience having been largely confined to working with blue-collar workers, union members and officials. Wendy suggested that working with her would provide me with valuable insights into a world where life was far more 'cooperative', with more collaboration between professionals than I had seen in my own work life.

So here we were, two months into this big community engagement job, which was to continue for several months and resume for a reporting stage in the following year. Despite reassurances, we had not received any written confirmation regarding disbursements for all the anticipated public workshops. We were having a meeting with a senior bureaucrat whom I'll call Leo.

We were sitting across from Leo in a high-rise office building in the city. Wendy broached the subject of the outstanding matter of the disbursements budget, explaining how wasteful it was to keep chasing the project team manager, as well as bureaucrats like Leo, for a simple budget allocation to allow us to continue our work. She further suggested it was discourteous of the client to avoid making a written

Continued

commitment and have us spend time on this topic, rather than focusing on organizing the public workshops. We had already conducted a successful stakeholders' workshop to agree on some issues, with resolutions to engage the wider local public through a number of public workshops, the first of which was only a few weeks away.

To this point, we had no budget for printing, advertising, mail-outs, catering, venue hire, training of facilitators and recorders. Nothing.

Wendy used an analogy to explain her position to Leo: the project's hazards analysts did not have to take the costs of the drilling equipment out of their hourly fee. For the expected 300 participants for the five-hour event that included a site visit, catering alone would cost several hundred dollars. And, given there were several public meetings planned, we needed a substantial budget allocation separate from our fee.

As the discussion proceeded, Wendy could see the writing on the wall. She excused herself, leaving me to listen to Leo and his plans for managing the catering aspects of the forthcoming workshop.

'Look Karl, how hard can it be to cater for this public meeting? I have no idea what Wendy is on about when she talks of "expenses",' he continues, while I am left speechless.

'I'll stop and buy a couple of packets of some "Nice" biscuits. What do you think, Karl, those with the sugar sprinkled on? Or some plain ones?'

My mouth must have been noticeably agape, for he continued, 'Don't you worry. I will get a large jar of instant coffee. And you could bring plastic spoons and cups. I'll get a litre of milk. And *voilà*, catering done.'

I composed myself as best I could, unable to comprehend this attitude, but feeling increasingly frustrated and perplexed. I began my response by asking him, 'Leo, is this all I could expect if you invited me to your place? Remind me not to go.'

I continued, 'Leo, are you aware of the timetable for this workshop? If you look, you'll see a 5.30pm start with a foreshadowed close about 10pm. Are you saying that instant coffee and the cheapest biscuits are your notion of catering for people whose participation requires them being there for four and a half hours after completing a work day?'

Continued

It was the union organizer in me talking now.

Leo hesitated. Now judging the situation to be annoying, he adjusted his manner.

'Look, Karl, this is how it is. If people want to come and have a say, they will do so. If they don't, that's not our issue. We make every effort to encourage public participation. That is why we hired Wendy. However, we are not going to spend money on non-essential costs. And don't worry, I'll bring lots of biscuits. About the rest, just talk to Don (the project manager). He'll allocate money for all reasonable expenses.'

By now, Wendy had returned and Leo spoke with her, reiterating his opposition to extravagant catering, assuring her that he had explained his plan to me, as well as outlining his reasons.

After Wendy and I left the building, we exchanged observations. We considered the cost of meetings such as this, endless hours chasing the project manager, who, when finally cornered, responded with the following advice, 'Karl, you don't know how this is. Ninety per cent of my work comes from those people. There is nothing you can do or say that would make me do anything to jeopardize my practice by upsetting the Department.'

Slowly, I came to understand. We were but a token in a charade intended to masquerade as a community engagement process. The client apparently cared little about the outcome. It wasn't about the catering. It was all about power. Having no catering budget meant that we could not proceed to do a good job.

We resigned the next day.

I don't know if they ever held the workshop but I do know that in the 15 years since that meeting, nothing much has happened on that site.

When Wendy and Karl explained what happened to Kelvin Walsh later that week, it was clear that something had to be done. Kelvin, from Melbourne, had made a commitment to work in Perth for several months. He and Wendy agreed that a better approach would be to write the *Workshop Checklist*. For Leo! This book is a direct descendant of that process.

Lessons from the first SpeakOut, December 1990

A few years earlier, Wendy Sarkissian and Andrea Cook undertook the first SpeakOut for the Adelaide suburban community of Salisbury. As the story in the 1994 *Community Participation in Practice: Casebook* explains, this event was highly successful.[1] Staff from almost every department of Salisbury City Council were involved in planning and managing it. The time frame was very rushed, with an unprecedented *two weeks* from initiation to the actual event. When the event was successfully concluded, Wendy and Andrea were breathless and grateful for the Council-wide support they received. The City Engineer installed the generator; the parks and gardens folk loaned pot plants to brighten up the drab parking lot; Community Services made available every possible staff member; the printer worked overtime preparing signs and handouts ... There was a lot of festive, good feeling and the results were undoubtedly valuable to the redesign of the town centre.

But while we initially basked in the good feeling of a pre-Christmas collaborative effort, the feedback we received through the grapevine was that, while we did a great job, we asked for too much help. This salutary experience reminded us of the necessity of explaining what is involved in a community engagement event.

We now believe that it seems to be a basic fact of human life that *people cannot imagine how much work is involved in a successful community engagement process.* Wendy and Kelvin recall a workshop in Melbourne in 1989 which was very difficult to manage because of complex local politics and antagonisms. The neighbours were incredibly angry with the Council. As Wendy and Kelvin collapsed into chairs at the end of the workshop, the client, a young project manager and a novice at these sorts of things, remarked, 'Well, that was easy, wasn't it?' Clearly, their efforts to make the processes appear effortless had failed to convince *that* client that a great deal of work was required to bring about a successful process.

An (almost) successful SpeakOut in Western Australia, 2003

One of our most unsuccessful SpeakOuts was held in Western Australia in 2003 for a developer client. In this case, budget restrictions were not a problem, as the project manager, a banker by training, was fully aware of the costs of 'disbursements'. All of our requirements were accepted and the whole project was proceeding without problems. But minutes before the SpeakOut was to open in a huge marquee, Wendy was unexpectedly called away.

A helpful colleague, unaware of the necessity for the rigid and formal SpeakOut structure to ensure that participants visit all stalls, rearranged all the furniture to look 'less formal' and 'more inviting'. When Wendy returned, the room was

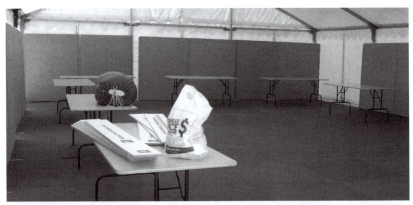

Figure 2.1 SpeakOut layout before and after set-up, with stalls poorly differentiated, 2003

full of people and she was unable to restore the formal format. Not surprisingly, this was not a highly successful SpeakOut. Participants complained that they did not understand what was expected of them. A SpeakOut manual may have helped that colleague, who was trying to help but did not understand the model.

A tragic email from Steph, 2007

One of our co-authors, Steph Vajda, has been designing and managing SpeakOuts for several years. He's often the Event Manager or Producer, with Wendy as the Coordinator or Director. Many of his projects are reported and illustrated in this book.

Steph has been a strong supporter of this book from its inception. There are good reasons for this, some of which are expressed in his 'tragic email', reproduced below.

Dear Wendy,

Here we go again! This SpeakOut was a shambles, inasmuch as William and John had no idea what was going on. I had been checking in with them weekly for the past six to eight weeks, asking for indications of their progress and getting very little. But William was always confident everything was in hand and that the materials were coming along. I had a little resentment about having our proposal reduced from running the event to just advising. So I wasn't that keen to overextend myself, given we were already busting our budget just advising them.

Same ol' same ol' … whether SpeakOuts or regular events: everyone thinks they can do it, easily and on a tiny budget.

Here's what happened.

I ask John a fortnight out to send me examples of the hundreds of different posters I'd suggested they design and get a few dodgy posters attached to an email, most in old software that isn't used much anymore, so I can't open them. John assures me it's all in hand and a team of people are working on them. I constantly remind them that they needed to be providing other departments with a clear idea of the information they need and am told that those requests have gone out and are being monitored.

Continued

So I get there on the Wednesday afternoon and sit down straightaway to a meeting with them. After about an hour, I realise they have no idea what is going on. William has never run an event before and so has just buried himself in logistics and given only little bits of time to the actual SpeakOut content. John is so upper management and 'big-picture': he's still trying to understand the activities. And they never do get that I had sent them a few activities per stall from which to choose the most appropriate and then redesign them as required.

So, at 8pm, three days from the event, they are telling me that they don't understand some of the activities I've designed and so haven't designed any materials for them. And they have no idea what information other departments are providing as background. They've been told they'll just bring it on the day. And, when they show me the display materials designed for activities and as background information ... you guessed it: mostly just the names of the displays from the list I sent them. In a big font – with absolutely no content.

So, I wrapped the meeting and told them I would take everything back to my hotel and work it out and come up with an action plan for the morning. Everything was due at the printer by 9am and nothing had been sent yet.

My take-away pizza defied description.

Started working on the materials at 9pm and redesigned mostly everything between 9pm and 4.30am and then turned up at the office again at 7am to finish the last two stalls. Over the next two days, William and John really took a back seat, focusing on logistics for the overall event and the facilitator briefing.

The briefing and training for facilitators on Saturday went really well. It's the first time I've done something like this and after staying up 'til 2.30am the night before (yes, about seven hours' sleep in two days), I cobbled together a mix of all those PowerPoints you sent me and some fresh stuff from the work we've been doing here.

On the day, there was confusion and mayhem. These are big-scale events with a lot of detail and so easily underestimated. I worked from 9am til 7pm, setting up the stall furniture and layout between 9 and 2. There was so little physical support from council, it was amazing.

As nobody had prepared a scale drawing of the site plan, there were some problems with layout and the proximity between stalls and activities.

Continued

Anyway, they loved it. About 5000 people came to the event and about 800 of them came through the SpeakOut. I spoke with some councillors and the Mayor and they were stoked and want to do it again. Local talkback radio the next day was positive and apparently continued for a few days after.

Next is a short report and then we're done.

So, Wendy, my lesson from this is: *no more just advising when people are doing their first SpeakOut.* We need to do more than give advice. And make sure we have a check-in visit two to three weeks before the event.

SpeakOut innovation

SpeakOuts are taking off all around the world. Andrea Cook has been designing and managing SpeakOuts in Melbourne for many years and is responsible for introducing interactive exercises, now a mainstay of the model (see Chapter 6). Interactive activities are being developed by Steph Vajda and Wiwik Bunjamin-Mau and others in a wide variety of contexts.

Wendy has been undertaking SpeakOut training in many Australian cities, as well as in Vancouver, Seattle, Hawai'i (Honolulu and the Big Island), Minneapolis and Thunder Bay, Canada.

A new champion of SpeakOuts: Wiwik Bunjamin-Mau

Talk Any Kine

While many SpeakOut reports have been produced and published, no research was undertaken about this engagement model before 2007. Inspired by successful SpeakOut stories (and the number and type of participants it has attracted), captivated by how colourful and lively the event can be and encouraged by Wendy Sarkissian, Indonesian-born community arts facilitator, Wiwik Bunjamin-Mau, working in Hawai'i, decided to write her Master's thesis focusing on the SpeakOut model. She submitted it to the Department of Urban and Regional Planning, University of Hawai'i at Manoa in 2007. The thesis explores the use of arts and cultural activities in a SpeakOut and involvement of local community networks in organizing a SpeakOut, as reflected in my case study of a SpeakOut in Chinatown, Honolulu (for more, see Chapter 4.2).[2]

Wiwik's reflections

My experience in organizing the *Talk Any Kine* Festival demonstrates the potential impact and reach of a SpeakOut as an engagement method. Responding to a festival-like event, participants not only engaged in neighbourhood issues, but also mingled with other community members. Many chatted with neighbours with whom they might not have connected otherwise.

My research on the SpeakOut model led me to believe that it has limitless possibilities. While the individual style and design of SpeakOuts vary, they consistently work and produce results when conducted with care. As long as the basic principles are followed, one can use as much creativity and imagination in designing their own SpeakOut as they wish. In the case of the SpeakOut in Chinatown, Honolulu, the infusion of extensive arts and cultural activities as a celebratory component was a natural response to the local community, whose members enjoy ethnic festivals as a form of cultural expression. Therefore, it worked ... and worked well. The celebratory component was also critical to change the somewhat uneasy and passive atmosphere of the local community to a much more positive, upbeat and hopeful energy. The effort was strengthened by directly involving many local organizations and agencies that rarely worked together in the planning, preparation and implementation of the SpeakOut.

I found that the SpeakOut, as a community engagement model, has great flexibility, approachability and clarity in terms of issue presentation. It is important to approach a SpeakOut as a culturally appropriate event and to pay attention to detail. After I followed the original *Workshop Checklist* and witnessed some 400 people attending the festival, my personal experience confirmed the effectiveness of the SpeakOut.

Why manuals?

Why manuals? Because people with good intentions still continue to design and manage community engagement processes that are ineffective and inadequate. Because people of goodwill need help to get it right. And because communities deserve better processes. To help those people get it right is our objective in this book.

SPEAKOUTS

*... a professional SpeakOut manager must be engaged
to coordinate and deliver an organization's first SpeakOut,
with the active involvement of staff to enable training and handover.
Then consultants can be engaged in an advisory role for future
SpeakOuts until agency staff has the skills to design
and produce future SpeakOut events themselves.*

Introducing the SpeakOut

Introducing the SpeakOut model

The SpeakOut is an interactive staffed exhibition that aims to provide an informal and interactive 'public meeting' environment where a wide range of people have a chance to participate. It is designed to facilitate structured 'drop-in' participation. Participants come to the venue, find the issues on which they wish to 'speak out' and have their say. Meanwhile, their comments are clearly recorded by a recorder and a listener pays close attention and asks pertinent questions.[1] It is primarily a 'listening session' where the community's views are clearly expressed. The staffing and facilitation components are what make it so distinctive, special and effective.

This is an inspirational participatory planning model that generates high-quality information, particularly for planning and design decisions, using community development and community education approaches.[2] It can also generate research findings, as we see in Chapter 4.5.

The first SpeakOut was designed by Andrea Cook and Wendy Sarkissian and held in suburban Adelaide, South Australia, in December 1990 to engage members of that large suburban community in issues surrounding the re-development of their town centre. In Australia, more than 20 SpeakOuts have been held in the past 19 years in a variety of Australian communities in five

Australian States: Victoria, South Australia, Tasmania, New South Wales and Queensland. The model has also been widely used in the American State of Hawai'i (see Chapter 4.2), as well as in Seattle, Washington and in Thunder Bay, Ontario, Canada (see Chapter 4.4).

Why there is a need for a model of this type

The SpeakOut model was originally developed in a context where (for time and logistical constraints) it was not possible to organize a public meeting or workshop. We were required to organize a public event immediately before Christmas in a town centre, the subject of the study. Constraints often experienced in the Australian context mirror those in other contexts internationally. We are aware of the well-known problems with meetings and workshops, as well as weaknesses with exhibitions and the Open House model.[3]

In formal processes, some people complain about limited opportunities to speak out on issues of community concern, whereas others find the tight structure of public meetings, workshops and focus groups restrictive, controlling and even intimidating. Sometimes, it is difficult to keep people on the subject and not all views may be heard. In the short time frame of most public workshops or meetings, attendees may only hear from a few people, whereas in the SpeakOut, as people come and go, more voices can be heard and views recorded.

Features of a SpeakOut

Staffing

This model depends on having one Listener and one Recorder at each issue stall, as well as other staff to assist with various aspects. Without this level of staffing, the SpeakOut will be nothing more than a staffed exhibition. It requires considerable staffing resources to design and mount the event, as well as for analysis of findings.

Accessibility

This model lends itself to wide community participation. The 'drop-in' format maximizes attendance, as people are free to participate at a convenient time. It is especially accessible to people in low-income communities where there may be low levels of formal literacy. It can provide training and paid employment for local people, as well as the potential for community enterprise development. The model also works well with a wide range of community groups, particularly if attention is paid to catering for local language/cultural groups (for example, engaging bilingual interpreters as listeners and recorders).

A SpeakOut is effective with those who rarely, if ever, are accommodated in more mainstream processes: children, young people, new immigrants, visitors to the area (shoppers or pub goers, for example), homeless people and so forth.

These processes work well for children and adults alike. Some features, including 'Vote with Your Hands' (see Chapters 6 and 8), enable community members (especially children and young people) to provide their ideas, even in communities with low levels of literacy or low proportions of English-speaking residents.

Physical accessiblity is also very important. We ensure that all stalls and the whole event are wheelchair accessible and we do what we can to assist people with other impairments.

Part of a larger process

We have never used a SpeakOut as a stand-alone process and emphasize the importance of building a SpeakOut into a wider community engagement programme. One event cannot perform miracles! Further, there are some issues that demand a 'town meeting' forum, where everyone can get together and be heard in the same meeting or workshop. Ideally, a process would include both such a workshop and a SpeakOut, among other processes. It can be used at the beginning, middle or end of an engagement process: for

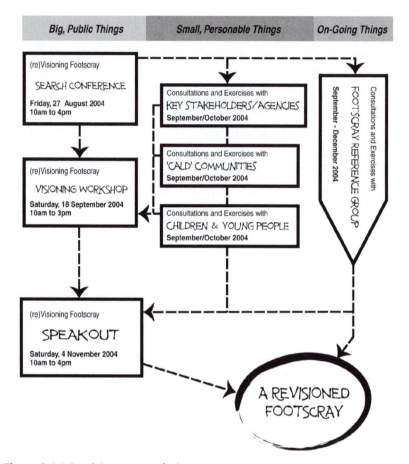

Figure 3.1 A SpeakOut as part of a larger community engagement process

example, in the early stages of a participation process to gather ideas (issue identification) or in later stages where the results of studies/planning are being communicated back to community members.

Figure 3.1 shows how a SpeakOut was embedded in a process in Melbourne in 2004.

Location, location, location

We have used this model in a wide range of different settings: indoors in rooms and halls, and outdoors using temporary venues such as tents and marquees. We have used one large marquee or several small ones, both with good effect. Finding the right location is a critical component of a SpeakOut. The idea is to take the event to the people, not to expect them to come to the event. A SpeakOut can occur in a train station, a mall or on the footpath. In one memorable event, the location was beside five bank ATMs. On a busy Friday afternoon, everyone came to get money for the weekend and they spoke out as well!

Displays

The individual stalls and the displays at SpeakOut stalls are the backbone or basic structure of the SpeakOut model. They can take many forms, including displaying information describing the stages and timing of the process, displaying information illustrating site analyses and other information or data about the site and the project, survey results, past planning, research and design work or other appropriate information. And, of course, there will be tailor-made displays designed for interactive exercises. It's critical that all of this material be produced using friendly and eye-catching graphics. It's important to resist the temptations of a 'one-size-fits-all' approach or standardized graphics. The highly successful graduate planning student SpeakOut described in Chapter 4.5 shows how effective hand-made signs and displays can be in a SpeakOut setting.

Bold, large issue stall signs (for example, *Vandalism, Traffic Safety, Children's Play*) and display space (pin boards, tables and chairs) are all important components discussed in detail later in this book. Adding to the effectiveness of displays can be issue 'prompts' (for example, annotated photos, provocative questions and points related to the issue), an annotated map of the study area with transparent overlays for community comments at each issue stall and, of course, props for the selected children's engagement process.

The formal graphic approach of a developer-led SpeakOut shown in Figure 3.2 is not preferable to that of a more 'funky' student-designed and managed SpeakOut display shown in Figure 3.3.

Figure 3.2 Formal SpeakOut graphics, Western Australia, 2003

Figure 3.3 Informal, student-designed SpeakOut graphics, Vancouver, 2007[4]

Logistics, tools and props

The SpeakOut is highly dependent on careful planning and logistical support. As some of the case studies in Chapter 4 illustrate, it's sometimes challenging for novices to design and manage a SpeakOut without expert advice. The props used to support a SpeakOut are described in detail in the checklists included in this book. It's important to pay attention to the design of materials such as participant sign-up sheets, green sheets for comments and sign-up sheets for membership of community advisory or reference groups.

Entertainment

Entertainment and special activities are important SpeakOut drawcards. To ensure balanced intergenerational participation, we provide engagement and entertainment activities for children and young people.

The step-by-step process of a SpeakOut explained

In this chapter we summarize the steps in a SpeakOut process, which are discussed in detail in the chapters that follow. In brief, the steps are as follows:

1 Undertake a research or scoping process to determine which issues are to be addressed at the SpeakOut.
2 Allocate sufficient time and resources to design and set up issue stalls.
3 Design a separate programme for children and provide the resources to support it.
4 Determine the issues on which you wish to have community advice and contributions.
5 Organize an 'issue stall' to display information about each issue (about seven to nine issues seem to work well).
6 Prepare visual prompts (for example, annotated photos of problems, annotated plans, other displays to encourage comment) for each issue stall.

7   Prepare the appropriate props for each issue stall.

8   Determine an appropriate time (such as a Sunday afternoon).

9   Find a convenient, central venue (preferably one within the study area).

10 Book it in advance. Or hire appropriate temporary structures such as marquees.

11 Ensure the venue has space for a separate children's participation.

12 Engage and train listeners and recorders for each issue stall, staff from the sponsoring agency to answer questions, people to staff a welcoming table and others to conduct the children's participation.

13 Advertise widely via letterboxing to community organizations, newsletters, posters, newspaper and other media coverage and/or other methods.

14 Advertise approximately ten days to two weeks before the event and then again perhaps four days before.

15 Cater with casual finger food (for example, a barbecue or sausage sizzle), ideally provided by a local community group (whom you pay) and make sure that it is culturally appropriate.

16 Be sure to welcome participants and give them clear instructions on how to be fully involved.

17 Provide a full briefing session beforehand and debrief all staff and volunteer workers at the end of the event.

18 Organize follow-up information (for example, an evaluation report, establishment of an Accountability Group, feedback to the participants and/or the wider community).

Five Successful SpeakOut Stories

Introduction

This chapter presents five recent SpeakOut case studies in three countries, focusing on methods and giving a sense of how the SpeakOut can be experienced in different contexts. These case studies illustrate how SpeakOuts have worked in various communities, using different settings and presenting a wide variety of issues. The style of each SpeakOut reflects the approaches of different organizing teams and produces distinct outcomes.

The first case study took place in Bonnyrigg, Western Sydney, in 2005, to encourage contributions from local residents about a local community renewal programme.

The second SpeakOut, the *Talk Any Kine* Festival, emphasized celebration and was conducted in Chinatown, Honolulu in early 2006, to gather community contributions to supplement the Mayor of Honolulu's Economic Summit.

The third case study, in Thunder Bay, Ontario, in 2007, aimed to engage citizens to voice concerns and offer suggestions about building a safe neighbourhood. The *Drop-In and SpeakOut* session was organized by several community groups, with the city's new Neighbourhood Office taking leadership.

The fourth case study discusses an innovative SpeakOut in Townsville, Queensland, in 2007, conducted by Townsville City Council. The *Townsville SpeakOut Festival* combined a large-scale SpeakOut with a general community event featuring a diversity of activities.

The last case study describes a SpeakOut conducted in False Creek North, Vancouver, in 2007 by a class of postgraduate planning students from the University of British Columbia. A version of the SpeakOut model was used as a component of a research model to gather information for a post-occupancy evaluation of a high-density city neighbourhood.

Together, these case studies demonstrate the flexibility of the SpeakOut model and how it can be successfully adapted in a variety of contexts to meet the needs of both organizers and local communities.

The Bonnyrigg SpeakOut, 2005

By Wendy Sarkissian and Yollana Shore

Background to the event

This chapter describes the *Bonnyrigg Community SpeakOut*, conducted in 2005 as part of the Living Communities Project for Bonnyrigg, a community in Western Sydney. While a lot has happened in that community since 2005, this story is only about the SpeakOut process held in April 2005. As a recent formal evaluation of the Bonnyrigg community renewal process has explained, Bonnyrigg is one of a number of large public housing estates in Western Sydney built in the 1970s and 1980s using Radburn urban design principles.[1] In 2004, when the engagement process began, it was argued that Bonnyrigg had much strength as a community, but the deteriorating condition of the housing stock and the high level of concentration of public housing had resulted in its shouldering a high burden of social and economic problems.

This community renewal process aimed to make Bonnyrigg a good place to live, offering good quality dwellings, facilities and services. Bonnyrigg is the first community in New South Wales to carry the 'Living Communities' brand, an approach representing recent thinking by the state government about the renewal of large, disadvantaged public housing estates. The Living Communities approach has three core objectives:

1   Providing better services and opportunities for residents.

2   Building a stronger community.

3   Renewing the houses and public areas.

The Living Communities' emphasis on community engagement focused on developing community support and enthusiasm for the project by offering Bonnyrigg communities important roles and influence in project implementation.

The Bonnyrigg site is shown in Figure 4.1.1.

Regarded as a 'pathfinder project', Bonnyrigg was the first large renewal project to feature the use of a Public Private Partnership (PPP), whereby a special purpose PPP company would be formed to manage all aspects of the project for a 30-year term. The company would undertake the redevelopment of the estate, build new public housing, build and sell new private housing

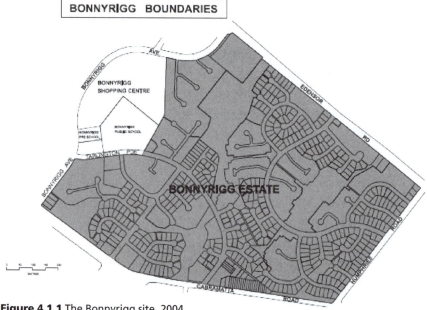

Figure 4.1.1 The Bonnyrigg site, 2004

and provide the full range of services, including tenancy management and maintenance of the public housing and provision of significant community renewal services. The New South Wales Department of Housing (Housing NSW) will pay for these services based on the achievement of specific Key Performance Indicators.

Community engagement was given a particular priority in Bonnyrigg but it was an uphill battle, at least initially. As the project began, the community engagement process faced challenges. Over half of the population was born overseas and almost half did not speak English or did not speak it well. Reflecting Bonnyrigg's role over many years as an entry point for refugees, residents spoke over 150 languages or dialects, with Vietnamese speakers the largest single cultural group. Many were from traumatized backgrounds. We found significant interaction and capability within individual cultural groups in Bonnyrigg (*bonding* social capital) but not much interaction between groups (*bridging* or *linking* social capital). Some regarded Bonnyrigg as a community with only limited community capacity.

The project will see replacement of the current ~840 public housing dwellings with 2330 new dwellings, of which about 30 per cent will be new public housing dwellings. The additional private housing adds to an existing somewhat over 100 privately owned dwellings. An additional approximately 134 public housing dwellings will be provided in other areas within Western Sydney to maintain existing public housing numbers.

Public and private dwellings will be scattered throughout the 81-hectare site and will be indistinguishable from each other. The redevelopment, undertaken over about a 12-year period, will include new high-quality parks and public domain improvements, a new community centre and, potentially, new retail and professional service facilities.

This chapter describes a SpeakOut in Bonnyrigg in April 2005. At that time, a snapshot of the community would have looked something like this:

- population: 3300
- 50 per cent born overseas
- south-east Asian community: 31 per cent (compared with 22 per cent in the wider municipality of Fairfield)
- Aboriginal residents: 5 per cent (compared with 0.6 per cent)
- Arabic residents: 6 per cent (compared with 8 per cent)
- residents under 18 years: 35 per cent (compared with 27 per cent)
- residents who don't speak English (well or at all): 43 per cent (compared with 32 per cent)
- public housing dwellings: about 840 (about 87 per cent of the housing stock)
- privately owned dwellings: somewhat over 100 (about 13 per cent of the housing stock).

In December 2004, the New South Wales Department of Housing advised the Bonnyrigg community that their estate would be the first to be renewed under the Department's Living Communities programme.

The *Bonnyrigg Community SpeakOut* was designed to maximize participants' opportunities to find out more about the Living Communities process, as well as to identify issues relevant to community renewal in Bonnyrigg and how it would affect the community. Emphasis was placed on identifying opportunities that would make community renewal successful, as well as seeking advice on the most effective way to consult with Bonnyrigg's diverse local communities.

The SpeakOut was one component in an ambitious series of consultations about the Living Communities Project, summarized in Tables 4.1.1 to 4.1.2.

The community engagement process

Community engagement began with an initial information phase from December 2004 to late January 2005. This phase centred on advising the community of the government's decision to undertake the Bonnyrigg Living Communities Project.

The next phase of the community engagement process had two broad strands: large- and small-scale community engagement events.

The large-scale events were the Stakeholders' Workshop on 24 February, the SpeakOut on 2 April and the two-part Our Bonnyrigg Dream Workshop on 10 and 14 May (see Table 4.1.1).

Table 4.1.1 Phase One: Large-scale engagement events

Date	Description	Estimate attendees	Regular/ specific event	Tenant/ stakeholder audience
24 Feb 2005	Stakeholders' Workshop	79	Specific	Mixed
2 April 2005	SpeakOut	300	Specific	Mixed
10 May 2005	Our Bonnyrigg Dream Work- shop	124	Specific	Mixed
14 May 2005	Our Bonnyrigg Dream Work- shop	90	Specific	Mixed

Throughout the same period, there were smaller community events, meetings of cultural and special interest groups and neighbourhood barbeques (see Table 4.1.2). A Community Reference Group (CRG) and the Bonnyrigg Residents' Group (BRG) were formed as important additions to the community's social infrastructure and to facilitate effective participation in the project.

Although not all the participants registered, an estimated 300 to 350 participants attended, or approximately 10 per cent of the total population. Participants included public and private tenants, children, young people, adults and older people, people with a disability and members of the Indigenous, Arabic, Vietnamese, Lao, Spanish-speaking, Khmer, Assyrian, Cantonese and Mandarin-speaking communities.

Table 4.1.2 Phase One: Small-scale engagement events

Date	Description	Estimate attendees	Regular/ specific event	Tenant/ stakeholder audience
11 Feb 2005	Vietnamese stall	10	Specific	Community
12 Feb 2005	Vietnamese stall	10	Specific	Community
12 Feb 2005	Chinese temple stall	10	Specific	Community
13 Feb 2005	Vietnamese stall	10	Specific	Community
16 Feb 2005	Lao language session	41	Specific	Tenants
17 Feb 2005	Khmer language session	35	Specific	Tenants
23 Feb 2005	Spanish language session	37	Specific	Community
3 March 2005	CRG meeting	21	Regular	Mixed
6 March 2005	Aboriginal session	15	Specific	Tenants
9 March 2005	Street BBQ	80	Regular	Mixed
14 March 2005	CRG meeting	20	Regular	Mixed
16 March 2005	Arabic language session	26	Specific	Mixed
16 March 2005	Street BBQ	35	Regular	Mixed
23 March 2005	Private owners info session	20	Specific	Owners
24 March 2005	B'rigg public school workshop	60	Specific	Children tenants
30 March 2005	Vietnamese language session	24	Specific	Mixed
30 March 2005	Street BBQ	85	Regular	Tenants
31 March 2005	St John's Park School workshop	112	Specific	Children tenants
4 April 2005	CRG meeting	20	Regular	Mixed
6 April 2005	Street BBQ	100	Regular	Mixed

Date	Description	Estimate attendees	Regular/ specific event	Tenant/ stakeholder audience
9 April 2005	Street BBQ	15	Regular	Tenants + Minister
13 April 2005	Street BBQ	19	Regular	Mixed
18 April 2005	CRG meeting	17	Regular	Mixed
27 April 2005	Street BBQ	37	Regular	Mixed
28 April 2005	Khmer language session	30	Specific	Tenants
4 May 2005	Street BBQ	27	Regular	Mixed
5 May 2005	Field visit: Browne St, Liverpool	8	Specific	Tenants
11 May 2005	Street BBQ	27	Regular	Mixed
18 May 2005	Street BBQ	32	Regular	Mixed
25 May 2005	Street BBQ	45	Regular	Mixed
30 May 2005	Fairfield City Council (FCC) Master Planning Principles	25	Specific	Stakeholders
1 June 2005	Vietnamese language session	36	Specific	Mixed
6 June 2005	Disability forum	7	Specific	Mixed
11 June 2005	Youth consultation	100	Specific	Young people
27 June 2005	Field visit: CityEdge, Canberra	53	Specific	Tenants

Objectives of the Bonnyrigg SpeakOut

The Bonnyrigg SpeakOut was an important event in the timetable of engagement activities. It was a public event, widely advertised to the local community and designed to build on previous engagement activities. It showcased the results of an earlier Stakeholders' Workshop, attended by 80 invited participants, held in February 2005, to seek guidance about issues concerning the renewal of Bonnyrigg and how the community engagement process should proceed.

The SpeakOut provided an opportunity to report to the wider community on consultations to date, on issues raised at the Stakeholders' Workshop and issues raised in a wide variety of information sessions, cultural and language group sessions and BBQs with local residents.

Another important objective of the SpeakOut was to build enthusiasm for the community engagement process and the proposed renewal of Bonnyrigg. It aimed to reassure participants that what was proposed in general terms was not merely a redevelopment of public housing, but rather a much more creative and wide-ranging process, incorporating all facets of the community and focusing on services and community capacity building, as well as physical renewal.

Inviting and assigning facilitators and recorders

The quality of a community engagement event such as a SpeakOut depends, to a large extent, on the impartiality and quality of facilitation and recording. Those who work in this capacity allow participants to concentrate on the subject at hand. All facilitators received extensive briefing and debriefing so that everyone was clear about their roles and responsibilities.

Although there was an unexpected shortage of listeners and recorders on the morning of the event, some listeners and recorders joined at the last minute and did a great service by their willingness to help out. Each of nine stalls was attended by at least one facilitator, often two or more.

The quality of facilitation is critical to the success of a SpeakOut, as this participant's comment illustrates: 'I found the one-on-one interview very useful. It put me more at ease to ask questions which concern me.'

Getting the word out

The SpeakOut was widely advertised and the marketing strategy entailed information prior to the event, information on the day, providing the means to get there and providing additional attractions as incentives for participation.

Information prior to the event

Residents and stakeholders were informed about the SpeakOut before the event by flyers for different language groups, press releases and newspaper announcements, community news radio announcements, a letterbox drop, invitations to people on the project database and participants of the Stakeholders' Workshop, announcements at all prior meetings/workshops linked with the project and five large signs displayed around the estate.

Information on the day

Community members were reminded about the event on the day by two very large signs advertising the event erected facing the main road and the car park. Invitations were also provided to the local library to hand out to Bonnyrigg residents. Two entertainers distributed balloons and flyers to passers-by. Four displays were erected at the local shopping plaza. Large laminated 'footprints' were placed on the ground leading from the plaza entrance to the SpeakOut site.

Three staff members encouraged people in the plaza and the car park to attend. During the four-hour SpeakOut, staff spoke to most people at the plaza and handed out 300 leaflets. Of the 300 participants at the event, more than 30 came because of encouragement from SpeakOut staff and entertainers working in the plaza and car park.

Transport to the SpeakOut

Residents of the estate were provided with free bus transport to and from the SpeakOut. The SpeakOut bus traversed the estate up to three times an hour for four hours. Invitations to the SpeakOut and SpeakOut bus timetables were posted at each bus stop on the first run. Although the bus driver also had flyers to hand out to pedestrians on the estate, he said he saw few people walking in the area.

Added attractions

A number of bonus attractions encouraged attendance, including a free barbeque and drinks, children's activities, balloons, children's collages and a lucky door prize. The free barbeque and drinks were seen as the most popular additional attractions provided. Everyone loved the balloons.

The SpeakOut layout and stalls

The SpeakOut, held in a large youth gymnasium, was structured around nine 'issue stalls', developed from issues raised at the Stakeholders' Workshop and during small group sessions since mid-January 2005:

1   What's important to children in Bonnyrigg?
2   The Living Communities Project for Bonnyrigg
3   How to become involved
4   Fairfield City Council planning
5   What residents want for Bonnyrigg
6   Community safety
7   Parks, recreation, public open space
8   Youth issues
9   Rebuilding Bonnyrigg: Houses, roads and services.

Figure 4.1.2 Interior view of the SpeakOut

There was also a reception desk, an interpreters' stand, a 'Vote with Your Hands' table, free barbeque lunch and free activities for children. There were interactive activities at nearly every stall and opportunities for informal discussion over lunch.

The reception desk

The reception desk in a small marquee outside was set up to welcome people, orient them to the SpeakOut, describe activities and provide the necessary materials for participation. Participants were asked to register so that they could be contacted for future events and were given an information sheet about the SpeakOut, a sheet for making comments during the day or at a later date and an entry form for the lucky door prize. The lucky door prize entry box was located inside the hall as a further incentive for participants to enter.

Although the SpeakOut was well attended, many participants signed in as a family or group and because of the crush at the reception desk, tracking accurate attendance figures became impossible. Whereas the registration showed that 140 households had attended, over one-third of households did not register. This experience emphasized the importance of a spacious and well staffed reception desk.

To help with welcoming the large number of people from culturally and linguistically diverse backgrounds in Bonnyrigg, interpreters were available at a table by the SpeakOut entrance with signs written in represented languages indicating the interpreters' names. The languages represented were: Spanish, Arabic, Khmer, Mandarin, Cantonese, Lao, Assyrian and Vietnamese. Interpreters circulated between the reception desk, the interpreter table and the stalls, meeting with participants who required interpretative assistance and walking around the SpeakOut with them, assisting them to make comments and participate in activities at the various stalls. Interpreters also greeted people from non-English-speaking backgrounds as they entered the SpeakOut and directed them to various stalls.

Figure 4.1.3 Egyptian-born interpreter Tawfik El Gazzar with an Arabic-speaking participant

The presence of interpreters added to the special feeling of 'individual attention' that participants at this SpeakOut were so grateful for: 'I prefer the individual attention at this SpeakOut rather than in a group where everyone may not feel comfortable raising their issues or having their issues heard.'

At the 'Mapping: Where do you live?' stall near the reception desk, participants marked a large aerial photograph of the Bonnyrigg area with a pink dot to represent where they lived and those who lived beyond the boundaries of the photograph put their dots around the border.

A 'Vote with Your Hands' activity was also held near the reception area. Participants could 'vote' for features that were important to them by placing their hand in a coloured paint and painting a large white sheet with their handprint. Each colour represented a different aspect of Bonnyrigg that participants valued, such as a clean environment, parks and playgrounds, people, public buildings, schools, churches and temples and shopping centres.

Figure 4.1.4 The 'Vote with Your Hands' stall

Children's activities were located in a separate room adjacent to the 'What's important to children in Bonnyrigg?' stall. Activities included mask making, paper collages, play dough and other paper crafts. Face-painting was also provided, as well as a unicyclist who kept everyone entertained with his magic tricks. Because the children's activities were very popular, they encouraged parents/caregivers to stay and visit the stalls in the main hall.

Stall 1: What's important to children in Bonnyrigg?

The stalls were set up around the perimeter of the gymnasium. This first stall displayed materials from the 'Week with a Camera' activity undertaken by 9 to 11-year-old students from two local schools. Over 180 children were given disposable cameras and asked to photograph what was important in their neighbourhood. The children were encouraged to photograph 'things that they would like to keep' and 'things that they would like to change'. Children provided valuable insights into the reasons they took the photos, both in log sheets and during the facilitated collage-making process.

The 'Week with a Camera' photos were combined into individual collages displayed at the SpeakOut. Because we were restricted to displaying only collages from students who were Bonnyrigg residents and who had returned permission forms, only about 15 collages were displayed. Nevertheless, some parents came to the SpeakOut specifically to see their children's collages.

This was the first stall that participants saw inside the building. It was bright, colourful and attractive and helped to communicate how a SpeakOut can be an easy and non-confrontational way to contribute in community engagement.[2] A face-painting fairy was located at this stall and asked children questions about what they liked about living in Bonnyrigg. And clowns provided engrossing entertainment.

This stall was designed to showcase the results of this work to both adults and children and to elicit children's views on what was important to them in their neighbourhood. According to the facilitator staffing this stall, children who

Figure 4.1.5 Display of 'Week with a Camera' collages

came to the SpeakOut needed some prompting to participate. Facilitators asked children and adults to reflect on what their impressions were from the displays of the children's collages. They also asked questions such as:

- What do you like about living in Bonnyrigg?
- What is important to you in this area?
- How would you feel if you had to move house?

Parents and other adult caregivers also made comments at this stall.

Stall 2: The Living Communities Project for Bonnyrigg

This stall presented information on the Bonnyrigg Living Communities Project, including the project timeline and processes, newsletter updates in eight languages, the Stakeholders' Workshop report (including answers to the questions asked at the workshop) and a leaflet with Frequently Asked Questions from public housing tenants. The stall was attended by senior staff from the Department of Housing.

Nearby at the Youth Stall (stall 8), participants were invited to view competition entries for the logo for the Bonnyrigg Renewal Project, select their 'top two' and vote by putting a green dot on the sheet attached to the bottom of the chosen logo. Participants could also make comments or suggestions about the logos.

Stall 3: How to become involved?

This stall presented the engagement processes to date and those yet to occur, as well as detailed descriptions of 24 different engagement processes. It offered an opportunity to engage in a survey about preferred styles of engagement. As with other SpeakOut stalls, participants could also make comments about engagement preferences, which were recorded on butcher's paper.

Members of the Community Reference Group, including local landowners, were present at this stall to help participants find out more about the Community Reference Group and join, if they wished.

A timeline activity ('When did you arrive to live in Bonnyrigg?') was also facilitated at this stall, where participants wrote the year that they arrived along a timeline posted on the wall.

Stall 4: Fairfield City Council planning

This stall was managed by Fairfield Council to support discussions about the new Development Control Plan and other planning protocols for Bonnyrigg. The stall displayed materials and photographs prepared by Fairfield Council staff. Individual comments or questions for the Council were also recorded with participants' names and telephone numbers so the Council could respond to each person individually.

Stall 5: What residents want for Bonnyrigg

This stall offered participants opportunities to speak openly about what they wanted in their community. Participants commented on a range of issues from community facilities to community safety and more, with all comments recorded on butcher's paper for other participants to see. This stall inspired much comment from participants so, by the end of the day, butcher's paper was overflowing in columns along the wall and along the floor around the stall.

At this stall, participants could also engage with an activity called 'Mapping Social Networks', creating a visual display of residents' desires, using symbols and words. The images were stuck to a large sheet of paper and residents or the facilitator wrote a brief statement about what each symbol represented.

Figure 4.1.6 What residents want in Bonnyrigg

Stall 6: Community safety

At this stall, participants communicated where they did and did not feel safe in the Bonnyrigg area. A summary of local crime issues and concerns about community safety in Bonnyrigg was provided in bullet points. A large aerial photograph of Bonnyrigg was also displayed, along with community safety and Neighbourhood Watch pamphlets and brochures.

In the 'Interactive Mapping Activity' at this stall, participants placed red dots on small individual maps representing where they felt unsafe and green dots indicating where they felt safe. Those dots were later collated and analysed to depict perceived community safety 'hotspots' in Bonnyrigg.

Stall 7: Parks, recreation, public open space

This stall was set up to facilitate contributions about parks, recreation and public open space, asking: Why are they important? And where should they go? The map is shown in Chapter 6.

Participants could also engage with an 'Interactive Arrow Mapping Activity' to determine why residents leave Bonnyrigg on a daily (or long-term) basis. For this activity, another large aerial photograph was displayed and participants wrote their reasons for leaving the area on arrows which were then placed around the edges of the map.

Stall 8: Youth issues

This stall aimed to engage young people in conversations about their ideas for Bonnyrigg. They were invited to comment on issues and opportunities and solutions relating to young people. Comments were structured around recreation and adventure, the Bonnyrigg Youth Facility, being involved in the Bonnyrigg community and employment and transport. For each issue, participants identified an issue/opportunity, where it was occurring and a potential solution. It was also possible to suggest solutions for other participants' issues. While this stall was designed primarily for young people, it was attended by both young people and adults.

Stall 9: Rebuilding Bonnyrigg: Houses, roads and services

This stall was designed to engage residents in thinking about the future of their suburb and to draw on their knowledge of what would improve layout and facilities. This stall, staffed by two multicultural planners as facilitators, presented an opportunity to represent ideas and aspirations for Bonnyrigg's future, particularly regarding street layout and housing density and siting. Participants worked with facilitators using coloured Lego™ building blocks to represent planning and design elements that they wanted to be included. The building blocks were placed on tracing paper (to permit annotations), over large aerial photographs of the area. Participants' models were photographed and their comments recorded on butcher's paper. Some participants also made comments about housing design at this stall without building a model.

Analysing the SpeakOut results

The butcher's paper record from the SpeakOut stalls, as well as outcomes of the many interactive activities undertaken at each stall, became the raw material that was analysed, taking into account comments from workers during the debriefing. In analysing the SpeakOut results, comments from the butcher's paper transcripts from each stall were categorized using a technique called 'lumping and splitting', where each comment was assigned a category and then all related comments under the same category were 'lumped' together. Sometimes, participants made comments not specifically relevant to the stall they visited. These comments were transferred to the relevant category on another stall.

Outcomes of the interactive activities were also analysed for quantitative and qualitative results, with methods of analysis differing according to the activity and outcomes. All this material is available in the final report and influenced the decisions taken later by all players regarding the community renewal programme for Bonnyrigg.[3]

The Bonnyrigg SpeakOut was marvellously successful by all accounts. One participant summed up the views of the organizers and other participants: 'I like events like today. Public meetings are a disaster. Individual feelings/needs are not met ... there's too much to absorb.'

Grateful acknowledgements

This chapter is based largely on a 2005 report written by Yollana Shore with Wendy Sarkissian, supplemented by a 2008 evaluation report by Bernie Coates and others (Coates et al, 2008). The community engagement processes held in 2004 and 2005 upon which this chapter is based are an ongoing and award-winning collaborative project of the NSW Department of Housing and Fairfield City Council, as part of the community engagement process for the Bonnyrigg Living Communities Project.

The 2004 and 2005 engagement processes described in this chapter were designed and managed by the Bonnyrigg Living Communities Project Consultation Team, supervised by: Bernie Coates, Manager, Community Building, Strategic Projects, NSW Department of Housing, and Lesley Unsworth, Senior Projects Officer, Place Manager, New Residential Neighbourhoods, Fairfield City Council. The generous support of Bernie and Lesley is acknowledged with many thanks.

The Consultation Team in 2004 and 2005 consisted of:

- *Sarkissian Associates Planners Pty Ltd*, consultants to the NSW Department of Housing: Wendy Sarkissian (Consultation Adviser, 2004–2006), Sophia van Ruth, Yollana Shore, Steph Walton, Elyssa Ludher, Samantha LaRocca, John Murray and Karl Langheinrich.
- *NSW Department of Housing*: Deborah Follers, Project Officer, Tawfik El Gazzar and Ann Bengele, administrative support, and Denis McNamara (Parramatta City Council).

- *Fairfield City Council*: Daniel Smith, Andy Chin, Karen James, Rodrigo Gutierrez, Josephine Roccisano, Andrew Mooney, Claudia Guajardo and Lisa Dang.

Staff from the NSW Department of Housing and Fairfield City Council were of great assistance in the preparation and management of the 2004 and 2005 engagement events. Other people and organizations contributed to the engagement activities, including Bonnyrigg Public School and St John's Park Public School staff, who assisted with the children's consultations.

About Yollana Shore

Qualified in environmental science, majoring in social policy and development, Yollana Shore is experienced in social planning and community engagement. An independent business owner and qualified personal development practitioner, Yollana has a passion for helping individuals and organizations address personal issues so they can engage more easily and effectively with sustainability. Located in Brisbane, Yollana is co-author of *Kitchen Table Sustainability: Practical Recipes for Community Engagement with Sustainability* (Earthscan, 2008). Yollana also helps business owners who want to make the world a better place, to grow a successful, soul-centred business doing what they love. To learn about that work, see www.soulbusiness.com.au.

Talk Any Kine Festival: Speaking out in Chinatown, Honolulu, 2006

By Wiwik Bunjamin-Mau

Background to the event

This chapter recounts how a community organized an innovative SpeakOut participatory process in Chinatown, Honolulu, in March 2006. The *Talk Any Kine* Festival was designed to elicit feedback from the Chinatown community as part of a community planning process initiated by the City and County of Honolulu. Chinatown is home to ten low-income affordable housing developments and has served as the entry point for many immigrants and refugees. The area has also attracted drug dealing and other criminal activities. Chinatown is a historic district, with many assets: heritage buildings, public parks, affordable rental housing, small businesses (including restaurants and shops with an ethnic 'old' Chinatown flavour) and traditional markets that sell fresh produce.

Until the late 1990s, Chinatown was underutilized, with many vacancies, especially in historic buildings. Early in 2000, arts-related businesses, such as art galleries, restaurants and cafés, began to develop and the area was designated as an Arts District. This recent introduction of arts and culture enterprises and activities has shifted the popular perception of the area from embarrassment and dismay to hopefulness and community pride. The result of the ongoing economic revitalization is a much safer neighbourhood that has become more attractive to visitors.

I chose to use SpeakOut as the community engagement model because it appeared suitable for addressing the many well-known limitations and weaknesses of conventional public engagement processes (and public meetings and workshops most notably). I am particularly sensitive to these needs, as I am in a unique position where I am versed in the 'language' of participatory planning, the arts and cultural sensitivity. I am a community planner and an artist, an immigrant from a multicultural society and I work for an arts institution (the Hawai'i Arts Alliance: *The ARTS at Marks Garage*). When I was introduced to the SpeakOut model by Wendy Sarkissian, I knew that this engagement model would be appropriate to implement in an immigrant community such as Chinatown, Honolulu.

The planning process for the *Talk Any Kine (TAK)* Festival formally began in January 2006 in anticipation of the Mayor's Chinatown Economic Summit, which aimed to engage Chinatown stakeholders in potential proposals for revitalizing Chinatown. The project was organized by *The ARTS at Marks Garage (Marks)*, a community arts project of the Hawai'i Arts Alliance.

The alternative engagement opportunity provided by *TAK* was critical in the Mayor's attempt to reach out to the Chinatown community, particularly immigrants who, like many hard-to-reach communities, often feel reluctant to participate in participatory processes.

The community feedback gathered at *TAK* was intended to inform the action steps of the Chinatown plan. Given that the day-long Summit was to be held at the Hawai'i Theatre Centre, local people and advocates were concerned that it would not be well attended by the majority of the Chinatown community, especially small businesses and local residents. Small businesses were unlikely to close during the day to allow staff to attend this type of forum, while residents might be intimidated by both dialogue with high government officials, as well as the 'palatial style' of the theatre venue. The *TAK* Festival was organized to capture the voices of small businesses and residents. The information gathered was presented at the Honolulu Mayor's Chinatown Summit.

Planning and design of *TAK* involved numerous community stakeholders, including non-profit housing developers, service providers, schools, artists, police, merchant associations, churches, local non-profit organizations and the Mayor's Office of Culture and the Arts. These stakeholders responded to an invitation to participate in the organizing and planning committee facilitated by *Marks* staff. Convening the community organizing committee in this way allowed community leaders to work together and share resources, as well as to build community capacity.

The Festival took place in the newest community park in Chinatown, conveniently located in the centre of the neighbourhood. The immigrant residents and small business owners, many of whom speak little or no English, were asked to share their thoughts, ideas, opinions, fears and hopes regarding various issues that occur in their neighbourhood.

Objectives and approach

This process was designed to be friendly to disenfranchised local groups by incorporating creative elements in the planning process and during the Festival. An artistic approach was necessary to provide all community groups with a myriad of ways to express themselves, as well as to create a celebratory atmosphere. Collaborative efforts were also emphasized in the overall process to capture community energy, project it in presentations and allow corroboration of findings.

Talk Any Kine Festival project design

In common with many communities, immigrant residents of Chinatown rarely, if ever, participate in public forums. Language is the main barrier. Further, most immigrants (especially newly arrived ones) are challenged by the new language, rules, laws and systems. This can result in isolation, disenfranchisement and stigma. This was the case with the majority of Chinatown residents officially invited to the Mayor's Summit. The *Talk Any Kine* Festival adapted the SpeakOut model to address these language and cultural barriers. It aimed to be welcoming and friendly to disenfranchised individuals and groups.

The Festival attempted to gather valuable contributions from as many Chinatown residents and small businesses as possible. It incorporated many arts and cultural elements to create a community celebration by adding live entertainment, art projects for children and free refreshments. An estimated 350 people actively participated, including local residents and businesses, children, elders and local homeless people. Astonishingly, 70 volunteers assisted with logistics, catering, art designs and projects, as well as facilitating interactions and recording responses and feedback.

At the Festival, participants were encouraged to 'speak out' and share their concerns and recommendations on a number of important community issues: 'Getting around Chinatown' (physical infrastructure), 'Homelessness', 'Affordable Rental Housing', 'Better Business Environment' (economic development) and 'Safer Neighbourhoods' (crime and safety). We chose these five topics because these were the top five issues that surfaced repeatedly at previous community meetings. Other issues included education, family strengthening, community identity and job training.

Interpretative materials at this lively and colourful festival were used to capture people's attention and imagination. It was art-focused and English as a Second Language (ESL) friendly. Participation did not depend in any way on an ability to read or speak English, as we had lots of visual displays and several interpreters on hand. All comments were clearly heard and written down by volunteers.

Planning processes for the *TAK* Festival

Planning for the *Talk Any Kine* Festival was a highly complex process. As explained earlier in this book, a SpeakOut planning process should always involve key community stakeholders. By obtaining community support from the very beginning, an event will have a better chance of being well received by the wider community. Similarly, staff at *Marks* needed to understand the concept of the public meeting in a SpeakOut format internally before it could be introduced more broadly to other community members in the planning committee. When we had achieved clarity about the SpeakOut concept, our next step was to make an inventory of community assets and use that information to determine the venue, scope and format of the Festival.

Gathering community support

As a result of *Marks'* networking and relationship building in the five years leading up to the *Talk Any Kine* Festival, many community members perceived the organization as a trusted community leader. Thus a wide variety of organizations, groups and agencies agreed to participate and collaborate in the planning, as well as to help design and implement the Festival. We began the process on a positive note, as representatives of most organizations invited attended the very first meeting, even though they were unfamiliar with the basic concepts of the SpeakOut model. These important community stakeholders included organizations involved with crime prevention and law enforcement, arts and culture promotion, faith-based homeless services, non-profit housing developers, resident and business associations, immigration services, churches, community development organizations, art galleries, restaurants and other businesses and tenant representatives from several affordable housing locations in Chinatown.

Taking advantage of their good community relationships, *Marks* optimized the opportunity for community capacity building by inviting many Chinatown stakeholders to help plan the community event. *Marks* designated this group of stakeholders as the organizing committee. They agreed to organize all necessary arrangements by bringing to the table their knowledge and resources. During the initial discussion in January 2006, it became clear that many of these groups were meeting each other for the first time, although they were practically next-door neighbours who had been conducting business in Chinatown for many years. Sadly, there had been few occasions or opportunities for these stakeholders to meet, let alone collaborate. Thus, our *TAK* Festival was important from the beginning because it provided a unique opportunity for these stakeholders to collaborate and share resources.

We were also conscious that these stakeholders were connected with group members, contacts and networks who could also contribute as volunteers at the Festival. We hoped (and we were not disappointed) that spreading the word in their immediate communities would increase attendance and participation in the Festival.

Specific techniques used

Timing

Adapting the SpeakOut model, the *Talk Any Kine* Festival was designed as an informal community-gathering event, held three months before the Mayor's Chinatown Summit.

Advertising for the *TAK* Festival

Before getting the word out in the community, the organizing committee wanted to find a creative catchy phrase for the Festival. The committee had many ideas and came up with several names. *Talk Any Kine* was finally chosen. This term is a local Hawai'ian slang term that means 'anything that is being said, goes'. The term conveys the informality and openness that everyone hoped would be communicated at the Festival. From the beginning, the committee agreed that what was needed was a community celebration, thus we chose to have a 'festival'. The committee felt the name truly projected the essence of the community event.

To advertise the Festival, the organizing committee relied heavily on its diverse constituents. We encouraged the organizing committee to work together to produce flyers and posters, using the creativity of local artists, who created large vinyl banners to hang outside the park two days prior to the event. Several resident representatives collectively wrote an article about the *TAK* Festival, which they translated into Chinese. It was then published in the *Hawai'i Chinese News*, a free newspaper widely read by the Chinatown community.

Animating public space

Smith-Beretania Park, a new park, was well maintained, although under-utilized. Most of the time homeless people occupied the park, which in the past decade had developed a reputation for unwanted and illegal activities that discouraged many residents (especially children) from using it. The Park was selected as the venue because local people wanted to activate and animate this new and underutilized public space. We argued that by bringing a lively community festival to the park, the community's positive experience of using it would change their perceptions and strengthen their resolve to take back ownership. We were correct on all counts. The result was a Saturday afternoon filled with diverse people, children running around, laughter and chatter, music and food and a meaningful community engagement process. As one local participant commented when he arrived, 'It's picture perfect!'

Layout and logistics

I soon discovered that one of the critical elements of organizing a SpeakOut model of public engagement was the selection and preparation of extensive materials. The presentation of materials required extensive use of different sized white and coloured papers, black and coloured markers, pens, tapes, foam boards, paint, tents, tables, chairs, easels, sticky dots and notes, cords (bungee and power), scissors and so forth. For the entertainment, a stage area and sound system set were provided within the park area.

Designing the *TAK* layout was probably the most critical part of the process because, more than anything, it affected participants' experiences. I felt that the more comfortable participants were with the atmosphere, the more they would be willing to share their thoughts. So we set up nine tents in the park to create a welcoming and informal environment that encouraged everyone to visit all the stalls. We erected the tents in specific places so that it would be easy for participants to navigate from one tent to the next.

We wanted entertainment to be a feature of the Festival, but not to drown out the other activities, so we located the entertainment stage and speakers

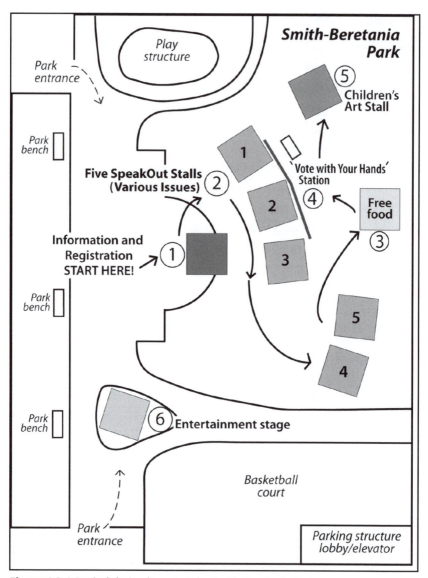

Figure 4.2.1 Festival design layout at the Smith-Beretania Park

as far as possible from the issue stalls so that they would not disturb the engagement process. We also wanted the entertainment to be visible so that afterwards participants could sit and enjoy it. The role of the speakers was somewhat different, as they had the function of drawing people into the *TAK* Festival.

Wendy had explained to me that in some of her SpeakOuts, participants came only for the food and did not stay to share their ideas. While we did not want our Festival to be overly regimented, we designed the pedestrian flow and located the food stall behind the issue stalls so that it was logical for participants to visit the food stall after leaving the last issue stall. Placing the *keiki* (a Hawai'ian word that means child) art stall next to the existing play structure made it convenient for both parents and children to spend their time between these two activity areas.

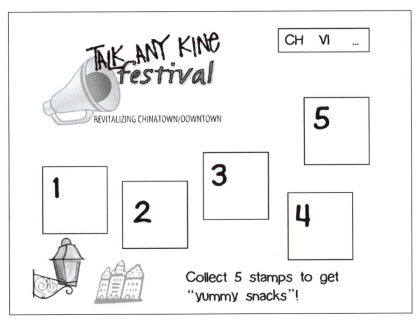

Figure 4.2.2 'Passport' for each participant to collect stamps

Figure 4.2.3 Welcome signs also presented in Chinese

Every participant was asked to sign in at the registration desk and leave some personal information. Each then received specific instructions on how to proceed and a 'passport' that was stamped at each issue stall visited. On the passport, participants could also indicate the need for an interpreter to accompany them through the process (the organizer would provide an interpreter).

To attract more participants during the event, especially passers-by, and to help them understand what to expect, large clear signs and instructions were posted by the entrance and throughout the rest of the festival area within the park. These signs and instructions were translated into Chinese to offer a warm welcome.

Presentation materials

We were convinced from the start that the overall presentation of the issues and other information at the *TAK* Festival needed to be very friendly and non-intimidating, particularly to non-native English speakers. True to SpeakOut principles, we avoided fancy or academic jargon and big words as much as possible. All signs and banners, as well as information and questions at individual issue stalls, were written and drawn in simplified terms. For example, instead of using the term 'economic development,' the phrase 'better business environment' was used. Further, some materials were translated into Chinese. Words were written in big, bold letters with the help of local artists.

To alleviate possible uneasiness people might have in sharing their thoughts concerning sensitive or contentious issues, we made sure that participants were not expected to communicate verbally or in writing if they preferred not to. Most questions at issue stalls were designed to be interactive. We used clipart and sticky notes, where participants needed only to place the

Figure 4.2.4 'Better Business Environment' exercise board

note in the appropriate spot. For example, one question required participants to imagine 'getting around Chinatown' to identify trouble spots in the
neighbourhood using a Chinatown map. Participants needed to draw a line
connecting the infrastructure items on the right of the map with the exact location in the neighbourhood. The interactive activity of visual identification of
issues surrounding physical infrastructure in the neighbourhood was popular
because it was fun, easy to imagine and, at the same time, straightforward.

An important task for the organizing committee was to compile relevant
information and write a set of questions associated with the issues to be
presented at the *TAK* Festival. We assigned these tasks to all committee
members, based on the strength of the organization and the types of services
they provided. For example, representatives from EAH Housing[1] and Mutual
Housing wrote brief summaries and a series of questions pertaining to affordable rental housing. The Honolulu Weed and Seed[2] and local police representatives addressed crime and safety issues, while the merchant associations
tackled the 'better business environment'. The River of Life Mission shared
their knowledge of homelessness in Chinatown. Other committee members
collectively wrote information and questions on 'getting around Chinatown'
and physical infrastructure.

One organizing committee member made this comment:

> This is truly a collaborative presentation on the issues in the
> neighbourhood. I'm glad to be a part of this process as the community
> can hold us accountable as we move forward with future solutions on
> problems.

Inviting and assigning volunteers

One of the keys to a successful SpeakOut event is having volunteers to help
with facilitating, recording and undertaking a huge variety of tasks required to
bring it all together. The *Talk Any Kine* Festival received an incredible amount
of support from community volunteers. The organizing committee recruited

many volunteers to help with the Festival and identified several institutions within and outside the neighbourhood whose members could potentially play a part in the process.

A couple of very excited volunteers shared their experiences:

> *It was very exciting to see so many community members coming out on a Saturday afternoon to participate in the **SpeakOut** process, including the seniors who don't speak much English! I can't believe they're really getting involved with the activities as they should!*

Several neighbouring schools showed their support by undertaking *TAK* tasks. A school principal and several schoolteachers helped as facilitators and recorders. Some students facilitated a hands-on voting stall and others swept the park for trash during the Festival as a community service project. A group of youth law-enforcement trainees supported facilitators and recorders and helped to maintain order. Several police officers provided added security. A group of university students set up tents, tables and chairs and worked as 'runners', handling logistical needs, especially with supplies for each issue stall. Several graduate students from the University of Hawai'i contributed by facilitating and recording at issue stalls. These volunteers received formal training prior to the Festival: they were briefed on how to facilitate by being an active listener who asks probing questions and clarifies comments. Some were briefed as recorders on how to record exactly what was being said by the participants. Others simply needed to understand their assigned tasks so that the event would run smoothly.

To help people not fluent in English, we recruited several interpreters who spoke Mandarin, Cantonese, Vietnamese and Thai. Participants who needed an interpreter's assistance could indicate their need at the registration desk. The support of these interpreters was critical to encouraging participation by many participants, particularly elderly residents.

One volunteer from the organization that helped provide the interpreters shared her observation of the SpeakOut:

It's unbelievable how many immigrant residents who would normally not show their faces in any community meetings are not only out of their homes to come here, but they're actually participating in the activities!

Arts and cultural celebration for the Chinatown community

Those of us who work in community engagement are aware that many people are disappointed with conventional public meetings, a result that can lead to a sense of hopelessness. The *TAK* Festival was purposely designed to ensure that positive energy and liveliness were maintained throughout the Festival. As most people in the Chinatown community are immigrants who continue to learn about and assimilate their new culture, we argued they would respond better to the invitation to participate in the *TAK* Festival than to invitations to other community engagement processes. Our research revealed that they trusted an invitation from a community organization with a reputation for positive and community-oriented initiatives. The familiarity of the presentations and many of the other components, including ethnic music and food, encouraged active participation by a variety of community members.

Refreshments and ethnic music

Pacific Gateway Center (PGC) is an organization that runs a kitchen incubator for low-income community members who want to launch catering and food-product businesses. They invited several of their kitchen incubator clients to cater at the *TAK* Festival. A group of high school students volunteered to help with serving. Participants could only claim their food after they had received stamps on their 'passport' from each issue stall. Wendy's experience confirms that providing appropriate and tasty food is a drawcard in attracting people to attend any community events. The *TAK* Festival was no exception.

Amplifying a sense of community celebration was an important objective of the Festival. We wanted participants to experience themselves as a vital part of their community and to feel that the processes were positive, despite the wide range of views about most issues. We wanted them to experience, as members of the Chinatown community, that they and their ideas were valued. Several ethnic musical groups were invited to join in the gathering, from a *keiki* group to a ukulele class, a Chinese string quartet, a Thai dancer, a classical guitar player and a well-known slack key guitarist. These performances created an attractive and inviting festival atmosphere, accessible to many ethnic groups. As one participant explained, 'The entertainment was definitely a great way to bring folks to spend time in the park on a Saturday afternoon.'

Children's art

Local children or *keiki* were also invited to participate in the Festival, where they could express themselves creatively through hands-on mixed media visual arts. The *keiki* art stall at the Festival allowed parents to participate freely, as they were relieved of worry about finding people to watch their children. Two community artists, who made the signs, banners and posters for the Festival, facilitated the hands-on arts activities.

For the Chinatown *keiki*, coming to the Festival and knowing that the community gathering was also a place for them, encouraged them to participate in much the same way as the adults did. With the help of parents and Festival volunteers, the *keiki* registered as individuals and were encouraged to visit issue stalls, share their thoughts and answer questions. The informal and friendly setting put the *keiki* at ease. They reported that they did not feel intimidated and were able to participate comfortably.

One mother with two children who participated in the SpeakOut shared her thoughts:

> Knowing that there's a children's art stall made it possible for me to come out and participate in the event. My children not only spent a lot of time at the children's art booth, but also visited the issue stalls with me ... it's truly a family outing for us! And a good use of the park!

REVITALIZING CHINATOWN/DOWNTOWN

Hawai'i Arts Alliance/
The ARTS at Marks Garage

VOTE WITH YOUR HANDS!

WHO ARE WE? WHAT IS THE "STORY" OF OUR NEIGHBORHOOD?

CHOOSE A PAINT COLOR NEXT TO YOUR PREFERENCE FOR WHAT YOU THINK IS YOUR NEIGHBORHOOD IDENTITY!

PLACE A HAND PRINT ON THE CLOTH IN THAT COLOR AND VOTE WITH YOUR HANDS!!

 Chinatown / (Re)Discover Chinatown

 Arts/Entertainment/Cultural

 Historic District of Honolulu/ Old Downtown

 New urban neighborhood; mix of different themes/business/activities

Figure 4.2.5 'Vote with Your Hands' themes

'Vote with Your Hands'

At the time of the 2006 *Talk Any Kine* Festival, the community was just begin-ning to address questions of community identity, partly because the emer-gence of the arts scene since 2000 changed some neighbourhood character-istics. Not only has the Chinatown area attracted more visitors, but it has also become a popular place for young people to hang out. Meanwhile, the core Chinatown area is still popular for the locals, mostly older people, seeking fresh green produce and authentic Asian food.

A couple of months before the *TAK* Festival, members of the business commu-nity attempted to 'brand' the area, thus giving voice to a critical question of identity that would be widely discussed by the Chinatown community. Different groups suggested themes that were presented to the wider commu-nity at *TAK* for voting and prioritizing at the 'Vote with Your Hands' stall. The themes were: Chinatown/(Re)Discover Chinatown, Art/Entertainment/Cultural, Historic District of Honolulu/Old Chinatown and New Urban Neighbourhood (mix of different themes/businesses/activities). We used this established SpeakOut method to try to find a sense of how community members related to their community identity.

One of the children who participated in the 'Vote with Your Hands' activities said, 'This is so much fun!'

By assigning a colour for each theme, participants (both adults and children) were asked to use their handprint to vote with the assigned colour for specific themes. The result showed that participants perceived their community as 'new urban', followed by 'Chinatown'.

Results of the *TAK* Festival

The report from *Talk Any Kine* was a 30-page document of raw data and information collected at the Festival. This material was distilled and a summary of findings presented. A short video was played at the Mayor's Chinatown Summit as part of the 15-minute 'Community Views' presentation by *Marks*.

It showed the diverse participants and how their feedback truly reflected community voices. A one-page summary was included in the handout. A positive summary article was published by the *Hawai'i Chinese News*.

Most findings identified the urgent need for changes to benefit the neighbourhood, including public restrooms, improvements to parking meters and continuing attention to addressing drug-dealing issues. Before presenting at the Summit, *Marks* staff met with city officials to discuss these findings so that they could begin to take action.

One participant made a comment on the overall event that seemed to be shared by many:

> *It's great to have this opportunity to come together as a community to discuss comfortably the neighbourhood issues and solutions. I think we need to do this more often!*

Drop-In and SpeakOut: Building and fostering a safe Fort William neighbourhood, 2007

By Frank Wilson

Background to the event

This chapter summarizes a variation of the SpeakOut model in Thunder Bay, Canada, to engage citizens in voicing their concerns and suggestions on building a safe neighbourhood. The public shared their contributions during drop-in sessions and by completing a survey in the spring of 2007. With 110,000 residents, Thunder Bay is the largest centre in north-western Ontario and the regional service centre for medical, educational, professional and government services. It is a significant transportation hub for highways, railways and ships. The United States border is 60 kilometres to the south-west. In spite of economic benefits, this location creates problems such as an active drug trade between the USA and Canada.

The City and region are in the midst of a major economic restructuring. Thunder Bay was created in 1970 by amalgamating two adjacent cities: Fort William and Port Arthur. Over time, most of the new commercial and office development has located to the area between these two former cities, while the traditional downtowns are reinventing themselves.

In recent years, a growing number of Aboriginal people have relocated to Thunder Bay from remote villages on First Nation Reserves. They are struggling to make the transition from village to city, from a close-knit Aboriginal society to a multicultural but predominately white society. Many are the most marginalized of the community's residents, tending to have the poorest health, education, employment and family stability prospects. However, a small but expanding segment is classified as middle-class and prospering.

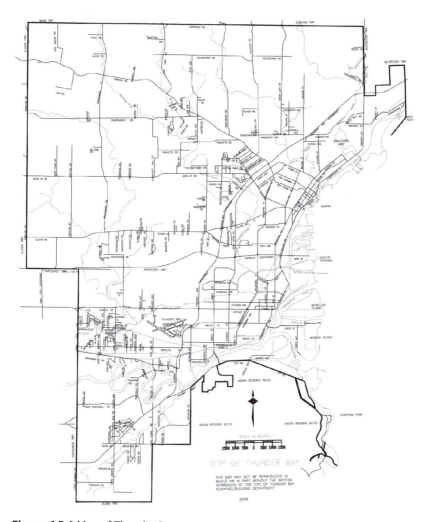

Figure 4.3.1 Map of Thunder Bay

Objectives and approach

Previous planning and renewal efforts

Numerous studies and reports have explored the potential for revitalizing the Fort William downtown and residential areas. There are 10,000 residents with most in the 50+ and under 19 age groups. Fifteen per cent are Aboriginal peoples. In 2003, citizens of the Fort William downtown area launched a public campaign called 'Downtown Now' asking the City Council to initiate a renewal programme for the area. A Neighbourhood Renewal Plan was subsequently developed with active citizen participation. People expressed a common concern: any renewal effort will be impeded if the area is unsafe or felt to be unsafe.

The City Council accepted the Fort William Neighbourhood Renewal Plan and directed administration to initiate actions on several fronts. A Neighbourhood Office was created and a Downtown Development Coordinator was hired to coordinate activities, including working with the City departments, citizens and neighbourhood groups. The new Neighbourhood Office was asked to coordinate a forum on safety. The Police Services launched an initiative of intervention and enforcement and held stakeholder meetings. The outcome was an acknowledgement that building and fostering a safe neighbourhood required the long-term engagement of the whole community.

A partnership approach

Several community groups, with the City's new Neighbourhood Office taking leadership, agreed to partner and organize a neighbourhood safety forum. The partners included the following: City Departments of Planning, Transit and Recreation; Police Services (Neighbourhood Police Office); District Social Services Administration Board (DSSAB); United Way via Action for Neighbourhood Change (ANC); Evergreen United Neighbourhood Association, a new grassroots citizen group that emerged from the Simpson Street area; Norwest Community Health Centre; the business sector; John Howard Society (for low-income housing and services); Ontario Native Women's Association; and the Urban Aboriginal Strategy.

Specific techniques used

SpeakOut training

In November 2006, the City Planning Division hosted a training session by Wendy Sarkissian on SpeakOut techniques for reaching to those who do not typically have their voices heard in public participation processes. Participants, including staff from Planning, Recreation and Social Services, learned about techniques for welcoming and interacting with participants, regardless of their communication skills and cultural backgrounds. Members of the partnering organizations then held a series of meetings to determine topics, presentation of topics and an event structure that would attract those most affected by neighbourhood safety.

The draft questions and drop-in format were tested in small focus groups of staff or others knowledgeable about the subject matter and participants with less familiarity with the material and plans. A guide and instruction package was prepared for each volunteer. Two training sessions explained the objectives, principles and operation of the *Drop-in and SpeakOut* session. Numerous 'what if?' situations were posed and addressed.

Public Drop-in and SpeakOut on safety

This partnership organized a unique and inclusive public consultation process, which employed different methods and attracted a wide range of participants, who expressed concerns, ideas and suggestions in a constructive manner. The event, called *A Drop-in and SpeakOut on Building a Safe Fort William Neighbourhood*, was designed so that everyone could be heard equally, regardless of cultural, personal, ethnic and language differences. Various methods were used to encourage and elicit contributions from those who might not normally be heard in a more conventional public forum.

Timing

Three distinct events were organized, beginning with the *Drop-in and SpeakOut* event on Friday 27 April 2007, from 11.00am to 2.30pm. To create a welcoming and relaxing atmosphere, there were refreshments, a children's area, Aboriginal drummers and a prize draw. A second opportunity, on Monday 30 April, from 11.00am to 6.00pm, was a low-key drop-in session. Participants were asked to complete a survey questionnaire and indicate on maps where crime was experienced and witnessed and where they felt safe and unsafe. Several volunteers provided clarification and guidance.

The third opportunity was a survey. Those unable to participate at either session were encouraged to complete a four-page questionnaire between 11 April and 21 May 2007.

Location and design of the sessions

The sessions were held at the Victoriaville Centre, a busy and accessible down-town mall, timed to coincide with the period of maximum visitors. The space consisted of a 20-metre wide corridor adjacent to the high-traffic corridor where the shops and restaurants were located. The space was divided into eight stations, each addressing one topic related to building a safe neighbour-hood. Trained listeners and recorders enabled participants to speak one at a time and to capture their comments on flip charts.

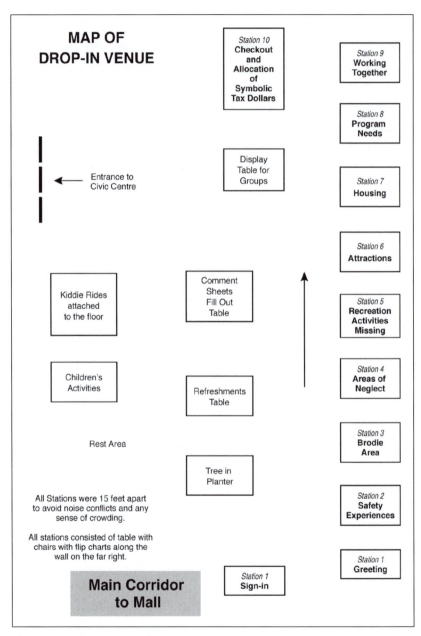

Figure 4.3.2 Drop-in venue layout

Promoting and marketing the issue and the venue

Meetings were held with target groups to explore their concerns and ideas and to encourage those people and their peers to attend. A meeting was held with a youth leadership group, information faxed to 300 agencies within the City, flyers were placed on city buses and an invitation was also placed in the City's bimonthly news bulletin, circulated to every city residence. The City's website on the Fort William Neighbourhood Renewal alerted people to this event several weeks in advance (see www.thunderbay.ca/fortwilliamneighbourhood).

In mid-April, the partners held a media briefing, attended by the Mayor, to explain the event and invite participation. Partners visibly working together demonstrated that a safe neighbourhood needed everyone's involvement.

Invitations to Aboriginal peoples

In Thunder Bay, there is a common view that Aboriginal peoples may be less inclined to participate in public meetings than other residents. To promote and encourage their feeling welcome and to explain the relevance of the event, visits were made to various Aboriginal organizations. At these meetings with the Executive Directors and their programme managers of the Aboriginal organizations, the Downtown Development Coordinator extended a personal invitation and explained the reasons behind the event and the need to hear from Aboriginal people about their concerns and ideas for improving safety. Organizers also sought their ideas on how the event could welcome Aboriginal peoples so that they could participate fully.

Initially, some Aboriginal leaders appeared unsure about the sincerity of these approaches. Many said, however, that they appreciated the face-to-face invitation and explanation, as evident by this comment:

> ... this is rare for someone to come and make the invitation in person, we get tired of being invited to someone else's meetings as though we have nothing better to do than be a token representative in a meeting where we will have no impact or influence on the outcome.

Dialogue with businesses in Victoriaville Mall

The management of the Victoriaville Centre responded enthusiastically when asked for their advice on how to organize and host this event, as they had recently decided that the Mall should welcome and cater for community functions. They aimed to make it a true meeting place. When they learned of the proposal for Aboriginal drumming and smudging ceremonies, some were initially apprehensive of disturbing merchants and office workers. These concerns were sensitively addressed, however, and no complaints were received about the event.

Assigning volunteers to topics and stations

Volunteers were carefully selected for each station to ensure objectivity. The three Neighbourhood Police Officers were also asked to wear civilian clothes, as they were attending as neighbourhood builders rather than law-enforcement officers.

Volunteers from the Aboriginal community

Of the more than 20 volunteers, five were visibly identifiable as Aboriginal persons. One volunteer, well known for her involvement in social issues and as co-chair of the Aboriginal Interagency Council, was especially effective in encouraging Aboriginal volunteers and participation by Aboriginal people.

Cultural recognition through music and ceremony

It is generally recognized that Aboriginal people in Thunder Bay (and throughout Canada) suffer disproportionately when it comes to safety and feeling safe. Many experience racism and can feel uncomfortable with the institutions, language and customs of the white society that has dominated them since European settlers arrived some 150 years ago. Some also feel alienated in their own land. In terms of certain kinds of crime, they tend to be disproportionately both victims and perpetrators of assaults and racism stemming from problems relating to alcoholism, drug addiction, poverty and despair. Thus, it was very important to conduct active listening and record the voices and contributions of Aboriginal peoples. Special efforts were made to ensure that Aboriginal and Métis people felt welcomed, valued and involved. Eight Aboriginal women drummers volunteered to perform traditional songs at the beginning and the closing of the *Drop-in* session. Playing on traditional hand-held drums and wearing traditional dress, they sang in their native language. The tradition of offering a packet or twist of tobacco was observed, symbolizing agreement between equal and willing partners. At both the opening and closing, an Elder performed a traditional ceremony consisting of a short prayer to the Creator to bless all participants, to recognize their constructive contributions and to protect everyone on their return home.

The Elder also recognized that participants were there in the home land of the Anishnawbic people and expressed thanks to the Elders for welcoming this event in their home land. The Elder then burned tobacco and sweet grass in a bowl. Participants were invited to cleanse themselves by fanning the smoke from the bowl over their head and upper body. This is a symbolic means of removing negative thoughts and clearing the mind and spirit before engaging in the next activity.

Figure 4.3.3 Drumming session by Aboriginal women drummers

These cultural performances were the highlight of the *Drop-in* session, as in Thunder Bay and across Canada, it is rare to experience these ceremonies outside of meetings hosted by Aboriginal peoples. Further, the Aboriginal people present appeared to respond with pride to the recognition of their culture. The spokeswoman for the drummers, when asked if her group would accept a financial gift or contribution, responded,' ... we are pleased and appreciate this opportunity to demonstrate and explain our culture to others'.

Topics organized by stations

The *Drop-in and SpeakOut* was designed to seek information on a wide range of topics related to building and sustaining a safe neighbourhood. Each topic had a separate station, consisting of a large table with four chairs, a listener and a recorder, and flip chart paper taped to the corridor wall. On the paper was an explanation of the topic and three or four questions. While the listener read out each question, the recorder visibly scribed the response on the paper. Participants were asked if their response had been recorded to their satisfaction. For a number of questions, participants were asked to place sticky dots on aerial photo maps in relevant locations. This approach aimed to equalize participation, regardless of levels of formal literacy.

Participants frequently expressed delight at seeing the neighbourhood on the aerial photo map and took pleasure in pointing out various buildings and lane ways that were familiar or that appeared different from above.[1] One person commented:

> Hey, I haven't ever seen the neighbourhood like this, looking down on it. Where did this come from!

SpeakOut stations

Station 1: Greeting and sign-in

The first station consisted of two separate tables. At the first, volunteers greeted and welcomed people. Potential participants were given a brief explanation of the event and encouraged to sign the guest book and provide contact information. They were given a ballot for the door prizes: a t-shirt and a two-week membership at the Recreation Complex.

At the second table, participants were provided with a further explanation of how to participate. Confidentiality was stressed: all information would be treated as confidential and used only in aggregate form. No concerns and suggestions would be identified with any individual. They were asked for some basic information such as whether they lived or worked in the area.

Station 2: Neighbourhood and personal safety

The second station provided more complete explanations, the Listener asked each participant to rate the neighbourhood in terms of feeling unsafe and being unsafe and to provide specific information about their experiences of feeling unsafe and encountering criminal situations. The recorder captured this information under a set of categories and on a map with a numbered dot. Volunteers were selected for this station because of their ability to demonstrate sensitivity, empathy and discretion. A surprising number of people provided vivid accounts of their experiences in witnessing or being victimized. An elderly woman said:

> A rough-looking man brazenly grabbed my purse, knocking me to the ground resulting in me having to be taken to the hospital for stitches to close the gash to my head. I am now very leery [wary] of using the terminal area unless there are other people around.

Station 3: Brodie Bus Terminal

Here participants were asked to categorize their familiarity with the bus terminal area and rate its safety. Recorders collected ideas for improving safety and comfort in and around the bus terminal. A large majority of participants frequented this area and were able to provide knowledgeable ratings of the degree of safety they felt during different time periods. The most common comments were similar to these:

- *...the area feels most unsafe in the evenings after dark.*
- *I feel uneasy when there are drunks and vagrants and gangs of youths are hanging around.*
- *Having to wait for a bus when there are no other people like myself around.*

Station 4: Neglect

Participants were asked to place numbered sticky dots to indicate areas of neglect and to note the type of neglect. Details were recorded on the flip chart with the number corresponding to the sticky dot. Participants were then asked for suggestions to address the neglect. Many people expressed a strong desire for action about derelict buildings and garbage, as this comment reveals: 'If we all did our part, then the area would change for the better in a short order.'

Station 5: Recreation activities

Here participants identified their age and the recreation activities they pursued, as well as assessing recreational activities missing from the neighbourhood. They mapped with numbered sticky dots where these recreational activities might be offered. Comments reflected the need for more activities for youths as opposed to the participants' own recreational needs or desires: 'I think that there is a lack of affordable recreational activities right at hand for the young people.'

Station 6: Attractions

Posing the challenge of how to encourage people to come into the downtown during non-business hours, participants provided suggestions about attractions that could be offered and how to establish such attractions. Suggestions revealed creative thinking, as evidenced by this comment: 'There should be live theatre where plays are performed during the summer months to mentor youth and attract visitors and tourists.'

Station 7: Housing

This station addressed local housing and sought assessments of the positive and negative qualities of living in the area from residents and others. Participants were also asked how to improve the area to attract new residential development and renovations of existing housing stock. Some of the suggestions were pretty direct:

> People don't want to live in an area with prostitution, violent crimes, drug addicts and rundown housing.
>
> Until we start tackling the real problems, then our image is not going to change and people won't see this as a place they want to live, unless it is all they can afford.

Station 8: Programme and service needs

At this station, participants identified behaviour and activities in the neighbourhood that made them feel unsafe and suggested programmes and services. Comments were generally constructive; people did not complain that existing agencies and programmes were overwhelmed, insufficiently funded or absent. However, many were not fully aware of the range of social programmes currently operating in the area, making comments such as: 'The local Health Clinic should offer counselling for youths on sexual health' and 'There is no drug addiction programmes for those living on the street.' Further, one said: 'We need police who work in this area and can get to know the neighbourhood.'

Station 9: Working together and respect

Participants were asked one simple open-ended but challenging final question: 'What should be done to help people work together and respect each other in the Fort William neighbourhood?' Of all questions, this one was viewed by organizers as having potential to befuddle participants or elicit racist comments. However, responses were positive and insightful. Written responses provided in the survey were also constructive. The following comments were typical:

We need to get to know each other so we can build trust and start working together to make this neighbourhood a better place for all of us.

There is much that volunteers can do to improve the neighbourhood if everyone is invited and welcomed to pitch in when and where they can.

... let's put together some form of a neighbourhood council to bring people together to work on the things we can do for ourselves.

Station 10: Check-out

Symbolic tax dollars

As each participant completed their visit to any of stations 3 to 9, the Listener presented them with a symbolic tax dollar. Those who attended all seven stations could accumulate seven tax dollars, plus three tax dollars received at registration. Participants were asked to decide where to allocate their tax money among the various topics discussed at stations 3 to 9. They then deposited their tax money in boxes corresponding to the seven topics. They also were encouraged to write a specific suggestion on the back of each tax dollar.

The hypothesis was that participants would invest a large majority of their tax dollars in projects related to crime enforcement, directly related to community safety and crime reduction. Participants, however, distributed their tax dollars among all seven topics, communicating that building a safe neighbourhood would require action on many issues and not simply an increase in enforcement.

This was a highly effective method and organizers were delighted by the strong positive reaction to it. Participants said it was relevant, interesting and encouraged them to think carefully about where to invest their symbolic tax dollars.

Some representative comments included:

Although this is make believe, I think it is worthwhile as it causes you to think and choose wisely.

... you made this into an enjoyable and engaging game. Thanks.

... well, I thought it was going to be a waste of time yet when I had to determine where to invest the funny money, I took it seriously.

Language services

The first residents of this region were the Anishnawbic Ojbway-speaking tribes of hunters and gatherers. The Fort William neighbourhood has subsequently evolved as a multicultural area with waves of immigrants from throughout Scandinavia and Europe, including Ukraine. Thus, while volunteers interpreted in French, Ukrainian and Ojbway, there were no observable needs or requests for these interpretation services.

Supervised activities for children

Participants with young children could choose to have trained recreation workers supervise and entertain their children within sight and calling distance. Children's activities were designed for their age groups in an area directly across the corridor from the stations. The four young recreation workers easily managed a scene of happy constructive activities, working well for children and parents, without causing distractions for others.

Refreshments

To reinforce the casual nature of this drop-in event, a refreshment table set up in the centre of the corridor, easily accessible to all of the booths and activities, attracted those walking along the corridor. Volunteers served coffee, tea, water, juice and cookies. A food voucher in the form of a $3 coupon (for use at any participating food outlet) was offered to participants on completion. This served to support local merchants and provided flexible options for participants.

Rest area

Off to the side, several chairs were arranged in a rest area. This proved invaluable, as some individuals found the activity of the *Drop-in* session to be pretty intense. As one participant explained: 'It's good to take a few minutes to step away from the activity and to gather one's thoughts.'

Liaison role regarding media and politicians

The Downtown Development Coordinator served in the role of liaison. Radio stations, newspapers and the local television station were invited and attended a media conference three weeks earlier. The Coordinator welcomed the media representatives and provided them with assistance in meeting and interviewing. Of 13 City Councillors invited to the media release and to the *Drop-in and SpeakOut* sessions, three attended.

Thank you

Upon leaving, all participants were personally thanked and presented with their $3 food voucher and offered a $2 bus token for a free bus ride home.

Debriefing of volunteers

Immediately after the 27 April *Drop-in* session and again on 1 May, all volunteers were invited to participate in a debriefing session to share observations and emotions and comment on what did and did not work and how to improve such a process. Their ideas were captured on a flip chart visible to all. Transcribed notes were sent to all volunteers for further comment. After the initial draft report was distributed for review, a meeting was held. The types of comments recorded from the debriefing sessions included:

... being a facilitator at this event has been the most demanding role that I have experienced.

I am pumped by how well things went, but I am very tired.

The people truly were feeling empowered.

The mood of the participants was overwhelmingly positive.

I can't get over how patient and constructive the participants were throughout.

People wanted the details of their idea noted even when repetitious of existing ideas.

People showed self-discipline in following the order of the topics by station.

Participants waited their turn to speak in the vast number of cases.

People didn't want to prioritize ideas as the list of ideas grew on the flip charts.

The roles of facilitator and recorder mixed and merged as things got busy.

Even though the roles overlapped it seemed to work out with no problems.

By giving a tax dollar at the end of their ideas, it signalled thanks for the input.

People were keen on the tax dollars even though it appeared to be a game.

We drew out our target audience ... most lived in the area ... many had no jobs...

The music set a friendly, welcoming and casual feel.

Lessons learned on methods and organization

The debriefing session revealed the following six lessons:

1   More space was needed between stations to reduce noise and accommodate more people.
2   It is wise to shorten shifts for facilitators and recorders to 40 minutes.
3   Ensure that each facilitator and recorder takes a formal break of 15 minutes every hour.
4   Select a site so that set-up can be completed the night before to avoid problems on the day of the event.
5   Have volunteers to serve in the explicit role of back-up in case others don't arrive or attendance is greater than anticipated.
6   Ensure that all volunteers are given orientation and training in advance about the overall event and their specific roles.

In summary, these inclusive methods were seen as relevant to all forms of community engagement, as they are people-friendly, regardless of the participants.

Information gathered

The questions asked at the *Drop-in* and in the survey captured similar information. Participants were asked two basic types of questions: 'What are your concerns?' and 'What are your suggestions for addressing these concerns?' At the main *Drop-in* session, participants could indicate their support on information previously captured on a flip chart or provide a new response or suggestion. Each topic had a series of as many as five questions. At the *Drop-in* sessions, participants were also asked to place dots on each of four aerial photos to show areas of crime and areas seen as unsafe, neglected or lacking recreational facilities or activities.

During the 27 April *Drop-in* session, each listener asked respondents to rate the ideas on the flip charts in terms of their first, second and third priority.

Although a sincere effort was made to gather this information, it did not prove practical. As the number of suggestions on the flip charts grew, the lists became too long for the respondents to review and prioritize. It also was impractical because of the congestion it created, as respondents took a long time either to read or have the list read to them before they could decide on their priorities.

Recording and grouping of contributions

During the 27 April facilitated *Drop-in* sessions, information recorded was visible to the respondent and to other participants. Respondents were encouraged to review and correct any errors. All responses and suggestions captured on the flip charts and submitted in the surveys were transferred into tables by staff who served as listeners and recorders during both sessions. These staff grouped similar comments recorded under each question and labelled each of these groupings with an appropriate heading. On the large maps from the *Drop-in* sessions, staff drew lines around areas where the dots were clustered and the areas were then displayed on maps in the report.

Outcomes of the SpeakOut process

Participation

In total, 188 participants attended the two *Drop-in* sessions and 123 completed the survey questionnaire between 11 April and 21 May. The drop-in approach and the survey yielded valuable insights and opinions from people who were knowledgeable and concerned about creating a safe neighbourhood. Participants were observed as patient, respectful, sincere and constructive as they shared their ideas. The majority of the 123 who completed the four-page questionnaire provided responses to each question.

As participants were not explicitly asked to identify their ethnic or cultural background, age, gender or income level, it is not possible to categorize participants. However, volunteers agreed that participants were representative of groups who rarely participate in public meetings. It is estimated that

Aboriginal people represented 15 per cent or more of participants. Aboriginal volunteers expressed satisfaction with the participation of Aboriginal people, the inclusive methods and that their concerns and ideas were recorded. Their comments included:

> ... *Aboriginal people were there and participating.*

> ... *it was good to see that Aboriginal residents of the area were there to contribute their particular concerns, suggestions and views.*

> ... *overall, the methods used were user-friendly and Aboriginals as well as other participants seemed to be engaged.*

> ... *glad to see the drumming and singing was well received.*

Given such positive feedback, the approach can be viewed as effective in engaging people who frequent the neighbourhood.

Review of the report

Feedback meetings held with various partners and other relevant agencies revealed that the findings validated and reinforced findings of previous public consultations and related studies. The partners indicated that the report format and contents accurately captured responses obtained from both processes. However, asking individuals to prioritize suggestions caused confusion and did not yield any clear or usable results. The volume and range of suggestions demonstrated participants' emphasis on the importance of building a safe neighbourhood. Agencies quickly discovered that their existing programmes and efforts were not well known and more public awareness or education was needed.

Use of the report

On 10 October 2007, two workshop sessions were held to discuss the report. Approximately 20 participants from a wide variety of groups attended. Especially valued were ways in which the report succinctly presented a large amount of information. The report confirmed many prior assumptions and observations and validated results of other reports regarding neighbourhood safety. Representatives of individual agencies recognized their responsibility to use the report and to follow up on the suggestions. Those present expressed overwhelming agreement to participate in a network to build a safe Fort William neighbourhood, to share information, to collaborate where possible and to exchange updates on programmes and initiatives.

Recognition and thanks

A large debt of gratitude is owed to everyone who participated in this project, including those who volunteered to initiate, host, facilitate and record, the agencies and groups who will take the work forward and, most importantly, citizens who shared their concerns and contributed their ideas about creating a safe neighbourhood. They deserve the greatest thanks. Hopefully, they will see in the outcomes a commitment that ideas can be transformed into actions.

About Frank Wilson

Frank Wilson is currently working for the City of Thunder Bay, a northern city at the top of the Great Lakes in the geographic centre of Canada in the Province of Ontario. His role is to coordinate activities to renew the downtown neighbourhood of Fort William, which grew from a fur trading post in the 1840s.

Working with him is a volunteer citizen Renewal Team composed of individuals spanning a cross section of the community. Together they are promoting, facilitating and linking individuals, groups and organizations that are working on or wish to work on activities that will sustain and revitalize the neighbourhood. Previously, Frank was the Executive Director of the Lakehead Social Planning Council. This role involved advocacy work on behalf of a variety of social issues affecting Thunder Bay. He was part of the pioneering efforts to implement a 211 information and referral system[2] for the city and region.

Following a long career in the provincial government of Ontario, Frank describes himself as a planner who facilitates the sustainable interaction of people with each other and the environment. He's benefited from the opportunity to live in nine communities, large and small, across the province of Ontario.

Contact:

Frank Wilson, Downtown Development Coordinator

+ 1 807-625-2410

fwilson@thunderbay.ca

www.thunderbay.ca/fortwilliamneighbourhood

Townsville Families SpeakOut, 2007

4.4

By Steph Vajda with Yollana Shore

Background to the event

This chapter describes an innovative SpeakOut held in Townsville, North Queensland in October 2007. Townsville City Council (TCC) engaged Steph Vajda, employed by Brisbane-based cultural planning firm, Plan C, with Wendy Sarkissian providing advice on design and production issues. Plan C specializes in community engagement, public space collaborative design and space activation. The SpeakOut was hosted by the Townsville City Council's Community and Cultural Services Division as a means of developing the Townsville City Council Family Charter into a Family Strategy and Action Plan. With the full support of Townsville's Mayor, the event was intended to engage a wide variety of local families.

The *Townsville SpeakOut Festival* combined a large-scale SpeakOut with a general community event featuring a diversity of food, music and dance performances, skate ramp, photographic displays, video blogging and a variety of activities for children. The location on The Strand, an expansive seaside parkland, provided access to seating, shade, play equipment, a basketball court and a protected swimming area.

The Council conceived the Family Charter to recognize, create, support and develop opportunities for the diverse families within the Townsville community. The Council has used a variety of ways to engage with the community to develop the Charter and gain insights into its practical implementation. The 2006 *Families Summit* was a significant engagement event that reported on previous contributions, combining this information with existing Council policies and strategies.

Objectives and approach

Broad objectives

The SpeakOut's specific aim was to gain information about how the Charter could be implemented through the development of a 'Family Strategy and Action Plan'. As one participant commented: 'The SpeakOut is a great idea and event for community involvement.' For the Council, broader objectives included:

- Continuing engagement with families about how the Council conducts its business.
- Providing the community with a response to their participation in the 2006 *Families Summit*.
- Synthesizing *Summit* outcomes and creating relevance among these outcomes, potential policy options and the Council's wider planning framework.
- Coordinating planning for a range of services, amenities, spaces and places to encourage family participation and health.

In working with the Council to design and produce the SpeakOut, Plan C's broader goals involved coordinating planning for a broad diversity of the Council's activities across departments and programmes. The SpeakOut model offers great opportunities for facilitating communication across agencies by using the information generated for the event as a means of encouraging broader discussion and strategic planning. The SpeakOut had three aims: to identify and clarify issues faced by families; to provide information and solutions with which the community can identify and understand; and to generate community contributions to the Family Strategic and Action Plan.

Early concepts for the Townsville Families' SpeakOut

The *Townsville Families' SpeakOut* was designed to appeal to every age group and to allow all members of a family to engage simultaneously by providing activities for each generation. By conducting the SpeakOut within a larger, community-wide event, it was anticipated that young people, parents, singles, grandparents – in fact, all people – could be encouraged to attend.

The event would also need to appeal to specific groups, including Indigenous people, people from culturally and linguistically diverse backgrounds, people with a disability and people from the widest possible diversity of family structures.

Some initial suggestions for this event included:

- Live performances: music, circus, dance, children's entertainment, other local performers.
- Video blogging: opportunities for people to share views in private.
- Sports and activity workshops: basketball competition, skate school, fitness boot camp, Indigenous games, rock-climbing wall, jumping castle.
- Community recreation/arts and cultural workshops: art workshops, henna tattoos, jewellery making, creating do-it-yourself magazines (known as 'zines').
- Food and drink: a variety of refreshments available.

Combining a SpeakOut with a larger community event also made sense to the participants. Perhaps taking advantage of a pre-existing event could have had an even greater impact, as one participant explained:

> *An ideal time would have been when the 'power boat' races were on or the Kite Festival, to attract a large number of people to the event and take advantage of the numbers present. The community events on the Strand are great. Great job. Well done.*

Approach to producing the SpeakOut

Initially, Plan C's role was to act in an advisory capacity, with the Council organizing and conducting the event with guidance and active support from Steph and Wendy. The event was designed and planned through email updates, phone meetings and two face-to-face organizing sessions, in addition to hands-on support on the day of the event. Our experience with event production (see Chapter 3) consistently reminds us that SpeakOuts, enormous events to organize, require months of planning, design and coordination – often across a range of government departments, as well as service providers, community organizations and individuals. The depth of organizing involved in meeting the demanding logistical needs of these events means that more intricate tasks, such as sourcing information, designing displays and activities and selecting and preparing facilitators, can often be neglected. The strategic and engagement opportunities that the SpeakOut model offers are most easily achieved with sufficient time to work across departments, projects and positions to produce information which represents a coordinated approach to the SpeakOut theme. It is also important to remember that a well-managed event should look as though it is happening effortlessly (although this can perpetuate the misconception that events are easy to produce).

Figure 4.4.1 Marquees before and after the set-up

In retrospect, Steph felt that it was a mistake to agree to act in an advisory role when no Council staff or elected members had experienced, let alone managed, a SpeakOut. We believe that a professional SpeakOut manager must be engaged to coordinate and deliver an organization's first SpeakOut, with the active involvement of staff to enable training and handover. Then consultants can be engaged in an advisory role for future SpeakOuts until agency staff have the skills to design and produce future SpeakOut events themselves.

The many tasks related to assisting the Council to run a successful SpeakOut event (undertaken or assisted by Steph) included:

- *community networking, finding service providers and facilitators* in the lead-up to the event
- design and implementation of a *marketing* programme, including *design* of materials, contacting service providers and coordinating placement and updating of materials
- *design* of the event, including specific stalls, activities, participant processes and tools for recording information useful to the development of the Family Strategy and Action Plan and other materials for the Community Services Division
- *graphic design* of display and interpretive materials for the event
- *content design* for display and interpretive materials
- coordination of *logistics* for the event, including venue, equipment, catering and materials for stall activities and recording of participant perspectives, as well as wider event management
- assistance with coordination of *set-up, management and pack-down of the event* on 7 October, 2007
- *organizing and training facilitators and recorders*
- organizing a *debriefing session* for facilitators, recorders and the Council
- using *film* to document the event and outcomes, including *video blogging.*

Involving the Townsville community

The initial stage of gathering community support for the SpeakOut was enormously helped by the Mayor's role as a key driver. As Townsville is a relatively small city, word spread quickly about what was happening and active participation by community service providers and community group members increased word-of-mouth discussion of the event. A marketing campaign was undertaken, and although it started late and not all higher profile elements (such as public bus promotions) came to fruition, it reached a wide diversity of people. As the SpeakOut was held at The Strand, a prominent parkland well used by the local community, banners and signs were effective in promoting the event. This comment illustrates how well loved the event location was:

> We think the things done on The Strand are fabulous, e.g., Culture Fest, Kite Fest. It's amazing what you do.

> The SpeakOut is a great idea – a very easy way to go to have your say.

Figure 4.4.2 The SpeakOut flyer

Not all advertising was effective, however:

The advertising for the SpeakOut was not as effective as it could have been – we were just walking along here and found it. The music helped.

Other marketing activities included a letterbox drop, local newspaper and magazine advertising, school talks and active local talkback radio. The Council's Community Services Division worked hard to link the upcoming SpeakOut with a range of other planning and engagement activities already under way in Townsville.

Organizing facilitators

Facilitators for the SpeakOut stalls, selected by the Council, were drawn from a range of TCC departments and community services and organizations relevant to the stall themes. Unfortunately, because of late design of stall materials and activities, information was not sent to facilitators before the training session held the day before the SpeakOut. While the volunteer facilitators were highly skilled, there would have been benefits to early communication with them about objectives, information and processes associated with their involvement in particular stalls. Early communication allows issues to be identified by those with expertise in the particular stall themes. It also allows the training day to occur immediately before the event so that information is fresh in each facilitator's mind. That session can also be an opportunity to clarify materials and processes, rather than being the first opportunity for staff to engage with them.

Animating public space: layout and logistics

The SpeakOut was held at The Strand because of its prominent location, easy accessibility, established activities and high level of existing support by the local community. The event layout at the site was designed by Steph with Abbie Trott, Plan C's event manager (using principles of public space activation) to increase exposure to passing traffic by locating the skate facility and

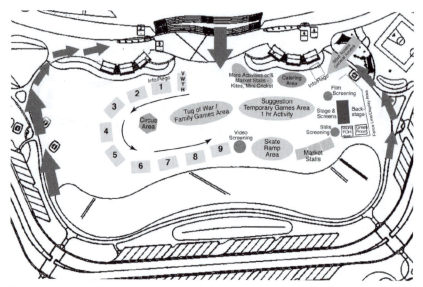

Figure 4.4.3 Site layout planning for the SpeakOut

stage close to the main road to maximize walk-ins from people using the site who weren't aware of the event. Specific access points into the whole event were designed to take advantage of locations that already promoted pedestrian and cycling activity, particularly along the Esplanade and the beach.

The site was ideal: a large grassy area that could be used to separate the SpeakOut stalls acoustically from other noisy activities, such as the stage and skate facility. A colourful 'Vote with Your Hands' stall was located near the registration stall, visible from both the street and the beachside walking paths, to entice people into SpeakOut stalls from the rest of the event. An extensive, undercover children's play area was to be located within the horseshoe design of the SpeakOut stalls, to enable parents to monitor children playing while they engaged with the SpeakOut.

Presentation materials

More than 230 interpretative materials and signs were required for this 12-stall SpeakOut. The interactive exercises and subsequent materials fostered participants' involvement in a variety of ways, including voting, drawing, talking, writing and even filming through the addition of a video blogging room.

On the day, the information materials probably did not completely represent or reflect the depth and range of the Council's current work in developing appropriate social, cultural, economic and environmental policy to meet the current and emerging needs of families. Nevertheless, they worked adequately and most interactive activities were highly supported. The hard work and commitment of facilitators listening to and engaging with participants, responding to queries and recording comments compensated for any weaknesses in displays. Further, as this was the Council's first SpeakOut, it was a learning opportunity. Production of information for display at future SpeakOuts could be improved over time, as more are conducted.

Designing the stalls

The SpeakOut aimed to build upon the work of the *Families Summit* and subsequent targeted engagement activities. Thus, the choice of topics for the stalls was strongly influenced by outcomes from the *Summit*, leaving organizers to determine the order of stalls and commonalities that would allow themes to be combined in one stall. Steph worked with the Council to develop activities for each stall to allow a diversity of age groups to participate beyond simply providing comments to be recorded. Interactive stall activities (see Chapter 6) offer a range of contribution options and, if done well, contribute vibrancy to a SpeakOut. In the same way that the 'Vote with Your Hands' activity enlivens an engagement event, activities within stalls combine games and creativity, while allowing participants to engage with relevant issues. Vibrant stalls attract participation from people who may not be interested in speaking with a facilitator. Selection of activities as simple as voting for a preferred element or writing a letter to another generation will depend on the outcomes sought for each stall.

Some of the interactive activities brainstormed for the Townsville SpeakOut included:

- 'Where do you live?' – a mapping exercise to gauge where people are travelling from. This requires a high-quality orthophoto map with main streets clearly labelled.
- 'How do you want to participate?' – a large printed table with a list of participation options in the left column and space in the right column to place dots to vote for that option.
- 'Modelling public space' – sandbox modelling exercise that can appeal to a variety of age groups.
- 'Training and mentoring' – a mapping exercise to determine skills people were interested in learning and sharing.
- 'Physical activity preferences' – using symbols representing different physical activities, people vote for their preferences and locate representations of them within a public space where they would like to engage in that activity.
- 'Hanging out in public space' – mapping where young people 'hang out' in public space and what they do and would like to do there.
- 'Intergenerational connections' – a diary- and letter-writing activity for comments to people from different generations about what it's like to share community, what their needs are and ideas for creating better relationships among generations.
- 'Transport' – mapping preferred transport routes and modes, including describing current problems and opportunities.
- 'Community events' – voting on types of community events, where they should be conducted and how often they should be held.

The stalls

The SpeakOut featured 12 stalls, including seven issue stalls, two project information stalls, a 'Vote with Your Hands' activity station, a registration desk and a video blogging space, coordinated by Shelley Waterhouse, Plan C's videographer. The stalls were located in a U-shaped formation (see Figure 4.4.3) to encourage participants to engage initially with the SpeakOut through the

'Vote with Your Hands', then to sign up at the registration table where the SpeakOut process was explained. Participants could then walk around the SpeakOut displays, reading background information and joining in activities or making comments on topics that interested them. At the end of the stalls was a video blogging room where people could share their feelings about being part of a family in Townsville. With participants' permission, these blogs were then projected at a stall at the other end of the event.

The stalls were set up as follows.

Stall 1: Vote with Your Hands

'Vote with Your Hands' is a simple voting exercise that creates colour and vibrancy at a SpeakOut entry. Participants vote for categories and issues that interest them using different coloured handprints for particular issues. In this case, the stall came to represent the importance of addressing all logistical details in such a large and important event. On the day of the event, the metal star pickets for mounting the 'Vote with Your Hands' display were not available. Thus, the stall, planned as a colourful entrance point to the SpeakOut proper, was located 25 metres from the entrance.[1] Nevertheless, it attracted attention and participants still found their way to the SpeakOut entrance.

Stall 2: Registration and reception

Staff at the registration desk aimed to explain how the SpeakOut works, record participants' contact information, find out where participants lived using a mapping exercise and give each participant an entry form for the SpeakOut competition. As part of initial planning and design, a 'SpeakOut passport' was suggested. Visitors would be provided with a SpeakOut passport that presented an overview of each stall and an opportunity to win a prize after each page had been stamped at each stall. (This model was successfully piloted by Wiwik Bunjamin-Mau in Honolulu in 2006.) However, time and resource constraints resulted in changes to the passport idea. Participants received an entry form for the prize draw, to be dropped into a box at the last stall.

In the *Where do you live?* mapping exercise, participants marked their home using a coloured sticker.

Stall 3: Background to the Townsville Family Strategy and Action Plan

This stall provided an overview of the project, including its purpose, process, time frames and relationships to broader planning objectives. A participatory voting activity used a large sheet of paper with a table showing a list of participation options in the left column (such as events, meetings, focus groups, surveys, etc.) and space in the right column for people to place dots to vote for that option.

Stall 4: Developing neighbourhoods for people

Material in this stall explained how people participate in their neighbourhoods and focused on how public space is managed, including material about park design and infrastructure and links between public and private spaces. A participatory activity used a sandbox where participants could model and remodel public spaces. This exercise, aimed particularly at children, was successful in

Figure 4.4.4 Sandbox modelling was a great success with all ages

attracting whole families, who completed their model together or assisted their children to engage. This activity was highly successful and could be used more broadly, with tables with different heights to enable all age groups to make separate sandbox models within the one stall.

Stall 5: Support for your family

This stall provided an opportunity to involve local support services that meet the needs of families. It addressed support for physical well-being and activity, nutrition, mental health, accessibility, disability services, financial planning and services for single parents. Activities were initially designed to elicit how people used currently available services, which services were not offered and where services should be located. One idea was a life-cycle interactive exercise, asking people to comment and vote on the availability of services over a whole life cycle, from birth to death. This somewhat complex activity was not used, although it could be used in other processes. An asset mapping activity enabled people to map skills they were interested in learning or sharing. Stall facilitators were well selected and briefed to explore these issues effectively with participants.

Stall 6: Healthy families

This stall, which focused on community, family and individual health services, issues and opportunities, invited contributions about physical activity, mental health, nutrition and other key areas of personal health. Originally, it was intended that a small stall beside the main stall would offer participants a basic health check. The initial concept involved participants firstly rating their own health in a number of areas and then receiving a basic health check by volunteering local general practitioners. The outcomes of both assessments would be anonymously mapped in the main stall, providing an idea of the accuracy (or not) of their personal appraisals. This innovative approach merits further development. Unfortunately, when the general practitioners were not available, this activity could not be implemented.

As an alternative, participants voted on preferred physical activities to stay healthy and provided comments on health services, public infrastructure to support healthy lifestyles and other health-related topics to facilitators who were currently undertaking studies relevant to health.

Some suggestions generated at this stall included:

- 'more free activities at events like today'
- 'more family events (not just for Mums and Dads)'
- 'ideas for families to do together'.

Stall 7: Being young in Townsville

Depending on the event, many SpeakOuts will have a stall for children and young people. Young people's specific needs can sometimes be missed in community planning. Being young can be challenging in what is often an adult-focused world. This stall was designed to be vibrant and appealing to young people and give them an opportunity to talk about issues that affect them. The stall focused on identifying the things young people do on their own, as well as things they do and want to do with their families. As with many stalls for young people or children at SpeakOuts, the comments at stall 7 often reflected a similar basic message: 'More activities for us', with many elaborating on the specific activities desired by young people in Townsville.

A participatory activity involved mapping where young people hang out in public space and what they do and would like to do. Colourful, cut-out symbols representing a variety of activities (from hanging out to seeing movies to playing sport) were used so that participants could glue them to a large map and write short comments within the symbol. This exercise mapped popular locations for different activities. Large sheets of paper were also available for young people to record what they would like to do and what prevented them from undertaking those activities.

Stall 8: Bridging the generation gap

Generational breakdowns are a common societal issue. This stall summarized how some intergenerational issues can affect families and the broader community. It generated ideas about how to promote healthy relationships between generations as a positive way of building better functioning communities. Diaries and letter writing encouraged participants to make comments to people from different generations about what it's like to share a community, what their needs are and ideas for creating better relationships. Some comments included:

> *To Whom It May Concern*
>
> *Stop chopping down our trees, we need them for shade and animals need them to live.*
>
> *Em M*

> *To Whom It May Concern*
>
> *In 20 years or so, I would like to see people being more inclusive and giving back to the community.*
>
> *Alex, 14 years. X*

> *Dear Tracey,*
>
> *I'm sorry to hear that you and your family had to leave your nice home in Kelso. I hope your mother is feeling better and recovering. It was good that your mother was able to access the Women's Shelter and they were able to help you and your sisters settle into a new school.*
>
> *Are you feeling safer now that your father is in gaol? Violence towards women and children cannot be excused under any circumstances. I know that it has been a time of upheaval and turmoil and I hope this will settle down for you and your family. I look forward to hearing from you. Take care,*
>
> *Regards,*
>
> *Heather*

> Dear Grandma and Grandpa,
>
> As I have been growing up, I have noticed a great change in many aspects of life. We speak differently to you – We write differently to you – We know how to use computers – We all have mobile phones and MP3 players. I've had the use of cars and electricity all my life – I've had computers and television all my life. The things that we are taught at school is different to you – we use pens and paper now not slate – Our teachers use white boards, not black boards – we don't get the cane anymore. It makes me wonder how much more the world is going to change by the time I'm a Grandparent. I just thought that I'd write to you and tell you that I have noticed the changes in society.
>
> Talk to you soon,

> Dear Children of Today,
>
> May you all have the opportunity to enjoy life, respect the people of today, both young, old (and yourselves) and remember to live life to the fullest and save for a rainy day.
>
> Beth.

Stall 9: Accessing your community

This stall addressed broad accessibility issues, including existing ones and ones that may develop over time. It emphasized a big-picture understanding of accessibility, beyond simply transportation, to encompass accessibility of marketing and communications undertaken by the Council, how parks and public spaces could be activated through events and activities and how the style of events affects their accessibility.

Among many comments, participants at this stall reported:

> Activities for kids on weekends (like the SpeakOut) are really appreciated.

and

> It's a good idea for people (not Council) to have their say on issues.

Participatory activities at this stall included voting on types of community events, where they should be conducted and how often they should occur. One activity addressed Townsville's public spaces that are currently underutilized, asking participants how these local, smaller-scale spaces could be better used. Participants were invited to map preferred transport routes and modes, while describing their current attitudes towards an experience of transportation.

Stall 10: Building sustainable communities

It is now widely accepted that sustainability is much broader than simply environmental factors. It encompasses social, cultural and economic considerations.[2] This stall emphasized how building sustainable communities in turn helps build cohesive families. It included an activity to map people's preferred transport options for the future, with facilitators recording comments after participants had voted. A second activity required voting on options for being actively involved in the community, through social action groups, gardening activities, advisory bodies and other options. Another activity initially aimed to provide information about community programmes, projects and groups. While that activity could not be produced in time, it is worthwhile idea. This stall was complemented by the late addition of a local sustainability group, whose stall beside stall 10 featured information and displays about sustainable technology and innovations.

Stall 11: Where to from here?

This unfacilitated stall provided participants with a sense of how their contributions could affect future Council planning. It provided information on the development of the Family Strategy and Action Plan, future engagement and review opportunities, time frames, project contacts and projected outcomes. Participants were invited to complete a *Postcard to Townsville*, which they displayed. In addition to expressing hopes for future participation opportunities, some participants expressed appreciation for the SpeakOut, making it clear that it should become a regular event (we think that's a great idea!):

SpeakOut is a great idea. I'm sure it will take off over time. Well done.

Outcomes

Comments about the SpeakOut were generally positive, although, as one participant suggested, timing is an important component of an event's accessibility:

> The 'Families SpeakOut' event needs to be for the day rather than only four hours, to give the broader community the opportunity to provide the feedback required.

Anyone who has been involved in the production of a SpeakOut will probably be shocked about the idea of one that lasts for a whole day![3] However, combining a SpeakOut with a community event creates broader opportunities, where a whole-day event could feature a four-hour SpeakOut within it, to maximize people's engagement with issues while enjoying food and entertainment activities.

More than 2000 people attended the Townsville event, held on a scorching spring afternoon. Between 500 and 600 participated in the SpeakOut component, offering contributions on the specific themes in each stall. The SpeakOut successfully created a space that both facilitated community engagement in the Council's policy and planning processes and allowed people to immerse themselves in their community through the activation of the public space itself.

Overall, the SpeakOut was a success. It generated great interest from the public and was widely appreciated on the day and in subsequent media reports. While analysis of contributions had not yet been completed when this book went to press, the wealth of information will assist in developing the Family Charter into the Family Strategy and Action Plan for guiding the Council's policy and implementation strategies.

Have Your Say! Day, False Creek North, Vancouver, 2007

By Christine Wenman with Nancy Hofer and Wendy Sarkissian

The SpeakOut as a qualitative research method

The SpeakOut is not only effective for community engagement; it is also a powerful qualitative research tool. The creative use of the model in Vancouver as part of a post-occupancy evaluation of housing was a resounding success, leaving no doubt about the many potential research uses for the SpeakOut method.

False Creek North background and history

In 2007, a class of postgraduate planning students set off to find out how the high-density, family-oriented, mixed-use community of False Creek North (FCN) in downtown Vancouver was meeting the needs of those who call it home: the residents. False Creek North is well known as a master-planned community. At the time of the study, more than 10,570 residents lived in 5450 households.[1] Thirteen per cent of the population were aged under 19. Although final construction was still under way during the study, the first residents had moved into the neighbourhood in the 1990s, providing enough time to warrant investigation of how the planned community had met its intended goals.

Before the current mixed-use development, the waterfront site was a railyard operated by Canadian Pacific Rail. The land was purchased by the provincial government, used for the 1986 World Exposition and finally sold in one large parcel to Hong Kong billionaire Li Ka-Shing and developed by Concord Pacific.[2] The sale to one developer meant that the City of Vancouver planners had a significant and unprecedented influence over the development of the land.

The City of Vancouver's community engagement process resulted in clearly articulated visions that continue to guide the development today: the concept of a vibrant, safe, inclusive and accessible downtown whose built form does not obstruct Vancouver's spectacular views or access to the publicly owned waterfront. The City required certain public amenities, including an extension of the Seawall on the FCN lands, public park space, public art, community centres and out-of-school care facilities. When the site construction is completed, approximately 15 per cent of the dwellings will be social housing units. The City's planning design principles and policies also inform the aesthetic expression of the site, reaffirming the street pattern as a central organizing principle, extending the urban fabric to the water's edge and paying attention to colour, texture and materials.

Despite general public acceptance of FCN, it is not without its detractors. The City acknowledges that in-depth sustainability analyses and projected social responses, now considered leading practice, should have been conducted. Further, the neighbourhood required more schools, daycare centres, places of worship and merited greater preservation of historic sites. Early building quality could have been improved and the built form could have been more diverse, as it has been critiqued for its 'one-generation aesthetic' and overuse of green glass.[3]

During the students' preliminary investigations, the following questions were raised by the development community, the City and other interested players:

- Have development pressures in neighbourhoods surrounding FCN created an affluent neighbourhood that may not meet the needs of those of moderate income?
- Are dwelling units meeting the needs of the full range of residents?

- Could dwelling units be improved to accommodate flexibility and adaptability?
- To what extent do the dense built form and the marketing of a leisure and resort-type aesthetic influence community interaction and social capital?
- To what extent does the mix of land uses (with its focus of activity and vibrancy) detract from the tranquillity and 'residential' quality residents seek?
- To what extent do residents feel that high-rise living is appropriate for raising families?

False Creek North provides a valuable case study of high-density down-town living. An internationally recognized project, it has guided subsequent developments in Vancouver and beyond and demonstrates the redevelopment opportunities of underutilized industrial land, as well as highly

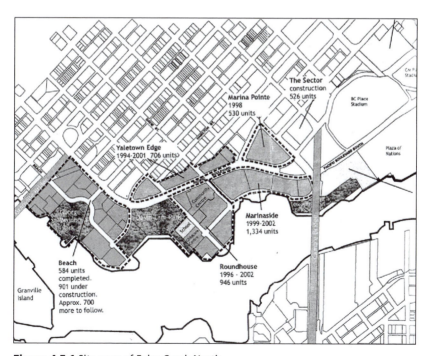

Figure 4.5.1 Site map of False Creek North

orchestrated and comprehensive urban design and city planning efforts. The post-occupancy evaluation (POE) aimed to explore these and other issues, as well as to evaluate the City's policy directions. It aimed to inform planning and development more broadly.

Speaking out as part of the False Creek North post-occupancy evaluation

The POE research was conducted by planning students at the University of British Columbia's School of Community and Regional Planning (SCARP). POE is the systematic evaluation of a designed and occupied setting from the perspectives of those who use it; it can be used to provide feedback throughout a building's (or in this case, a community's) life cycle. Over the course of 18 months, two professors, Larry Beasley CM and Dr Wendy Sarkissian, worked closely with 24 student researchers, who developed a mixed-method research approach to gauge measures of resident satisfaction. In October 2007, 4000 of the 5450 households in FCN received a self-complete questionnaire in the mail. Of these, 497 were completed and returned, representing a respectable response rate of 12.4 per cent.

On 3 November 2007, a version of the SpeakOut model, called a *Have Your Say!* Day, was held at the Roundhouse Community Centre in the FCN neighbourhood; more than 70 residents attended. As with all SpeakOuts, participants responded to the comments of other participants and visual and auditory prompts facilitated by a student listener. As they spoke, verbatim notes were recorded by a student recorder and later analysed. A second, more intimate workshop was held later the same day, based on the World Café model.[4] A dozen participants, facilitated by a student, explored concepts of home, community and quality of life in FCN.

Shortly after the SpeakOut, researchers facilitated a 'Week with a Camera' exercise with primary students at the local elementary school.[5] Finally, through 20 in-depth interviews with residents from diverse backgrounds and demographic profiles, students elaborated on the information gathered by the other methods, exploring contradictions and gaps emerging in the initial investigations. The multi-method approach was found to be highly effective in ensuring a deep analysis.

This chapter summarizes the *Have Your Say!* Day at the Roundhouse Community Centre on 3 November 2007 and explains the method's use as a quantitative research tool, in this case as part of a larger methodology.

SpeakOut and post-occupancy evaluation

Following Wendy Sarkissian's introduction of the SpeakOut model to SCARP students in a training workshop in October 2006, students decided to use this model in 2007 because it permitted a wide cross-section of participants and respondents to express satisfaction with a range of community issues and contexts. The SpeakOut allowed discussion and evaluation of issues of research importance that might not have been identified by the students using more formal research methods.

The SpeakOut design followed the basic principles set out in this book, with the added component of academic rigour. Themes for each issue stall, for example, were chosen based on research areas of inquiry and specific target participant groups identified during the development of the overall research methodology. Comments from participants were transcribed under each stall category and tabulated and coded through a standardized analysis identifying common and recurring themes, using a 'lump-and-split' method of simple categorizing. These thematically grouped comments within the major themes served as the basis for summarizing participants' opinions and experiences.

Presentation materials and stalls

Although the students had received adequate and repeated warnings from Wendy, they found it difficult to imagine how long the SpeakOut preparations would take. And, although logistical planning had begun months earlier, the design and creation of the stall displays was left to the last two weeks. The

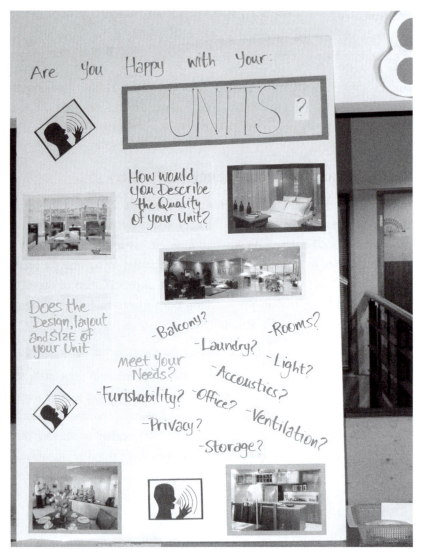

Figure 4.5.2 Hand-crafted display

students who worked closely on this aspect of the event spent most waking minutes together over the course of several days, often working into the early morning hours. Despite the time demanded, the students resisted the temptation to use computer graphics or print display material. Instead, they heeded Wendy's advice to make as many of the visual props as possible by hand.

The results were worth the sleepless nights. Using felt pens, construction paper, scissors and glue, the students created displays that were not only colourful and appealing but also warm, informal and inviting. Although computer graphics appear 'professional' and can often be made more quickly, their formality can reinforce the distance between planners and researchers as 'experts' and the participants as 'witnesses', possibly with little to offer. The home-made, down-to-earth feel of the graphics helped everyone to feel relaxed and encouraged participation.

In spite of dozens of checklists, it seems in such events some detail is always overlooked. On the morning of the *Have Your Say!* Day, volunteers realized that the lighting in the SpeakOut room was inadequate. While some volunteers purchased refreshments, others posted signs and display boards, some prepared the children's activity room and a carload zipped off to Ikea in search of inexpensive floor lamps to save the day. With minutes to go before participants would arrive, volunteers completed their tasks and suddenly, the room was ready for action, enlivened by the displays, brightened by lamps and made welcoming by refreshments. Seamlessly.

As this book points out, a well-planned SpeakOut looks easy. The *Have Your Say!* Day SpeakOut certainly was not easy but participants would not have known that. Having enough time and volunteers during the set-up time ensured that the (inevitable) forgotten details could be quickly handled.

Specific stalls

The *Have Your Say!* Day SpeakOut stalls were designed according to nine key research areas. Listeners and recorders were given a set of initial questions as prompts and each stall had a page of directions for participants.

False Creek North Community stall

Photographs of people of different ages and cultural backgrounds decorated the community board. Some questions were intended to stimulate initial discussion: 'Why did you move here?' 'Does False Creek North meet your expectations?' 'Does False Creek North have a community spirit?' Residents were asked to place a sticky dot on a huge aerial map indicating where they lived. The activity allowed researchers to see the spatial distribution of participants and invited residents to begin the SpeakOut process by locating themselves spatially.

Shops and services stall

Photos of local shops and services decorated this stall, with large colourful letters inviting public comment, asking: 'Are your needs met locally? Medical services? Entertainment? Shops? Schools and Daycare?' 'What are your experiences with community services and activities in False Creek North?' 'What are your experiences operating a business in False Creek North?'

Buildings stall

This stall was home to skyline views and close-up photos of apartment buildings. Researchers carefully selected a mix of building types, including towers, condominiums and medium-sized buildings. Several photographs reminded residents to consider life *inside* their buildings: a swimming pool, a work-out room and a pool table. Again, some questions prompted residents: 'What are your impressions of the architecture in False Creek North?' 'How are the common spaces in your building?' 'Do you feel there is community spirit in your building?'

Parks and plazas stall

The parks and plazas stall was complemented by a second interactive exercise, where residents were asked to 'Vote with your sticky note' for a quality of a park that was most important to them.[6] Residents were asked to elaborate on their votes by writing a comment on the sticky note that they placed in the appropriate section. The stall displayed photographs of several local parks, with these prompting questions: 'What are your favourite outdoor places? If you could redesign the Roundhouse plaza, how would you change it?' 'Do you find False Creek North Park suitable for your needs as: an active person? A parent? A senior? A dog owner?'

Safety stall

Images representing community safety issues included: gates left open, a bicycle tyre locked to a bicycle rack, signalling that the bike had been stolen and some photographs highlighting lighting around buildings. Written prompts included: 'Would you walk alone at night?' 'How safe do you feel in your unit? In your building? In the parks? Going into your building?' 'When and where do you feel vulnerable?' 'Do you feel False Creek North is safe for your children?'

Families and children stall

Photographs included the local elementary school, a neighbourhood daycare centre and park facilities for children and parents with young children. Prompting questions asked: 'How suitable is False Creek North for raising a family?' 'Will False Creek North meet the evolving needs of your family?' 'How well does False Creek North meet the play needs of your children?'

Adolescents and youth stall

This stall aimed to attract and engage local youths with a hands-on mapping activity. They were given a map of the neighbourhood and asked to place a sticky gold star on their favourite spot, a red sticky dot on any place that they did not like and a green spot where they lived. Comments were recorded on maps displayed for others to see. The stall also offered candy as an additional enticement. Perhaps most importantly, the stall facilitators were experienced in working with youth. With their fun and casual attire of baseball caps and

Figure 4.5.3 Renée welcomes youth and their parents

glittery t-shirts, both knew how to approach youth and how to allow youth to approach them. A board invited additional comments with photos of youth of a variety of ages and ethnicities. Questions prompted: 'How do you like living in FCN?' 'Where do you hang out and what do you like to do?' 'What would you change about FCN to better suit the needs of your age group?'

Dwelling units stall

Photos of typical dwelling units decorated this stall, with questions asking: 'Does the design, layout and size of the unit meet your needs?' 'How would you describe the quality of our unit? Privacy? Acoustics? Ventilation? Light? Furnishability? Office? Laundry? Storage? Balcony? Rooms?' The units stall also offered an interactive activity. Several sample floor plans of False Creek North units were displayed. Residents were invited to compare those floor plans with their own. Floor plans were an effective tool to stimulate detailed conversation about residents' units. The plans drew participants' attention to dwelling details that they may otherwise have omitted.[7]

Mobility stall

This stall featured photos of the heavy traffic along Pacific Boulevard, cyclists and rollerbladers along the Seawall and some wayfinding signs. Questions prompting residents were: 'Can you find your way around?' 'What modes of transport do you use and for what purpose? Car? Bus? Skytrain? Ferry? Cycling? Rollerblading? Skateboarding?'

Specific approaches taken in the SpeakOut

How participation was encouraged

SpeakOuts are designed to facilitate structured 'drop-in' participation. In this study, students recruited a wide range of advertising and publicity approaches. These included:

- 3500 mailed questionnaires arrived in residents' mailboxes the day before the SpeakOut and included an invitation to the event.
- One week before the *Have your Say!* Day, an invitation was included in a school newsletter sent to parents of Elsie Roy Elementary School students, almost all of whom live in the area.
- The day before the event, volunteers distributed flyers to students at St James High School, many of whom live in FCN.
- During the days leading up to the event, advertising posters were placed in all local stores whose management agreed to participate.
- Building managers were contacted; some posted the advertisement on lobby news boards.
- A press release was sent to local newspapers. The *Vancouver Sun* published a short article about the research project on 31 October 2007. The event poster was published in the *Georgia Straight* one week before the event.
- Larry Beasley spoke on CBC radio on 2 November 2007.
- During the event, volunteers with flyers circulated throughout the neighbourhoods and invited the public to attend.

Have Your Say About The Neighbourhood!

What do you think about living in False Creek North?

Saturday 3rd November, 2007

10:00am - 4.00pm

Roundhouse Community Centre

Drop in For:

Interactive Displays
Kids Activities
Refreshments & Door Prizes!

We are also looking for volunteers to participate in:

A **Group Discussion** between 2:00pm - 4:00pm on 3rd Nov.

An individual **In-depth Interview**

Contact Nancy from UBC via email at ndee@interchange.ubc.ca or by telephone on 778 239 8733

Figure 4.5.4 The SpeakOut poster

At least 70 residents participated, including adolescents, families, single people and seniors. Men and women participated equally. Among ethnic minorities, Chinese and Eastern Europeans were well represented. Several participants, especially families, self-identified as living in subsidized housing or cooperative living units. In spite of the participation of a diverse cross-section of residents, the overall participant profile may have disproportionately represented those in higher income groups and English-speaking residents. Given the questionnaire results, this bias appeared to be reflected throughout the entire research process. Although time was a limiting factor, researchers regretted not cooperating more with local schools and community centre personnel to develop strategies to reach youth, those living in subsidized housing and those for whom English is a second language. Promotional strategies should have focused on engaging members of these groups from the initial planning stages.

Layout and logistics

Wendy had explained to the students that 'the devil is in the detail'. The aphorism rings true when planning for any public event, especially a SpeakOut, where success relies on the degree to which participants feel welcomed, relaxed and free to express their opinions. In this SpeakOut, the small upstairs room quickly filled with people and the resulting intimacy and energy were contagious and inspiring. Several residents, who said that they came 'only to take a look', left surprised at how much they had contributed. The students, initially nervous about how to prompt participants, later commented that it had been surprisingly easy – even the quietest person readily chatted about their home and neighbourhood. Many participants commented that the friendliness and focus of the listeners and recorders and their ability to *really listen* encouraged participation. The refreshment table invited residents to linger, chat and feel at home.

The child-care activities were in a room adjacent to the SpeakOut on the same floor. Their proximity, a certified and experienced child caregiver and a host of available children's activities reassured parents that their children would be happily and safely occupied. Children's activities included face-painting, bean ball throwing and painting on large sheets of paper.

Despite enthusiastic facilitators and participants, the SpeakOut was not flawless. The room was simply too small, meaning that not all participants' comments could be displayed. Further, not all interactive exercises had their own identifiable space and some were overlooked by some participants. The reception desk was at the bottom of the stairs, whereas the stalls and displays were upstairs. This layout disrupted the flow and created some confusion. Although the SpeakOut room initially felt very large and empty to the researchers, it quickly filled as people entered and their comments were hung on the walls. Had the students had more experience and faith in their ability to transform a space, they likely would have chosen a larger, more appropriate venue. The interactive activities, often overlooked because volunteers were trying to manage too many activities, needed to be separated with their own listener and recorder.

Inviting and assigning student volunteers

Well over 30 volunteers helped to make the *Have Your Say!* Day a success. However, more were needed. The SpeakOut method's effectiveness relies on its intimacy, which requires one listener and recorder per stall, as a minimum. In this case, two stalls had only one volunteer. The interactive activities were incorporated into the stalls, still using only two volunteers. Although volunteer numbers often cannot be controlled, this case study reiterates that organizers must plan for this constraint. The researchers regretted not using existing relationships with the community centre and elementary school staff through which volunteers, especially youth, could have been easily recruited. As it was, volunteer numbers were high because of interest from other students in the School of Community and Regional Planning. As such interest and ownership may not be present in every research scenario, volunteer recruitment must be treated as a process that begins as early as possible.

Outcomes of the process: The SpeakOut as a powerful qualitative research tool

As part of a mixed methodology, the SpeakOut complemented the questionnaire, where detail, comprehensiveness and length must be sacrificed for statistical significance and brevity. The student researchers came to perceive the questionnaire as the skeleton of the research and the SpeakOut as the flesh. The intimacy and the energy of the *Have Your Say!* Day brought the community alive for the students who had been studying it for so many months.

The SpeakOut results complemented, expanded and triangulated information gathered from the quantitative questionnaire. For example, the questionnaire asked residents:

- How often do you visit the parks, plazas and open spaces in False Creek North?
- What is your favourite park, plaza or open space in False Creek North?
- To what extent do you feel the parks, plazas and open spaces in False Creek North serve most of your recreational leisure needs?

Questionnaire respondents were given predetermined options: a list of frequencies, a list of parks or a satisfaction scale of 1 to 5. Such information proved invaluable; surveying such a high percentage of residents at once provided statistically significant data and an overview of residents' satisfaction levels and living habits. However, any one of these questions introduces an array of others. Why is that park your favourite? What do you like about it? How do you use the park space? The SpeakOut results served to explain in greater depth many questionnaire results. Residents spoke about features of different parks, explaining why they may prefer one over the other. The SpeakOut, with its verbatim transcription, also captures nuances, energy and passion that can be lost in other processes. Here are some particularly rich statements about parks as examples:

- *People need to control their dogs!*
- *Dog parks and children's playgrounds don't go together.*
- *Dogs can be dangerous.*
- *Cut the bushes! It's a safety issue!*
- *We have two baby parks around here but nothing for us [parents of youths]. What about a summer waterpark?*
- *I use [the Seawall] daily; that's why I'm here.*
- *One of the best things about False Creek North is that you can round a corner and see a vista and you feel alone.*

Only a few short statements can make it clear which issues are most contentious, especially when they are repeated by several participants. Although volunteers expected park use by dogs to be a significant topic, the importance of the issue had not been clarified before the SpeakOut. It was tempting to disregard the problem as inevitable and petty until the emotion in participants' comments revealed the degree to which the conflict degraded user enjoyment of the parks and contributed to resident dissatisfaction.

Other comments that are particularly descriptive can reveal much in a few words. Residents' descriptions of 'feeling alone' and seeing 'vistas' highlights the value of waterfront access, intentional building patterns that accentuate views and landscaping to create a sense of space. Without using any technical jargon, participants affirmed the success of many of the City of Vancouver's and Board of Parks and Recreation's policies. From scores of sheets of paper filled with such comments, the researchers discovered a wealth of information that would not have been possible without the SpeakOut method. In particular, the careful verbatim recording, displayed for others to read, captured and validated emotion, allowing others to respond reflectively and honestly.

Summary of findings

Parks were not the only topics to elicit such responses; each stall revealed a wealth of information – too much, in fact, to include here. However, a brief summary suggests the potential of the SpeakOut as a research tool.

Community

A sense of community is strong among certain groups of people: dog-owners and parents of young children for example; however, the neighbourhood has not yet developed a sense of self typical of established residential areas. Nonetheless, residents experience a sense of place and ownership resulting from access to many local amenities and seeing familiar faces in shops and cafés. In particular, the community is growing because of the number of children living in the area; many residents noted that the cooperatives and subsidized housing units dramatically improved the quality of the neighbourhood for the better because of the increased number of families.

Shops and services

Local shops and services are inadequate. Many residents complain of high prices and few options, forcing them to do much of their shopping outside of the neighbourhood and with a car. Those who do shop locally tend to be retired seniors with time to take buses into more affordable neighbourhoods. The community centre is well used and greatly appreciated but does not adequately serve teenagers, adults and seniors.

Apartment buildings

Apartment buildings are seen as safe but several already have problems relating to construction quality, including leaking. Amenities in buildings, such as pools and weight rooms, are generally well used, maintained and appreciated.

Parks, plazas and public spaces

Parks are loved, well used and the reason many residents chose to live in FCN in preference to other downtown high-density communities. Most popular is the Seawall for local commuting, leisure strolls and active sports. Dogs in parks are emotional issues for many. Amenities for young children are plentiful and of high quality but residents feel that older youths have been largely overlooked.

Community safety

Most residents feel reasonably safe in the neighbourhood but some comments about landscaping and lighting suggest that improvements are merited. Residents feel particularly safe inside their buildings but not all are comfortable outside at night. Homelessness and the perceived threat of discarded syringes from drug users cause some residents, particularly parents, to feel unsafe. Several parents also worry about off-leash dogs in the parks.

Families and youths

Youth appreciate the proximity of their school to their home and feel a sense of community, as many of their friends live nearby. However, almost unanimously, older youth and their parents complain of insufficient activities and space. Many parents of young children are not convinced that they will be able to stay in FCN as their children grow older because of limited space in the schools, in their own dwelling unit and in neighbourhood parks.

Dwelling units

High dwelling unit costs mean that most residents are living in spaces that they feel are too small for their needs. Residents complain about insufficient storage and little flexibility in how to furnish their unit. Private outdoor spaces, patios and balconies are loved by those who have them and greatly missed by those who do not.

Mobility

Residents appreciate accessibility to many shops and services on foot or by bus. Almost all report using diverse modes of transportation and walking frequently within the area. Many, however, regret that they have not been able to give up a car completely, as they use it for work, for grocery shopping or to access other areas in metropolitan Vancouver.

Constructing knowledge by speaking out

The SpeakOut elicited a wealth of invaluable research material. Without it, the post-occupancy evaluation would not have achieved its depth and richness of detail. The SpeakOut provided a forum where residents could identify subjects of importance and elaborate to their hearts' content. The newest reiteration of the original 1990 SpeakOut leaves no doubt that the method is an effective tool for qualitative research.

Acknowledgements

We are extremely grateful to everyone who helped with the False Creek North Post-Occupancy Evaluation. In particular, our funders: Concord Pacific Group Inc, Hillside Developments, Amacon Group, City of Vancouver Planning Department, Beasley and Associates and Sarkissian Associates Planners. From the School of Community and Regional Planning at the University of British Columbia, a special thanks to the leadership, teaching and administrative support of Professor Leonie Sandercock, Professor Penny Gurstein, Dr Wendy Sarkissian, Larry Beasley CM and Patti Toporowski.

The POE was a collaboration of 24 students, who worked extremely hard over many months. Deepest gratitude to all of them: Michelle Babiuk, Rebecca Bateman, Robert Bateman, Claudia Bialostosky, Debra Bodner, Courtney Campbell, Renée Coull, Jeff Deby, Eric Doherty, Jana Fox, Peter Giles, Jeff Ginalias, Nancy Hofer, Charlotte Humphries, Dianna Hurford, Brendan Hurley, Jay Lancaster, R.J. McCulloch, Haley Mousseau, Kathryn Quinnelly, Marian Thomas, Christine Wenman, James White and Zheyu Zhou.

We are also indebted to the entire Grade 6 class of Elsie Roy Elementary School, their teacher, Duncan Coo and their Principal, Isabel Grant. Thanks also to our advisers and helpers, Dr Stephanie Chang, James Cheng, David Ellis, Emeritus Professor John Friedmann, Michael Gordon, Diane Guenther, Terry Howe, PC David Krenz, Dr Betty McGill, Gordon Price, Professor William Rees, Piet Rutgers, Gregory Saville and Professor Jacqueline Vischer, for their generous professional contributions.

For further information

The following references provide further information:

- City of Vancouver (undated)
- Price, G. (2008)
- Preiser and Vischer (2005)
- Wenman et al (2008).

Christine Wenman

Christine is a graduate student in planning at the University of British Columbia, studying community planning, inclusive engagement methods and resource management. Her previous studies in environmental sciences reflect her passion for exploring the interface of social and environmental sustainability and led her to professional work in community development as the Water and Sanitation Program Coordinator for a non-governmental organization, *Caminamos Juntos para Salud y Desarrollo, AC* in Mexico. Through her experiences working with a community struggling against generations of imprinted oppression, she has become interested in societal structures that perpetuate power inequities and how change can occur. She is a co-author of *Creative Community Planning*, forthcoming from Earthscan, 2010, and recipient of the Amacon-Beasley Masters Student Award for 2009 at the University of British Columbia.

Nancy Hofer

Nancy is a final year master's student at the School for Community and Regional Planning, University of British Columbia. She brings to this degree a background in ecology and natural resource conservation. Upon completing her undergraduate degree, Nancy spent close to a year in Freiburg, Germany where she worked at the Albert-Ludwigs-Universität and gained an appreciation for German settlement patterns that are denser, public transit oriented, lively and on the whole more pleasant to be in than typical contemporary North American towns and cities. It was this experience of living in Freiburg that tweaked her interest in planning and the need for it to be based on ecological principles. She is a co-author of *Kitchen Table Sustainability* (Sarkissian et al, 2008), an earlier book in this Earthscan suite of books, and recipient of the Amacon-Beasley Masters Student Award for 2009 at the University of British Columbia.

Designing and Managing a SpeakOut

This chapter sets out the steps and requirements for preparing a SpeakOut. It contains basic information about the logistics of preparing for a workshop. While this chapter addresses the requirements for SpeakOut design, many considerations apply equally to community workshops or meetings, discussed in detail in Chapter 9.

The *outer circuit*

We have often likened organizing a SpeakOut to a wedding reception: the organizer needs to consider many details to be prepared to host hundreds of guests. In all the SpeakOuts we have organized, seen or heard about in many different settings and venues in different types of communities, one thing has remained consistent: having an *outer circuit* and an *inner circuit*.

In most cases, the *outer circuit* serves as the general area that greets participants as they first enter the SpeakOut. It is critical that participants feel welcome and accepted there. It is also important that when they arrive, participants learn what to expect, what to do and what is likely to be expected of them. Any confusion at this critical first stage can lead to weaknesses in the SpeakOut. We explain in detail below the components to consider in creating an effective *outer circuit*.

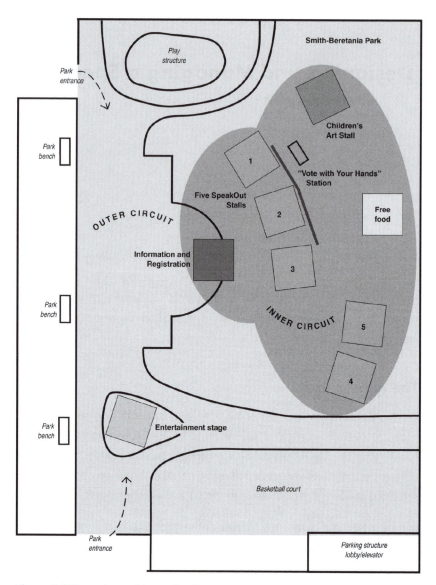

Figure 5.1 The *outer* and *inner* circuits

Location: Selecting a venue

Location is everything with a SpeakOut, as for a workshop. When considering a venue, it is important to have a clear idea of the type and possible size of the SpeakOut or workshop. Keep in mind all stages of the event and try to predict accurately what participants will be required to do at each stage. We try to imagine how participants will feel when they first arrive.

Think laterally about how available resources can be used. Some venues are simply unsuitable, whereas others that may at first seem unsuitable can be modified with a little effort. For example, an acoustically dreadful room may be improved simply by hiring a carpet to dampen noise.

Similarly, a marquee or tent may be added to the side of an existing building to provide room for refreshments or children's activities. Or marquee linings can be hung inside larger buildings to dampen reverberation and create a visually more attractive atmosphere. In addition, a small canopy at an entrance can protect people queuing in bad weather. We recommend that you plan well in advance, as there are always some things that cannot be rectified at the last minute.

The drawing in Figure 5.2 shows the arrangements of stalls and the flow of pedestrian activity in the Footscray SpeakOut (which employed small marquees for issue stalls in a pedestrian mall) in Melbourne in 2004.

When assessing a venue, we recommend that the issues of *shape, size* and *accessibility* be paramount considerations.

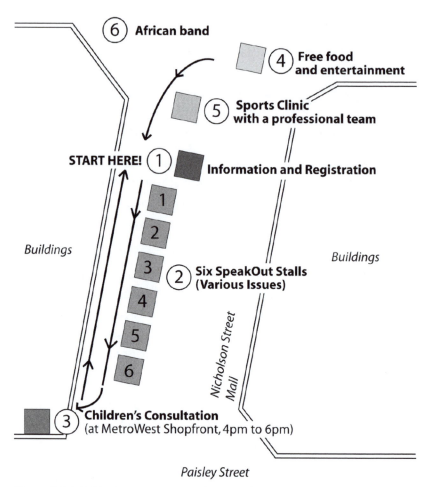

Figure 5.2 (re)Visioning Footscray SpeakOut, Melbourne, 2004

Rooms and halls

Finding the right room is always a challenge. A room is often too big, too small or too expensive. While adjoining rooms are invaluable for set-up, storage, children's activities, catering, briefing and debriefing sessions, we believe it's better to work together in one large room (providing acoustics can be managed well), rather than having workshop groups break off and go into separate rooms.

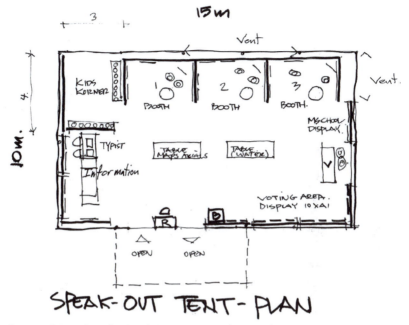

Figure 5.3 Drawing of a SpeakOut marquee where voting was to occur

Item/issue	Comments	☐ √
Adequate room for all anticipated participants (plus a few unexpected ones)		
Storage room for equipment		
Area for a separate children's consultation process		
Kitchen facilities adequate for catering		
Acoustic isolation from noisy food preparation and serving		
Sufficient electrical outlets		
Obtain accurate dimensions of all venue spaces. Prepare an accurate floor plan		

With respect to room size, 'too big' can generally be overcome with amplification or partitions. Too small will always be too small.

Make sure you obtain the dimensions of the room and tables either from the hirer or by taking along your own tape measure and checking the venue yourself. This will help you determine whether your furniture arrangements will fit. It's important to ensure that the venue is accessible for all possible participants.

Adaptable venues: Tents and marquees

Where there is no suitable venue for a large workshop or SpeakOut, adaptable environments can be the solution. Marquees or tents can be used to make a space larger by extending a small room, for catering or children's activities or providing a covered entrance. Take care, however, to check all requirements carefully.

Marquees and tents pose special problems. They can get very hot in summer and the walls are not suited to provide stable backing for displays (although some material can be suspended from roofs and ceilings). They need heating in cold weather (and heaters can be very noisy). They also need a suitable power supply. Lighting is especially important for evening workshops.

Room size and shape

Although the venue manager may tell you that the venue seats 100, often the venue you're assessing will seat only 60 people in the format that we recommend for workshops (called 'cabaret-style' seating). And the circulation space required for a SpeakOut will mean that even more space will be required. They'll tell you it's fine acoustically. We recommend that you check it out anyway, remembering that what works for a 'meeting' may not be suitable for people working at tables or SpeakOut stalls. It's often very difficult to hear discussion at your table when people at a neighbouring table are making a lot of noise. When interpreters are used, noise levels will be even higher, placing greater emphasis on space and acoustic controls.

Item/issue	Comments	☐ √
Can it be attached to an existing building?		
Does it need a floor? Does this need to be ordered separately?		
Ensure it will not blow away in strong winds		
A security guard may be necessary if the marquee is set up overnight		
Check with hiring company when marquee will be set up and taken down (confirm in writing)		
Find out who from the hiring company can be contacted at any time during the event in case a problem arises. Get mobile telephone number and check that after-hours numbers are correct		
A small canopy at an entrance can reduce the problem of participants getting wet or hot while having to queue in bad weather		
If a marquee is to be erected in a public park, a permit may be required, as well as a rental fee or cleaning deposit		
Check all requirements for public liability insurance		

When assessing the room for its suitability, it's helpful to think through the workshop or SpeakOut process step by step. Will the building be large enough to accommodate queues for drinks or meals? Is circulation between tables or SpeakOut stalls really possible when the room is full? How will you accommodate an overflow crowd? What if everyone comes at once?

We cannot overemphasize the *qualitative* aspects of a space. Does the room feel right? Would you like to spend an afternoon or an evening slogging through planning details or listening to scientific evidence in this space? Can you possibly make it welcoming? If it feels dreadful, despite ticks in all the boxes in this book, we advise you to keep searching. Trapped there for hours, participants (and your SpeakOut workers) will soon sense those qualities, which will affect their comfort and the effectiveness of your workshop.

Accessibility and parking

Accessibility is a prime consideration and includes being able to get to the venue, through it, to access amenities in a *mainstreaming* and not separate way. Participants need to be able to move freely, feel comfortable and not feel out of place. Our populations are rapidly ageing and many people are living longer and with a disability. Many people report difficulty accessing public events. This can be a major disincentive to equitable participation.

Figure 5.4 An accessible reception stall

Item/issue	Comments	☐ √
Access to the venue: • easy to find and enter • by public transport[1] • by bicycle • on foot		
Safe and even path between the public transport stop and the workshop venue		
Safe, accessible and well-lit parking		
Temporary signs between parking, transit and the venue (may require a permit to be posted on the nearest utility poles, etc.)		
Parking available close to venue for set-up people		
Access for participants with a disability: includes a continuous accessible pathway to public entrance e.g., ramps and rails provided instead of steps and doorways wide enough to accommodate a wheelchair (760mm or wider)[2]		
Continuous access from main entrance to the function room, including no steps and accessible ramps and lifts		
Is there a contrasting strip on step edges?		
Do all steps have handrails?		
Clearly labelled and unobstructed fire exits		

A suitable and comfortable environment

Often there is little or no choice of venue and it is necessary to use the local hall or the one closest to the development site. We have found that it's wiser to consult people on their own turf than to select a more comfortable venue in an inconvenient location.

Item/issue	Comments	☐ √
Heating and insulation from cold weather		
Fans (and air conditioning if absolutely necessary) in hot weather		
Carpeted for comfort and to reduce noise, particularly if the room has high ceilings and/or wooden floors		
Check that heating/cooling works and is not noisy. Know where the controls are and how to operate them		
Fresh air, if possible. What can you do if the room gets stuffy?		
Does the room smell pleasant? Can it be easily aired out? Be careful about room fresheners, as many people are allergic to them		
How windy will it get if the door or windows are open?		

Layout and acoustics

Workshop participants often complain that they can't hear what's going on, despite our attempts to consider acoustics. Selecting a large room can help reduce the problems of discussions at workshop tables being overheard. We try to avoid rooms with timber floors (although often we are in a gymnasium). Carpeting a noisy room can make a world of difference. Providing several roving microphones can counteract problems of voices being heard only from the front of the room.

As traffic noise is a familiar complaint, it's best to check out your venue at a peak hour to get a sense of the impact of traffic on conversations at workshop tables.

We cannot overemphasize the need to test all equipment before use and to learn how to deal with feedback from microphones and speakers. Starting a workshop with an ear-destroying blast from the speakers is not wise.

Item/issue	Comments	☐ √
Check timetable for neighbouring rooms: will the aerobics class or band practice affect your participants' ability to participate?		
Large enough so participants can talk at tables without problems with hearing or being distracted by conversations at other tables		
Toilets and washrooms clearly labelled and accessible		
Adequate room for serving food. Remember that a queue will form for meals and drinks. Determine all queuing arrangements in advance		
Locate the focus of the room so that all participants can see easily. Often this will be at the centre of the long wall of a rectangular room		
Locate the focal point along the long side of the room to reduce viewing distances		
Avoid rooms with many large pillars or columns		
Avoid odd-shaped rooms where one group has to sit apart from the others and may feel excluded		

Lighting and electrical power supply

We often have 'electrical' difficulties at SpeakOuts or workshops. Working in old buildings, in rural areas, in industrial areas with unreliable power supplies or in marquees and tents requires awareness of our power needs. Often there are simply not enough electrical outlets to support all the technology required for a public workshop. So we need to bring our own extension leads, power boards and double adapters and gaffer (or duct) tape to tape cords to the floor so that people do not trip over them.

Or it may be that the venue has inflexible 'romantic' lighting – designed for weddings and parties. If the lighting cannot be increased to permit people to read materials at their tables (and recorders to see to record what people say), you may need to provide some additional lighting, as the students did in Vancouver.

Using a projector requires that the room be darkened for best effect. Often rooms described as 'darkenable' do not have curtains that cover the full length or width of the windows. If the windows are the only form of ventilation on a hot day, will you still be able to see the slides and not suffocate? It's good to check for awkward backlighting and glare from windows that can make it difficult to see projected images.

Skylights are a particular problem. We have had to send a person up onto the roof of two gymnasia we have worked in to tape black garden plastic to the skylight. On one occasion, the outside temperature was 42 degrees Celsius (or 108 degrees Fahrenheit)! And it was a metal roof ...

Item/issue	Comments	☐ √
How will power be supplied to the venue?		
Ensure enough power for your needs – all your needs		
If you need to rent a generator, make sure you can either locate it some distance from the activities or rent one that is low-noise		
Check all electrical outlets and bring extension cords (including appropriate tape to protect cords if required)		
Ensure the fuse box is unlocked. Spare fuses or fuse wire?		
If lights are the mercury-vapour type, they need time to reheat when switched on		
Natural light is more pleasant to the eyes and not so tiring to participants as artificial light		
Avoid fluorescent lights if possible unless they are full-spectrum fluorescents, as they can tire participants or contribute to headaches		
Is the venue darkenable for slides, video and overhead projectors? Do the blinds or curtains really keep the light out?		

Washrooms, toilets and storage

In inner Sydney in 1998, we were organizing a SpeakOut workshop to discuss a highly contentious local issue. Temperatures were running high in the neighbouring community. We had been negotiating for several months between Indigenous and non-Indigenous people about the future use and development of strategically located community land. The night before the workshop, which was to be held in an old building on the site, one of our helpers asked if there were toilets there. A quick last-minute phone call to the hiring company averted that potential disaster. In spite of all our carefully designed checklists, *we* forgot the basics. In the rush of organizing a SpeakOut or workshop, it's an easy thing to do, which is why we've made a separate category for toilets.

Not all portable toilets or washrooms are accessible for people with a disability but it is certainly necessary to have some toilets on the site of your workshop.

It's always good to provide a place where participants can hang their coats and for the organizers, in particular, to be able to store their belongings (such as handbags, briefcases and laptop computers) in a secure place. This is particularly important in high-crime areas.

Item/issue	*Comments*	☐ √
Are there enough toilets available (especially if using an adaptable venue such as a marquee)?		
Is there an accessible toilet, preferably on the same floor as the function?		
Does the toilet have grab rails?		
Are all the toilet facilities e.g., hand basin, hand dryer, paper towels and toilet paper, within easy reach of a person using a wheelchair?		
Circulation space in the toilet to turn a wheelchair?		
Secure storage space for valuables		
A place to hang long coats		

Telephones

This section is really about communication. We have given telephones a heading simply because of the importance of communication while organizing and managing a community engagement process. Today, almost everyone is a mobile (cell) phone user. But even mobile phones get lost. Once we had to go to a pay phone to ring our mobile phone, which had been buried under a large pile of workshop materials and plans.

Item/issue	Comments	☐ √
Ensure access to a telephone preferably with long distance access. (Make sure that the phone is not in a locked room)		
Produce a list of telephone numbers of all workers and those who may need to be contacted (like police, ambulance and emergency services) on a laminated card that all organizers can carry		
Make sure you have all the relevant telephone numbers with you		
Let the relevant people know your intended movements and ensure that you can be contacted		
Consider hiring a mobile phone if you don't already have one. Ensure that people know your mobile phone number, that it is switched on, fully charged and within range		
Ensure the public phones in the building or on the site are working and have some spare change or a phonecard for participants' calls		

Furniture and other equipment

While furniture is often included in the cost of venue hire, sometimes it needs to be rented separately. It is essential that the hired furniture meet your needs. Long trestle-type tables (over 2m in length) which often come with venues, are a real problem: the distance from one end to another makes conversation impossible without speaking very loudly. This creates acoustic problems for other groups. It can also create the sense of a 'hierarchy': who is in charge or at the 'head' of the table?

Remember that comfortable furniture (especially seating) can greatly increase your participants' ability to engage with the material you are presenting to them and to work collaboratively. And it is a mark of respect to consider their comfort.

Item/issue	Comments	☐ √
Round tables for workshop sessions (not too large) Avoid long, rectangular tables		
Small lectern for speakers		
Small tables for SpeakOut stalls that do not take up too much space in front of displays		
Small raised stage or podium for workshops and meetings		
Comfortable chairs		
Tables for drinks and food		
Reception table		
Access to a photocopier		
Tables to lay out materials and equipment before distributing to tables		

Registration desk

The welcoming process

At its most fundamental, a workshop or SpeakOut is a welcoming process: new residents are welcomed by organizers and the listeners and recorders (in a SpeakOut model). Feeling 'received' is an essential ingredient. You may be dealing with fairly large numbers of adults and children, so some measure of queuing design and 'crowd control' will be necessary to ensure that there is not a long line of people waiting (possibly in poor weather) to come inside.

At the registration desk, new arrivals will have to be advised of how a SpeakOut or workshop works. You will need to have a staffed welcoming desk in a highly visible position. Participants will also need to be confident that their children are being well taken care of. Your helpers should be trained to allay these potential fears.

The registration desk is often the first point of contact for the community with a public forum, workshop or SpeakOut. Listeners and recorders must be on hand to welcome participants and assist them to settle in. The people staffing the registration desk must be hospitable, friendly, efficient and welcoming. It's good to have extra people to assist with orientation, as most workers will be occupied at their SpeakOut stalls.

Congestion is always a problem at the registration desk. One way to handle this in a workshop context is to ensure that workshop table facilitators and recorders 'hover' around the registration desk and escort participants (whom they identify by coloured dots on their nametags) to their tables. In this way, participants are assisted in finding their workshop table, while clearing the space around the reception desk. This approach will not work for SpeakOut processes, however.

Figure 5.5 Welcoming smiles and pre-dotted blank nametag labels for a workshop

Item/issue	Comments	☐ √
Locate the reception desk to facilitate queuing and reduce congestion		
Locate the desk to permit surveillance of it from the main room once the workshop or SpeakOut has started so that a separate person is not required to 'mind' it		
Provide protection so that participants do not have to queue outside in harsh weather		
Have people who speak key local languages available to interpret and ask them to wait around the reception desk		
Have at least two friendly and welcoming people at the reception desk		
Clear signs ('please register here')		
Labels or nametags for participants. Don't pre-prepare them, as it's far quicker to write them as participants show up or ask participants to write their own names		
Thick pens for nametags		
Coloured dots to identify different table allocations for workshops		
Information for participants to read while they are waiting for proceedings to begin		
You may wish to hand participants a short questionnaire to fill out before proceedings begin		
Take-home material for participants		
Summary of project objectives or summary of how the SpeakOut or workshop will work		

Depending on the expected size of the workshop or SpeakOut, two tables and at least two people to assist with registration may be required. In small communities, everyone may come at the same time (especially if lunch is provided). So it's wise to have lots of people on hand to greet them and explain the process.

We have found that preparing nametags in advance is more trouble than it is worth. Unless it is a very formal occasion, most people are quite happy making their own nametag.

Drinks on arrival

We have found it useful to have drinks available when people arrive. Often people come to these events after a rushed day at work, dinner preparations or with their families and need a 'cuppa' to settle them down. The volunteer can offer a cup of tea or coffee as a welcoming gesture. An urn can be bubbling away in a corner of the room at the beginning of the workshop.

Moving the registration desk inside after the workshop begins

There will always be late arrivals. In a workshop situation, after the workshop begins, the registration desk should be moved to an indoor location (with appropriate signs from the outside identifying its location) so that the person staffing the desk can also help with other duties, as directed by the Coordinator (or Director) chairing the workshop. This is because you will almost certainly not want that one person to be totally occupied staffing the desk. For example, they could take notes from that position or even act as a second photographer.

In the case of a SpeakOut, essentially a drop-in event, you can't move the registration desk, as people need to be able to see it when they are deciding whether to participate.

Audio and visual equipment

Unless available for hire from the venue, most audio and visual equipment will need to be hired from an outside provider. This can be an expensive option, so it's best to exhaust all other options before hiring equipment. The venue may have a preferred or regular supplier who knows the location well.

Make sure that all equipment is carefully tested. This applies particularly to borrowed equipment, which may have been damaged in transit.

For details of audio and video recording, see Chapter 13.

Item/issue	Comments	☐ √
Check well in advance that all A/V systems operate correctly and have helpers available		
Projector (check the quality and compatibility with the laptops you intend to use)		
Overhead or other projector		
Public address system (microphones and amplifiers)		
Roving microphones for audience participation in workshops		
Screen, white sheet or panel on a wall to project images onto. Screens are often awkward and something simpler (like a sheet) can work just as well		

SpeakOuts have very specific furniture requirements which differ from those of workshops.

A box of essential materials

During a SpeakOut or a workshop, the success of staff and volunteers in carrying out their tasks depends largely on having the essential materials provided and ready to use. A checklist of necessary materials below has helped us in creating a successful event. Having a volunteer to help as a gofer who is constantly checking whether facilitators or recorders need more materials throughout a workshop or SpeakOut can be a tremendous help.

Figure 5.6 A box of essential materials

On each workshop table or at each SpeakOut stall:

- cardboard or plastic boxes to hold equipment and materials
- ball point pens for sign-up and feedback sheets
- coloured dots
- reusable adhesive
- scissors
- wedge-tipped, thick markers (black, green, red and blue)
- pencils and crayons[3]
- masking tape
- glue sticks.

In reserve:

- adhesive contact (clear)
- drawing pins
- Velcro dots and strips
- gaffer (duct) tape is great for sticking down cables. Use bright colours such as yellow for additional safety
- coloured paper or card for cutting up
- tracing/detail paper
- rulers/scales
- hooks and eyes for hanging materials
- butcher's paper
- hammer and nails
- sheets of letter or A4 sized paper
- sheets of A3 sized paper
- large and bold badges to identify: staff; project team members; facilitators or listeners; recorders; and participants (names and perhaps the group or community they represent)
- extension cords
- double adaptors.

The *inner circuit*

Once participants arrive, receive a warm welcome and explanations about what to do and expect in the process in the *outer circuit*, they will start visiting the *inner circuit*. In a SpeakOut, the main component of the *inner circuit* is the issue stalls. As mentioned earlier, a SpeakOut is usually organized as one stage in a larger or wider process. Thus, for the most part, issue stalls in a SpeakOut display work in progress, pose related issues or problems and probe related questions to gain feedback. Each component in the *inner circuit* is explained in the remainder of this chapter.

Presentation and display boards

In community planning and design, one of the objectives of participatory processes is to share basic and important information pertaining to the plan or design under consideration. In our experience, presenting information using big and bold letters, as well as images and interactive activities, is effective. Any reports need to be summarized and big words or jargon need paraphrasing to help communicate a clear message. This type of presentation appeals to participants, as it is easy to understand and in many cases can trigger more meaningful discussions than can complex material.

Use foamboard, cardboard or large sheets of paper on walls to create display boards that can be written or drawn on.

Issues and questions

Depending on the communities for which the SpeakOut or workshop is organized, it is important to rephrase issues and questions to reinforce clarity. This is particularly critical in multicultural communities (which is now almost every community in which we work!) for participants who may have language and cultural barriers that keep them from fully understanding complex issues and questions presented in English. Presenting these issues and questions using simple images, pictograms or clipart helps to communicate the message. This is because most people process visual images faster than they process the printed word. These representations are particularly useful for interactive exercises or activities where they are presented in the form of questions.

Item/issue	Comments	☐ √
Convert all technical language and jargon into plain words		
Translate key material into local languages		
Use images, clipart and pictograms wherever possible		
Ask for advice about presenting material in languages other than English		

Moving through the *inner circuit* of a SpeakOut is a process of participants determining what to pay attention to and what to ignore. In our SpeakOuts, we design and create every issue stall to make it easy for participants to make decisions about how to participate. They will want to decide which issue they want to learn more about and share their thoughts on. Although all participants are encouraged to visit all issue stalls, some may choose to visit only one or two. Therefore, selecting stalls needs to be a simple decision from the start. It's critical that participants do not feel that they are being forced to wander through a long route to reach those stalls (and speak out about the issues) that most interest them.

For participants to have the most enjoyable and satisfying experience, they must be able to follow easily the sequence of displays and activities at each issue stall. Directions from each stall's listeners and recorders can foster an easy circulation of participants. It's important to design a diagram of the flow (or circulation), as well as a diagram for each issue stall before putting up presentations and display boards. A clear diagram helps lessen confusion on all sides.

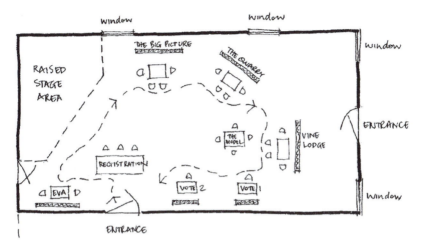

Figure 5.7 A simple issue stall layout where voting will occur

Figure 5.8 SpeakOut stalls offering some privacy, Redfern, 1998

Stall essentials

A SpeakOut stall is not a complex matter. As the following images show, the components are very simple:

1 A stall number and sign
2 A place where illustrative materials pertaining to one topic can be displayed
3 A place for vertical scribing of participants' comments
4 A small table and seating
5 Displays of photographs, materials and summaries of previous studies or engagement activities
6 Display of participants' comments from this SpeakOut
7 Space and materials for interactive activities (see Chapter 6).

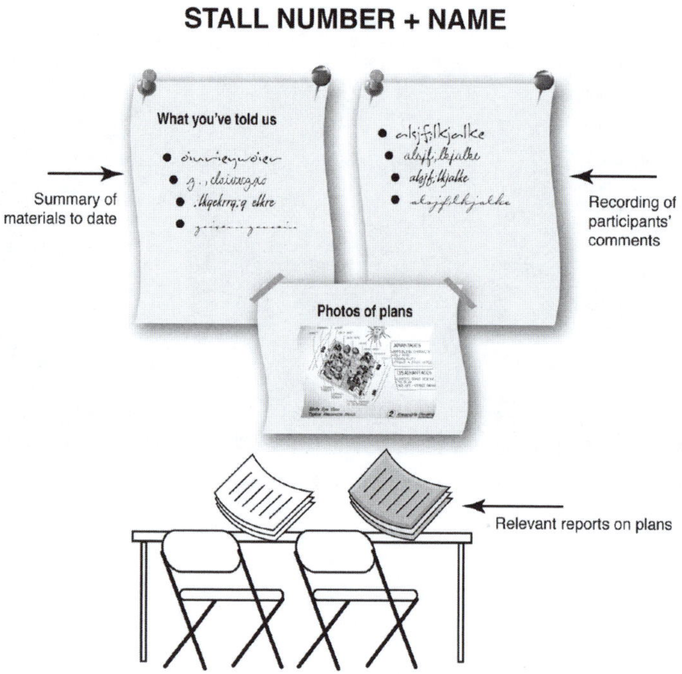

Figure 5.9 The basics of a SpeakOut stall

Interactive activities

At each stall, interactive activities are an essential part of the SpeakOut process. They are discussed in Chapter 6.

Figure 5.10 A huge amount of recording at the safety stall, Eagleby, 2000

Ending on time is important

People who still want to talk

In our experience, there are always people who do not want to leave workshops of this type. Listeners and recorders in SpeakOuts and workers in workshops will have to leave for their debriefing meeting. Thus, the best advice we can give is to use the 'green sheets' (comment sheets) for this purpose to conclude: ask these participants to fill out their concerns or comments and a responsible person will get back to them. Ensure that all 'green sheets' are placed in the questionnaire box or given to a facilitator.

Ending, debriefing and socializing phase

Some facilitators and participants will want to stay and speak to participants who linger. This often creates a problem with the timing of the debriefing session, as other facilitators and those who have worked through the day are tired and wish to leave. It may be possible to have a volunteer deployed to speak to 'hangers-on' while others are being debriefed. When the time comes to begin the debriefing meeting, all participants will have to have left.

Arrangements for debriefing

Debriefing is regarded as an essential part of the SpeakOut or workshop process. It must not be left out of the process, as this is where very important process and content issues which do not come up can be raised. The improvement and eventual refinement of any model depends on the information that these trained people can give directly after a SpeakOut or workshop. Some guidelines will ensure that the debriefing session is as effective as possible:

- Select a quiet table away from noise and cleaning up: in a separate room or at least in a corner.
- Select one person to take notes (preferably someone who has not been recording throughout the event).
- Ensure that all listeners, recorders, facilitators and others are paid for debriefing.
- Put a time frame around the debriefing so that people will know how long they will have to spend.
- Use the debriefing time to hand out payment sheets so that workers can write down their hours and, if possible, receive cheques on the spot for their work.
- Acknowledge that these people will be exhausted. Therefore, try to get feedback in 'advice' or 'recommendations' mode as quickly as possible, so that they can leave. Ensure that everyone who facilitated or worked on the event has some way to give feedback, even if they fill out a short form.

Arrangements for cleaning up

A separate person (from the SpeakOut or workshop manager) should be responsible for supervising and ensuring that cleaning up occurs, as the other two will be too exhausted. It is critical that the clean-up be carried out thoroughly. Often you will be relying on the hospitality of an organization which owns or operates the venue; they are likely to be very concerned if it is left in an untidy state.

Losing things

At this stage precious things get lost, especially signs and props which are intended for reuse. The clean-up person would have a list of all things which are to be reused. If participants want to take 'mementos' they should be dissuaded and site plans and other information can be sent to them later (use green sheets for this).

Interactive Activities

By Wendy Sarkissian with Andrea Cook and Steph Vadja

In Chapter 5, we described the essential components of a SpeakOut. Refinement of the model has yielded many changes and innovations.[1] Interactive activities can be highly effective during a SpeakOut or as components of other processes. They offer a variety of enjoyable and informal ways to collect information and perceptions, while building community capacity. Figure 6.1 shows how they could be set up in a SpeakOut stall.

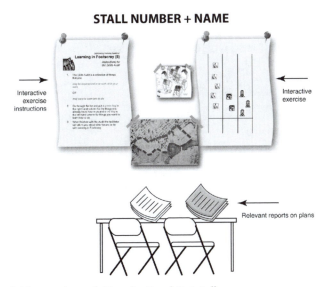

Figure 6.1 Interactive activities at a SpeakOut stall

A smorgasbord of interactive activities

Described below are interactive activities that could be used in a SpeakOut context, as well as in a workshop.

Audits and other information-collection activities

Accessibility audit

This interactive activity focuses on areas within a community that are not accessible because they are not known about or seen. This is especially useful when completing needs assessments and services audits.

Building a 'fun' graph

Participants are invited to build sections of a large 'bar graph' with picto-graph symbols representing how they enjoy different types of recreation. Each participant is given a symbol, with a space to write comments; these are added to the 'bar graph' under the category. This provides an indication of preferred ways of enjoying community life.

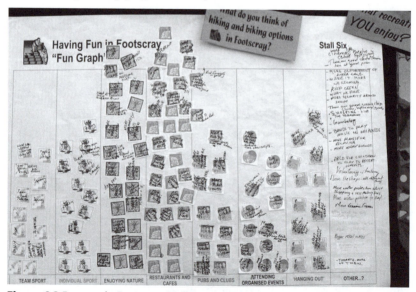

Figure 6.2 Fun graph, Footscray, Melbourne, 2004

Skills audit

Based on principles of Appreciative Inquiry (AI) and asset-based community development (ABCD),[2] this participatory activity enables participants to identify skills they are interested in learning and/or sharing. This is achieved via an interactive graph showing a comprehensive range of skill areas. Participants are invited to place a tick next to areas of interest and also indicate skills they wish to share. A recent modification has new categories to reduce the risk of exclusion: 'I am *highly skilled* and I could possibly teach it', 'I am *moderately skilled* and would like to become more "expert"' and 'I am a *keen beginner* at this and would like to learn more'.

Figure 6.3 Skills audit, Braybrook, Melbourne, 2005

Children's activities

Face-painting interviews

Using face-painting, we can gather general information on a one-to-one basis about children's activities and perceptions of their everyday environments. The sensation of paint being applied to the face helps the child relax and helps to engage the child's imagination. It is best used when comments are required from younger children. It is a perfect technique to undertake a detailed discussion or interview. Young children aged between 3 and 7 years enjoy participating in this process. One facilitator (face-painter) is needed to work with each child.

Children are invited to have their faces painted. The face-painter engages the child individually in a conversation about their environment or the issue being discussed, referring to a set of pre-prepared questions. The facilitator gains inspiration for the painted design from the conversation. A digital or tape recorder is used. The face-painting takes about 15 to 20 minutes, including the discussion. Facilitators are debriefed after the event and the transcript analysed.

Film interviews

Interviews with children can be conducted indoors, under a tree or in a convenient quiet or shady area separate from the busy SpeakOut. Interviews are sought with all participating children to maximize their opportunities to explain why particular ideas are important and relevant to the SpeakOut topic. Permission must be sought from parents or guardians to film and photograph children.

Neighbourhood drawings

This activity involves younger children (and children waiting to build models) in creating a neighbourhood drawing. It is best to use a pre-printed drawing sheet with half devoted to a drawing of how they see their neighbourhood now and the other half devoted to how they wish to see it in the future. Careful note-taking aids further analysis.

Random object modelling

Facilitators help children create three-dimensional models of their design and spatial preferences using random objects such as clay, sticks, glitter, Plasticine, dirt, etc. The outcomes can be astonishing. Using a trained arts facilitator increases opportunities for developing models that truly reflect children's values and interests and in eliciting spoken or written descriptions. Modellers can also be interviewed on film, discussing their model or telling a story about it.

Sketch interviews with children

Here children describe their engagement with Nature, open space needs, priorities and location of features in open space, as well as their overall planning and design preferences. Facilitators record children's stories and explanations as they draw. The sketch interview stall should be located away from noisy activities to reduce distractions and ensure that conversations can be heard and recorded. Sketches can be posted up in the SpeakOut for all to see.

Figure 6.4 Drawing by Bella, age 9

Facilitator summary: Bella depicts the street across from the SpeakOut with shops, the road and the fence in front of the community house. In her future drawing, Bella wants to see a pool, as there is only an outdoor pool now. Bella would like a playground (swings and a slide). She would like school to be closer to where people live so they don't have to travel so far (Bella goes to school in Lilydale where her mum works.) She would like people to come and stay and a big welcome sign and a motel are in the future drawing.

A 'Week with a Camera'

A 'Week with a Camera' activity is usually undertaken in conjunction with one or several primary schools during a community engagement process. In one example, more than 180 children were given disposable cameras and asked to photograph what was important to them in their neighbourhood, following a briefing session in the classroom. The children were encouraged to photograph 'things that they would like to keep' and 'things that they would like to change'.

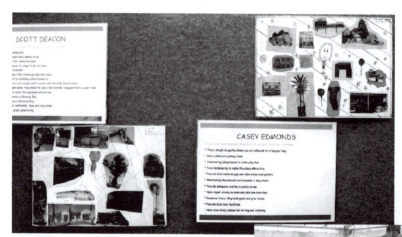

Figure 6.5 Display of children's 'Week with a Camera' collages, Port Kennedy, Western Australia, 2003

'Week with a Camera' photos are then incorporated into collages in an intensive, facilitated workshop and displayed at the SpeakOut. This display works well to attract parents specifically to see their children's handiwork.

Recording children's SpeakOut and workshop results

Drawings, paintings and models are always photographed before children take them home. Children are always given a certificate of appreciation to acknowledge their participation.

Design games

Design games can take many forms and are often helpful at the 'options' stage of a project. For example, they can be used for working on a preferred option and then work 'on the plan' to refine and annotate the option. Annotated notes from each participant's redesign are then summarized in the reporting and used to assess community responses to options. Sometimes this approach reveals a new option that had not yet been considered.

Health check

A small stall near the SpeakOut entry could allow for participants to take part in a basic health check. Results of the health check could be anonymously mapped and displayed, thus allowing individual participants to compare their perceptions of their state of health with health check results.

Housing 'building block' exercise

Density block modelling

The activity is well suited to exploring site-planning, housing layout and density issues. Participants work with facilitators using coloured Lego™ building blocks to represent different heights, densities and design elements they want included in the future vision or project. Building blocks are placed on tracing paper over large aerial photographs, which can then be annotated.

Figure 6.6 Density block modelling, Bonnyrigg, Sydney, 2005

Participants' models are photographed and their comments recorded on large sheets of paper.[3]

After each participant builds their density model, it is photographed and the base map cleared for the next participant. This proved a useful exercise in a neighbourhood with redevelopment and planning pressures for increased densities and community concerns and anxieties. It allowed participants to express their views about where higher density development was acceptable and what they saw as appropriate height limits.

Housing survey

Participants share basic information, such as household size and the percentage of their income spent on rent or mortgage by building a bar graph.

Another housing survey activity invites participants to share their reasons for living in their community (the things they like and dislike). Using a list of reasons, participants place a plus (+) symbol next to the reason they like and a minus symbol (–) next to the reason they don't like or would like to change.

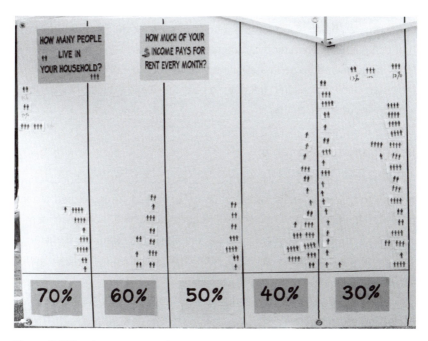

Figure 6.7 Housing survey graph

Intergenerational letter-writing

Participants explain to people from different generations what it's like today to live in a community, what their needs are and to explore in a creative and visionary way their ideas for creating better relationships among members of different generations. Letters and diaries can later be analysed.

Interviews with parents

Interviews can be held at tables and chairs set up in front of the SpeakOut space. Interviewers use 'input sheets' and interpretative materials to develop an understanding of parents' perspectives related to the children's environments (in one case, a children's garden) and children's needs in general.

Questions can be aligned with the inquiry framework guiding the project so that comparable information can be received from both children and adults. Listening to the adults separately allows facilitators to work with children on their own, allowing children freedom to be creative and express their personal views without adult 'editing'.

Issues/opportunities table

Participants are invited to comment on issues, opportunities and/or solutions relating to the topic under consideration. Comments are structured around predetermined issues and objectives. For each issue, participants can identify an issue or opportunity, where it occurs and a potential solution. Participants can also suggest solutions for other issues. This activity is suitable for young participants, as well as older ones.

Mapping exercises

Many mapping exercises can be used at SpeakOuts. The two essential components are a facilitator familiar with the local area and a high-quality orthophoto map with streets and landmarks clearly labelled. Participants' preferences can be drawn on a laminated map, with a photo taken before the map is wiped clean for the next participant.

Annotated maps are valuable for revealing personal perceptions and assessments. We have encouraged participants to map 'preferred' retail precincts (i.e., what they would like to see in the future). Mapping exercises often contribute to SpeakOut stalls being extremely busy.

Mapping 'where you live'

At the registration desk, participants can be asked to place a dot on a large, labelled, laminated map or aerial orthophoto to show where they live. Participants living beyond the boundaries of the photograph put dots around the border. This is a surprisingly effective exercise, a good 'ice breaker' and introduces participants to the interactive format of the SpeakOut and the role of facilitators. This process has the further advantage of identifying gaps in the geographical representation of SpeakOut participants.

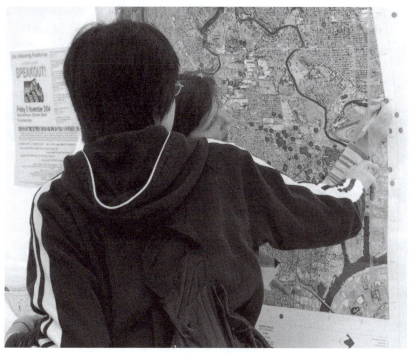

Figure 6.8 Marking where I live, Footscray, Melbourne, 2005

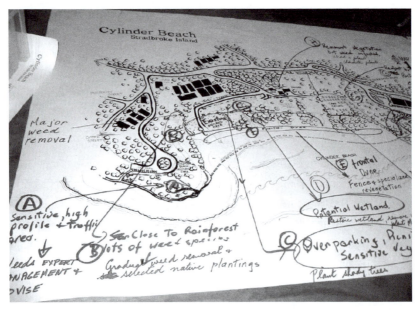

Figure 6.9 An annotated map of recreation issues, Cylinder Beach, Queensland, 2003

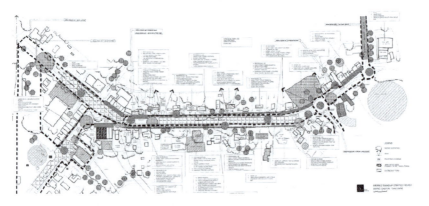

Figure 6.10 Summary of community mapping advice, Emerald, Melbourne, 2007

Interactive community safety mapping

This activity provides a good indication of perceived safe and unsafe areas. Each participant places red dots on small maps representing where they feel unsafe and green dots representing where they feel safe. The dots are later collated and analysed to show perceived community safety 'hotspots'.

Mapping sacred spaces and hated spaces

In a redevelopment context, participants are prompted with instructions to consider 'sacred spaces' (elements of the community or the environment to keep) and 'hated spaces' (elements of the community or environment to change) and their ideas for change. Participants' comments are recorded onto maps or plans of the local area.

Mapping social networks

Participants can map their social networks relevant to their language groups. This requires the help of a bilingual facilitator.

Roaming range maps

Participants are asked to map out their 'roaming range' (i.e., where they travel to on foot, by bicycle, on public transport). This is a useful tool for developing composite pictures of how public spaces are used (or avoided). Participants are invited to mark on individual A4 size (or letter size) maps their usual and preferred routes for walking, cycling and for using public transport, while describing current issues or difficulties they experience with local transportation modes. Maps can then be posted in the SpeakOut stall.

Why I leave my community

This mapping exercise encourages participants to determine why they leave their community on a daily (or long-term) basis. For this activity, a large, high-quality aerial photograph is displayed and participants write their reasons for leaving the area on arrows that are then placed around the edges of the map.

Figure 6.11 Roaming maps, Footscray, Melbourne, 2004

Figure 6.12 Why I leave my community? Bonnyrigg, Sydney, 2005

Young participants' maps

In this participatory activity, young participants can map where they hang out in public space, what they do and would like to do there.

Mind mapping

Mind mapping lends itself well to numerous community engagement contexts. In SpeakOuts, participants can be asked to provide their ideas about the guiding principles for a project. They can add their own information to a large posted 'mind map' and/or add a coloured 'vote' dot to a principle already raised (at previous workshops or at the SpeakOut itself).

Postcards to this place

At the 'Where to from Here?' activity stall, a 'postcards to this place' activity could be used. Participants record their final comments as they leave the SpeakOut. At this stall, participants could leave their entry form, received at registration, for a prize draw.

Sandbox modelling

Drawing on the powerful therapeutic sand-play model, this activity allows participants to model and remodel parks or public spaces. Or even their whole imaginary environment, visualized and then created in the small sandbox. While this activity is often used with children, it can easily be tailored for adults. In one exercise children were asked to build a perfect community.

The activity is facilitated and each model is annotated and recorded by a facilitator. Where permission is given by parents and caregivers, we take photos of the child with their sandbox model. Alternatively, a photo is taken of the annotated model by itself. Great care must be taken in selecting the objects used in the sandbox. Lots of small objects are needed to maximize creativity. Warning: as these small items are prohibitively expensive, it's good to keep an eye on them throughout the process.

Figure 6.13 Preparing for sandbox exercise and the actual exercise, Braybrook, Melbourne, 2005

SpeakOut passport

To help explain to participants how the SpeakOut works and encourage participation at each stall, visitors can be given a 'SpeakOut passport', which explains the issues covered at each stall and offers an opportunity to win a prize. Participants tear out the last page (which has been stamped at each stall) and deposit it in a box. A prize draw occurs later.

Spending your tax dollars

As each participant completes their visit to a SpeakOut stall, the facilitator presents them with a symbolic tax dollar. Before they leave, participants are asked to decide where to allocate their tax money among the various topics discussed at stalls. Participants can deposit their tax dollars in boxes corresponding to the SpeakOut stall topics. They are also encouraged to record a specific suggestion on the back of each of their symbolic tax dollars. This helps organizers understand community preferences related to how community funds should be allocated.

Timeline activity

This activity is centred on the question: 'When did you arrive to live in this community?' Participants write the year or place a sticky dot by the date they arrived along a timeline posted on the wall. As the SpeakOut progresses, it becomes clear how long community members have lived in this locality.

Visual preference survey

This can be an extension of a more comprehensive photo and preference survey conducted in public spaces. The survey is visual in that participants are asked to examine photographs of spaces and respond to them. This initially involves a straightforward rating exercise, where participants rate the space on a scale of 1 (really dislike) to 10 (really like). In the second part of the survey, participants indicate their preferences for three sets of photos, stating where they would most like to live/shop/play and where they would least like to live/shop/play.

This form of information gathering can also be successfully used with children and young participants. This exercise is also useful in communities with high proportions of non-English speakers.

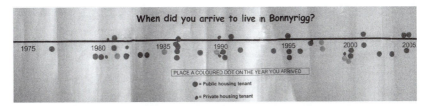

Figure 6.14 When did you arrive to live in Bonnyrigg? 2005

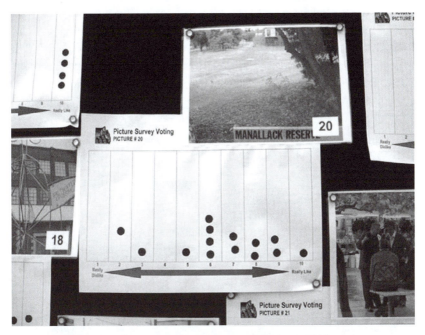

Figure 6.15 Visual preference survey, Footscray, Melbourne, 2004

Figure 6.16 What residents want in Bonnyrigg, Sydney, 2005

Picturing what residents want

In picturing what residents want, participants chose from a range of symbols representing some thing or things that they particularly want (or don't want) in a project, a public space or in their community generally. The images are then affixed to a large sheet of paper. Participants or the recorder record a brief statement about what each symbol represents.

Voting

Many of the SpeakOuts we have organized have had formal voting components. In one Queensland community, participants selected among competing proposals for the design of a city square. In another SpeakOut, in a small village in rural New South Wales, participants voted for their preferred development options. A very formal process of counting ballots was held at the conclusion of the SpeakOut.

Engagement voting activity

The question here is: 'How would you like to be engaged with this project or process?' A participatory voting activity uses a large piece of paper marked up with a table showing a list of engagement options or issues in the left column and space in the right column for participants to place dots to vote for that option or issue.

Another engagement activity involves the use of symbols to represent different physical activities that are possible in local public spaces. These symbols could also be placed on aerial photos or maps to identify specific preferences for activities or facilities in public spaces.

Voting for preferred ways of participating in the community

Voting exercises can include voting for preferred ways of engagement, voting for types of community engagement processes and events, where they should be conducted, who should be included and how often they should be held.

Voting could also be used to assess public spaces that are currently under-utilized, asking participants how these local, smaller-scale spaces could be better used.

Video blogging

As one of the final SpeakOut stalls, a video blogging space can be set up to offer individual or group privacy so that people can talk about their issues and needs to an inconspicuously placed video camera. Participants can speak for as little or as long as they like and be left alone if desired. With participants' permission, video blogs can then be projected onto a screen located in a small marquee on the other side of the event.

Using film, particularly where there is opportunity for private space for the camera, provides another medium for participants to share their perspectives and also provides great marketing materials. Getting participants to sign permission forms is a vital component of successful video blogging within a SpeakOut.

'Vote with Your Hands'

This simple voting exercise creates colour and vibrancy at the start of the SpeakOut. The process is briefly described here and in detail in Chapter 8.

Participants can vote for categories/issues that interest them most using different paint colours to represent those issues. Participants create a hand-print in a specific colour to indicate their interest in an issue (for example, arts and culture). A legend corresponds to each colour and participants annotate their handprint with comments about their 'vote'. Participants can also use colours corresponding to the 'Vote with Your Hands' to mark a small map to show the desirable locations. Each colour can represent a different aspect of the community which participants value, such as: a clean environment, parks and playgrounds, people, public buildings, schools, churches, temples and other religious buildings and shopping centres.

Speakouts for Children

By Steph Vadja and Yollana Shore

Introduction

This chapter introduces SpeakOuts for children and describes a successful SpeakOut conducted in Queensland in 2007.

Sadly, children are often excluded from formal community engagement processes or 'entertained', rather than being truly engaged. This is not only sad for the children, but also sad for the developers, the council, proponents and communities, including all adults, who miss children's unique, creative and insightful perspectives. A huge body of literature from research and practice reinforces the validity and importance of community engagement processes with children. It has been summarized well in other publications, including an earlier volume in this Earthscan suite of books on community planning, *Kitchen Table Sustainability: Practical Recipes for Community Engagement with Sustainability* (2008). In this chapter, we accept that there is no need to restate the case for engaging with children. Rather, we present a recent, successful example from practice.

Participatory processes for children

Considering SpeakOuts from a child's point of view can enhance the SpeakOut for adults. It involves making things simpler and more fun, which, in turn, makes them more accessible and engaging. We have found that **S**imple, **A**ccessible, **F**un and **E**ngaging (**SAFE**) activities appeal to people of all ages and backgrounds.

SAFE SpeakOuts for children

In addition to incorporating child-friendly and accessible activities in SpeakOuts, it is possible to design **SAFE** SpeakOuts specifically for children. (Activities from the children's SpeakOut can be adapted back into adult SpeakOuts.) In the **SAFE** SpeakOut, we take each element, apply the **SAFE** test and seek creative ways to make it simpler, accessible, fun and engaging.

Keep it simple: silly!

The process of designing interpretative materials for a children's SpeakOut, as well as the activities and the SpeakOut itself, is an engaging and creative challenge. Adults sometimes have a way of complicating things. The truth is, if we cannot rephrase in simple language, we are not that clever after all. Interpretative materials for a children's SpeakOut need to be simple to allow children to be creators of complex outcomes that can be interpreted on a number of levels.

Accessible and age-appropriate

When planning a children's SpeakOut, it is important to be clear about the ages you plan to cater for and how you will do that. Considering children's motor skills, coordination, attention spans, heights and weights ensures that both the range of processes adopted and the physical design of the space are suitable for your target age group. With interpretative materials and signage, again, if it cannot be said simply, it's not worth saying!

We need to acknowledge different stages in children's knowledge and under-standing of Nature when designing environments to suit their needs. While children, like adults, are not a homogeneous group, they nevertheless do exhibit common characteristics related to their ages. The stages in knowledge relevant to children and their uses and perceptions of the urban environment can be summarized as follows:

1 *Pre-operational period*, from age two to seven: The child forms a mental representation of the environment; there is a gradual development of knowledge of spatial properties: their 'action-space'.
2 *Concrete operation period*, ages seven to ten: The child makes map-like representations and can reverse routes.
3 *Formal operations period*, early adolescence: The adolescent coordinates thoughts about the spatial environment, engages in abstract thinking and can take short cuts.

Exploratory behaviour is very important to the child. As the young child grows in confidence, it draws away from 'mother' in ways that are antithetic to attachment.

Accommodating different types of play is an important function of any environment. While some types of play are essential for socialization (parallel, associative and cooperative play), children of all ages also have a strong need for solitary play. We must provide for a variety of play to enable children to develop to their full potential.

Our planning of SpeakOuts for children must support four types of play, listed below and explained in Table 7.1.

- physical play: skill practice, control, experimentation
- social play: social skills, language, cooperation
- creative and cognitive play: test ideas, exercise ingenuity, manipulate objects, use curiosity
- solitary play: quiet retreat, playing along, intimate spaces, away from noisy, boisterous activities.

Table 7.1 What are children learning as they play?

Every kind of play is a learning opportunity for children. Here are some typical play activities and what children learn through them:

Age group	Type of activity	What's being learned
Infants	Play and inter-action with others	• Peek-a-boo and other interactive games: Children learn 'object permanence': that objects do not mysteriously disappear into thin air just because they cannot be seen • Back and forth interaction: Children, adults making sounds, imitating baby, singing, talking back and forth, is amusing for babies. They learn language and the give and take of being social
	Play with objects	Children learn that their actions get a response: shaking, squeezing, tapping objects can produce sound or make objects move (cause and effect)
Toddlers	Finger-play and singing games	Children learn rhythm, counting and eye–hand coordination. These types of games also teach cultural norms. Many young children know childhood songs and games by the time they are in preschool or kindergarten

Age group	Type of activity	What's being learned
Preschoolers	Blocks	Block play teaches many maths concepts and skills such as: counting, length, height, patterns, symmetry
	Manipulative toys	Materials such as Play-Doh, threading beads, and stacking and nesting toys help children with their fine motor skills and eye–hand coordination
	Sand and water play	While being fun and soothing to the touch, sand and water play teaches maths skills such as measurement and helps children practice pouring skills
	Puzzles	Puzzles help children with abstract thinking skills and visualizing space and how shapes fit together
	Dramatic play	Older children love to pretend they are heroes, parents, or other adults doing 'grown-up' things. Dramatic play helps children with their language skills and can be a creative outlet. Children can practise life skills like grocery shopping or having a party. It's a good way for children to learn to cooperate with others as well
School-age	Group games	School-age children engage in more group play, which is usually more structured and may have rules. These are team games such as soccer, baseball, or less organized games such as hide-and-seek, tag and kick ball. Children this age also like board games with rules. These games allow children to develop independence, yet learn cooperation with others and to be part of a group
	Dramatic play	School-age children also engage in dramatic play or fantasy play. Still pretending and acting out real life or 'fantasy' play, dramatic or pretend play gives children a chance to be creative and interact with other children

Source: www.childcareaware.org/en/subscriptions/dailyparent/volume.php?id=50

Fun, fun fun!

You cannot design a children's SpeakOut without being in touch with your inner child! Children are playful, silly and eager to explore, discover and create. They are also fast workers and easily become bored. It's important to design a range of activities that are creative and fun and allow children to feel they are discovering something new.

Engaging

Gaining the most from children requires engaging processes. Participants need to be interested in the activities and content, the ways they interact with it and the potential outcomes. Activities that are colourful, textural, changing, involve interaction, manipulation and a combination of thinking and physically creating are highly successful with children. While all children's SpeakOuts should include these basic *SAFE* elements, they can vary greatly in terms of size and number of stalls, design style, types of activities and involvement with other events or activities. The case study described below illustrates one example of how a children's SpeakOut can unfold.

Case study: A children's SpeakOut in Australia

As far as we are aware, the first child-focused SpeakOut was held in 2007 to assist the Gold Coast City Council in South-East Queensland to gather community contributions for the design of a children's garden to be created as part of the Gold Coast Regional Botanic Gardens in Benowa. It was designed and managed by Plan C, a Brisbane-based cultural planning firm by which Steph Vajda was employed. It aimed to be a child-friendly variation of more traditional SpeakOut approaches. With the assistance of Council officers Amanda Lake and Kate Heffernan, the Plan C team, including Jim Gleeson (managing director), Steph (SpeakOut manager), Abbie Trott (assistant manager), Scott Shearer (engagement assistant), Hayley Ward (engagement assistant), Shelley Waterhouse (film) and Tasmin Waterhouse (photography), designed, planned, conducted and evaluated the SpeakOut. Specialist arts facilitators also managed specific activities.

More than 150 children and 30 adults participated in the children's SpeakOut, held to coincide with the *Gardens Alive Festival*. Facilitators reported that 'the children loved it!' and that adults truly respected the process and valued their children's participation.

Through this SpeakOut, the Council sought contributions about:

- spatial design, including opportunities and constraints related to the site
- children's general environmental and activity needs
- visions for the elements of the garden that were most valued and required
- a vision for the overall garden's design, location and relationships to other elements of the Botanic Gardens
- development of design briefs for future development of the garden.

The event was also designed to activate people's interests in the children's garden by making the site accessible to children, their families and friends.

Developing the framework

Through initial research into concepts such as biophilia,[1] synaesthetic response[2] and colour theory, Plan C developed an inquiry framework to ensure that engagement processes sought information consistent with the framework's themes. These included plants, textures and scents, health, built things, secret places and discovery, formal education, accessibility, wildlife and environment, water features, activities and events and materials. This framework was applied to all SpeakOut activities and interactive materials were designed for the entire SpeakOut, as well as associated engagement activities.

Facilitation

A team of facilitators, including sketch artists, modellers, filmographers and photographers, was engaged and Steph worked with them to design creative processes. It is vital to select facilitators who are experienced and skilled in using their creative practices to work with children. We believe that it is more important to select facilitators experienced in working with children than those experienced in using creative processes for planning purposes. Great skill is needed to keep children engaged and productive while still having fun and being stimulated.

The SpeakOut layout

The SpeakOut marquee was located near the future site of the children's garden, in the new Gold Coast Botanic Gardens, a location that helped generate interest and activity in an area that did not yet have everyday use. The SpeakOut was almost entirely housed within a 6 × 9m marquee, with both sides of one wall used for a preference survey inside and a 'Vote with

Figure 7.1 Inside the SpeakOut marquee

Your Hands' activity conducted outside. Film interviews were conducted with children underneath a tree located approximately 10m from this marquee, providing acoustic isolation for high-quality audio recordings.

The *Gardens Alive Festival* included approximately 15 other stalls featuring various gardening related products, processes and information and a stage for announcements, interviews and musical performances. All activities were conducted within the one space, rather than the 'separate stalls' design used for other SpeakOuts.

Design of the marquee

As people approached the SpeakOut, they were met initially with the 'Vote with Your Hands' display. In this activity, children voted for their favourite elements of a children's garden, including native animals and plants, built components, educational activities, edible plants, colours, textures, water features, seating and shade, play spaces, secret spaces and solitary and group spaces. As there was no 'reception desk' as such, facilitators positioned at activities near to the entrance, including 'Vote with Your Hands', needed to be vibrant and engaging, with a 'good spiel' to explain the SpeakOut process to visitors and encourage them to enter.

Figure 7.2 The visual preference survey

Signage at the front and throughout the SpeakOut was large, simple and clear, printed on coloured paper in blocky, comic-style fonts. Inside the marquee were a number of 'stations' for facilitated activities. The visual preference survey, set up around the entranceway and inside three walls, presented images of other children's gardens, play spaces, various plants and colours, general garden layouts, natural and built elements and other related topics. They were used to stimulate children's interest and association about how the garden could look, feel, smell and touch and could be engaged with by adults and children of all ages.

Random object modelling involved facilitators helping children to create three-dimensional models of their garden preferences. A variety of media were used: clay, Plasticine, sticks and paper; the colourful, creative outcomes represented children's priorities for outdoor spaces. Each modeller was filmed discussing their model after it was built.

Sketch interviews with children encouraged children to express their engage-ment with Nature, open space needs, priorities and placement of landscaping and play elements and overall design preferences. Sketch interviews were

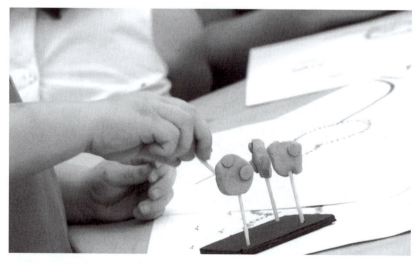

Figure 7.3 Children using their creativity to produce models

located at the opposite corner of the marquee, away from the noisier random modelling activity, to reduce distractions and ensure conversations were audible. The back wall of the marquee was rolled up to maintain ventilation and light, but was roped off to prevent children ducking out. Some sketches were posted up in the SpeakOut afterwards and most drawings, paintings and models were photographed before the children took them home.

All material prepared by children and young people was identified with the child's name, sex and age to facilitate later analysis.

While children were engaging with the activities, parents were able to sit with other facilitators at tables approximately 5m from the front entrance. The *parent interviews* involved facilitators using 'input sheets' and interpretative materials to develop an understanding of parents' perspectives and needs related to a children's garden.

Film interviews

Because of noise and lack of space in the small marquee, *film interviews* were conducted under a tree about 10m from the back of the marquee: a quiet, shady area separate from the busy tent. Interviews were sought with

Figure 7.4 Film interviews under a shady tree behind the SpeakOut marquee

all participating children to maximize opportunities to explain the relevance of their ideas.

Entertainment

Using interactive, organic music as a workshop activity helps children stay in a creative mode, while providing a fun and physical activity as a break. A local percussionist added music to the creative process. This proved highly successful, as children loved the instruments and how they provoked their imaginations.

After the SpeakOut

The remainder of the engagement programme involved interviews with key stakeholders, discussions with Council officers, school workshops and meetings with the Regional Botanic Gardens management, informed by SpeakOut outcomes. Finally, a *Tea in the Park* event was held to present initial findings to the community and to receive further clarification and contributions. More than 100 people reviewed information displayed around the marquee, spoke with facilitators and enjoyed light refreshments.

Subsequent analysis of SpeakOut contributions occurred using the inquiry framework and other processes:

- *children's drawings*: qualitative analysis of each drawing
- *film interviews*: transcription of interviews and analysis of children's needs
- *annotations on the visual preference survey*: compiling of annotations to be included in analysis of preferences
- *voting*: for elements and for the Vote with Your Hands (tallied)
- *input sheets*: lump and split and analysed according to framework
- *photos of models*: qualitative analysis of each model.

Key points emerging from evaluation and debriefing and featured in the report by Plan C for Gold Coast City Council, included:

- A larger space would have been more comfortable.
- Some unmoderated drawing/modelling space would have been valuable as free play space.
- Sandbox modelling would have allowed for design of overall garden size and location.
- Better signage was needed for 'Vote with Your Hands', especially colour coding.
- It's essential to manage printing in-house or be absolutely clear about printing requirements for materials and signs (e.g., the 'Vote with Your Hands' code sheet should not be laminated so that colours mixed on the day could be painted on it).[3]

The children's SpeakOut: How to ...

The overarching aim of the children's SpeakOut is to produce a vibrant, engaging and informative space for children to provide vital contributions to their environments. This case study shows how this process can create a child-friendly, creativity-focused space for children's participation in planning, design, development and community development.

A basic framework for producing a children's SpeakOut is set out below in a manual format.

Participants

This model lends itself to participation by children from age 3 to 12 and for parents, grandparents and other guardians or caregivers. The 'drop-in' format maximizes attendance, as people are free to participate at a convenient time and for as long they wish.

A diverse range of activities within the children's SpeakOut (including drawing, speaking, directing, voting and generally engaging with creative activities) allows children of all ages to participate in ways they find most comfortable. There are great advantages in combining the SpeakOut with other events:

increased attendance, decreased marketing costs and the opportunity to focus primarily on the SpeakOut instead of other logistics (like restrooms, catering, parking and access).

When to use

The children's SpeakOut works well where specific feedback or contributions are sought from children, particularly where this involves spatial or conceptual design of public space or the built environment. It is most effectively used in tandem with an existing community event, especially where this is developed to attract family involvement by providing activities for young people and children.

Designing the event

Developing a children's SpeakOut requires the design of processes that interest children to conceptualize the world around them and how they would like it to be – and to do that in creative ways. Tapping into children's senses can be facilitated on a number of different levels, from the initial design of the inquiry framework to achieve the project's objectives, to assembling a team of facilitators and designing the SpeakOut's layout, flow, stalls and activities.

Our model of a children's SpeakOut requires organizing in four main areas through seven key stages, as follows.

Planning

1 Set a date, time and venue for the event.
2 Effective design of an inquiry framework and resultant core themes and activities.
3 Assemble a diverse team of facilitators able to work effectively with children.

Producing

4 Design the layout of the event.

5   Organize logistics including display materials, activity and general management needs, set-up requirements and event management priorities, including how information is to be displayed to maximize children's understanding and engagement.

Conducting

6   Conduct the event.

Evaluating

7   Transparent analysis of event outcomes (including both quantitative and qualitative analysis) to translate children's contributions (without editing) into information relevant to the project deliverables.

Planning a children's SpeakOut

In this section, we provide a summary of points to remember.

Stage 1: Set a date, time and venue for the SpeakOut

Date and time

- wherever possible, combine with other events that are children- or family-focused events
- weekend afternoons work well
- have at least 12 weeks' lead-time from initial concept design.

Venue

- accessible for families with sufficient parking
- pram and wheelchair access
- changing venues for parents with young children
- appropriate spaces for food and drinks
- natural shade
- wet weather protection or option
- electricity supply if required (particularly for catering).

Stage 2a: Establish an inquiry framework

Developing an inquiry framework ensures continuity of information received from engagement activities throughout an entire programme and maximizes the effectiveness of children's participation by focusing on generally understood and interpretable norms, including symbols and colours, to inform project outcomes.

- Establish clear goals aligned to the project outcomes.
- Incorporate use of theory to underpin processes (biophilia, colour theory, etc.).
- Develop information themes to achieve these goals.
- Ensure themes can be translated across all age groups, for overall consistency.
- Develop themes related to core objectives:

    - developing children's understanding of space
    - growing awareness of identity and belonging
    - building children's social understanding
    - building children's connection with Nature
    - gaining contributions that are relevant, applicable and aligned to goals. And

- Test the framework and revise as required with:

    - the project team
    - an advisory/reference group
    - community organizations
    - parents
    - children!

Stage 2b: Design a range of activities

SpeakOut stall design should incorporate a variety of activities to activate children's imaginations and connection to their environment. Activities should be designed for:

Children

- *Visualizing*: via facilitated creative processes that encourage children to imagine beyond what is often considered possible.
- *Creativity*: using processes to produce tangible outcomes, such as a model or drawing, while linking with a narrative to describe the intent, the process, the outcome and its relationship to their view of the world.
- *Preference selection* in relation to project objectives, using a variety of tools such as a visual preference survey, 'Vote with Your Hands' and other voting-style activities to link design with ethics, the natural environment and local and personal priorities.
- Allowing for different *communication styles*: activities involving talking, drawing, selecting, listening, debating and modelling with a variety of ingredients.
- *Quantitative summary* of participants' characteristics, including age, gender, home location, use of project venue/site and any other relevant information (via registration or survey process).
- Giving *children something to take home* to acknowledge their participation: balloons, stickers or interpretative materials. Copies or photographs of drawings or models children created allow them to show their parents or other children how they participated. Older children should be offered opportunities to receive a copy of the report. A child-friendly summary report could be produced for this purpose.

Adults

- Include adults in the planning and management process.
- Often parents or grandparents will participate with children in activities, but sometimes it is useful to have at least one activity that children can complete simply with the facilitator with no other adults present.
- This frees up adults to talk with facilitators, complete surveys, vote for preferences or engage with creative activities themselves.

At this stage, it is important to compile all interpretative materials and signs into a list to enable design to begin as soon as possible. Ensuring signs and materials are designed and printed early maximizes time available for last-minute organizing, marketing and trouble-shooting.

When the framework and activities are developed, an extensive marketing programme can begin. Now it's time for the vital stage of finding facilitators with an appropriate range of skills and experience. While Stage 2b involves some preliminary design of activities, they will not become finalized until facilitators are engaged, as their skills and ideas influence activities that can be conducted.

Stage 3: Assemble a multidisciplinary team of facilitators

- An Event Manager is always required to produce a SpeakOut. The children's SpeakOut is no exception.
- Look for skilled facilitators, experienced in working with children.
- Types of facilitators to engage with:
  - *modellers*: sand, clay, random objects
  - *sketch artists* to interview children and draw what they describe
  - *film interviewers* to capture children's and parents' spoken comments
  - *questionnaire facilitators*, mostly with adults but also with children
  - *painters* and *'Vote with Your Hands' facilitators*
  - *clowns or other costumed characters* who are also able to work within the inquiry framework and engage with children.
- It is generally a legal requirement that all facilitators and event workers working with children have current and valid certification to do so. This needs to be resolved well before the event, as the application process can be time-consuming.

- After assembling a team of facilitators and organizers:

    - hold a briefing and organizing meeting with all facilitators at least four weeks before the event to discuss project goals, inquiry framework, appropriate processes, spatial requirements and materials
    - base the design of interpretative materials and signs on this meeting
    - list all materials, stationery and props required at this time.

Producing a children's SpeakOut

Stage 4: Determine a layout to accommodate traffic and activities

- Incorporate children's desires to explore, discover and to feel they are within a 'secret' space.
- Accommodate traffic flow between different activities.
- Ensure the main approach to the space is vibrant, colourful and active yet clearly communicates the SpeakOut's intent and how people can interact with it.
- If a registration space is included, ensure it is not daunting for children: it should be warm, unimposing and clearly signed/ coloured.
- Where possible, allow for free, unmoderated play areas that are safe for activities such as:

    - drawing and painting
    - modelling
    - collage making.

Stage 5: Organize logistics

Detailed venue design

- *Produce accurate scale drawings* of the interior and exterior space to ensure that all activities and associated equipment, furniture and traffic flow will actually fit.

- Ensure *refreshments* for all ages.
- *Shade*: natural and built.
- *Furniture*: tables and chairs for activities need to be child height.
- *Display* SpeakOut outcomes around the space to increase vibrancy and communicate that children's creations are valued.
- A colourful *exterior* to the event space: clear signage, use 'Vote with Your Hands' to attract attention to main entrance, particularly for passing traffic.
- *Entrance, exit and flow*: allow for constant and sometimes unmoderated movement throughout spaces, particularly around the entrance and exit. Try to make the entrance and exit the same to maintain control of the space and so that children can be left unmoderated.
- *Space for play*: an area for general play separate from spaces where moderated activities occur.
- *Signage and materials*: use bold, chunky, colourful text and colourful paper and a hierarchy of signage to indicate importance. Ensure signage is located in obvious places that relate to what is being described. Locate signs at appropriate heights for children.
- *Facilities for adults*: consider child supervision, seating and shade, catering requirements and processes specifically designed for adults.
- *Risk management*: have a risk management plan in place well in advance.

Involvement of the community and governing body

- Engage and involve child-support agencies: to facilitate the general flow and to assist with facilitating activities.
- Council and government involvement, including collaboration among departments to achieve strategic goals.
- Marketing and communications.
- Local event producers: if possible, combine with an existing event that is child-friendly or, preferably, child-focused.

Materials

- Develop display and interpretative materials according to activity needs.
- Develop instructional signage: clear hierarchy, clear design, consistent and easily distinguishable from interpretative materials.
- Use decorations to brighten up the space, but make sure there is still sufficient space to hang participants' contributions where they do not impede traffic flow.
- Stationery: child-friendly, non-toxic and safe.
- Printing: complete well in advance to allow time for corrections if required.

Conducting the SpeakOut

Stage 6: Conduct the event

- *Pre-event preparations*: may include organizing access and electricity, signage in the local area and ensuring that delivery agencies have the correct address.
- *Set-up*: includes setting up main structures, all activities and signage.
- *Briefing*: facilitators and organizers will need to be briefed by the Event Manager and to share information and discuss approaches to managing the space, activities and children's participation.
- *Event management:* ideally, the Event Manager should not be tied down to a particular task. Their priority should be to ensure everything operates smoothly and to solve problems as they occur.
- *Permissions*: get signed permission forms from parents to allow use of images taken for reporting and future marketing associated with the project. Space on the form for a description of the child's appearance and clothing permits easier identification of images, particularly when a parent has refused permission.
- *Music*: can be good for atmosphere but may be distracting in spaces where conversations need to be heard and recorded.

Locating musicians and sources of music some distance from the main SpeakOut space, facilitated by someone who is energetic and playful, creates another engagement space for children to maintain their enthusiasm.

- *Checking in*: opportunities for facilitators and organizers to discuss how the SpeakOut is progressing, whether logistical or spatial changes should be made and other management concerns are important. The Event Manager should manage this.
- *Debriefing* immediately after the SpeakOut: it is critical to make time (even 15 minutes) for debriefing all facilitators. Basic questions such as, 'What worked?', 'What didn't?', 'What were the highlights?' and 'What would we do differently next time?' are valuable to elicit thoughts fresh in facilitators' minds.
- *Pack-down*: one person should be responsible for storing all participants' contributions safely in an accessible spot, making sure they are not likely to be damaged. Pack-down is a time- and energy-consuming process that should occur quickly and easily, as workers are likely to be tired and want to go home.
- *Data and information storage*: all participant contributions should be transcribed as soon as possible to ensure that where writing is indecipherable or where a specific facilitator's contribution is required in analysing a drawing: this can be resolved while details can be remembered.

Evaluating the children's SpeakOut

Stage 7a: Debriefing

- Establish the goals of the debriefing session early to avoid wasting time, particularly if debriefing occurs directly after the event when people are tired.
- Design criteria for the debriefing and circulate them before the event, so that facilitators are familiar with what will be discussed and can observe the SpeakOut accordingly. If there is time only for

a short debriefing session immediately after the event, schedule a group debriefing soon after (via a specific meeting, workshop, teleconference or templates to record comments by email).

- Outcomes should feed directly into ongoing reporting processes and design of future engagement activities.

Stage 7b: Compiling and evaluating the outcomes of the SpeakOut

- Data storage is important, as loss of primary documents before they have been transcribed or analysed can be devastating.
- Use the inquiry framework to evaluate all outcomes, to maximize consistency.
- Analyse all outcomes using both quantitative (e.g., number of drawings that suggested a water fountain) and qualitative (e.g., analysing drawings for relationships among elements).
- Compile outcomes.
- Prepare the report, which can then be distributed, with client permission, to interested stakeholders. A simpler version can be produced for schools, students and child participants.

Conclusions

The insights and level of detail that emerge from engagement processes involving children and young people often surprise some adults. These processes are always great fun and very rewarding. Frequently, a fresh perspective on a project or a site emerges. For processes to be both efficient and interesting for children and provide valuable information for planners and designers, however, four factors must be taken into account. First, the process must be specifically designed for the age group of participants. They must not be treated as 'small adults'. Second, objectives must be clear and facilitators selected and briefed to achieve those objectives. Third, the process must be well resourced, especially in terms of materials, equipment and personnel. Finally, the results must be carefully analysed and integrated into the results of other engagement processes.

About Plan C

Plan C is a Brisbane-based collaboration of built environment and creative industries professionals who specialize in creating and activating amazing public spaces with the community. Working in partnership with diverse communities, Plan C seeks to increase the range of infrastructure and activities within public spaces and build connected, active communities and richer places. The cross-disciplinary consultancy works across a wide range of public space settings at scales ranging from site-specific to city-wide, including natural areas, parks, car parks, streetscapes, lost spaces, civic, urban, community spaces and buildings. The team also specializes in working with diverse groups: children, people with a disability, older people, Indigenous people, migrant and refugee groups, young people and the broader community. Plan C's core practice areas are VOICE (community engagement), SPACE (public space conceptualization and design collaboration) and ACTIVATE (using tools such as events and programmes that enable a greater diversity of the community to continue to engage in public spaces).

Plan C's experience of the SpeakOut approach is that it is flexible and adaptable. Because a variety of engagement approaches ranging from the highly creative to quantitative can be accommodated within a SpeakOut methodology, it can be readily adapted, depending on the project, activity or group being targeted.

Contact:

Jim Gleeson

Managing Director

PO Box 7754, East Brisbane, Queensland, Australia 4169
jim@planc.com.au, www.planc.com.au

Vote with Your Hands

Introduction to the exercise

'Vote with Your Hands' is a method for recording preferences and suggestions. It has been used with adults, young people and children, often in association with a SpeakOut, community event or celebration. First pioneered by a community artist at a community festival in Bridgewater-Gagebrook in Hobart in 1997, this activity is appropriate in communities with low levels of literacy or where children's views are sought.

Used with a SpeakOut, this process has the following features and advantages:

- It advertises SpeakOut issues (for example, at a festival).
- It draws people inside a room or marquee.
- It is bright and engaging.
- It does not rely on participants' ability to read or write.
- It is especially effective for shy or hesitant people.
- It is great with children: they can make their mark with little supervision.
- The results of the 'voting' can be analysed if votes are annotated and/or allocated systematically.
- It provides great visual material for later advertising and promotion of issues.

Figure 8.1 Some annotated votes, sample of voting choices and preparing paint

This is an engaging way to conduct a survey about a specific topic. The 'Vote with Your Hands' (VWYH) station displays a question and several responses for people to consider. Participants are invited by the facilitator to choose a colour corresponding to each response, dip their hand in the colour tray and leave a handprint on a large sheet of fabric as a vote. Votes can then be annotated.

Table 8.1 'Vote with Your Hands' checklist

Action
• Make sure you have shade or are located to the south or east side of a building or marquee (in the southern hemisphere)
• A sign that explains the steps and instructions
• A large white sheet or calico that can be used for the painting
• Large coloured sign displaying 'Vote with Your Hands'
• Sturdy backing for behind the calico to protect marquee, walls or glass
• Nine colours of non-toxic children's paint. It needs to wash out of clothes and off marquee walls. You will need enough to fill the takeaway containers a couple of times
• Nine takeaway food containers (large enough for a man's hand) to put paint in
• Nine thick sponges that fit well in the takeaway containers
• Tarp(s) or drop sheets to protect the floor
• A large bucket
• Water on tap
• A safe place to dispose of the paint-contaminated water afterwards
• Rags or wet wipes or old towels for washing hands
• Wedge-tipped black pen for extra signs
• Bullet-tipped black pens for annotating handprints
• A stepladder would be hugely helpful to help with tying things to a marquee's high walls
• A long table and two chairs for this stall. It would be best to cover the table also – it can be covered with paper or you can tape butcher's paper to it
• Materials to fix the fabric to the marquee. Perhaps ropes are needed

This method also allows everyone else to see the votes. It is fun, inclusive and informative. Children can participate and see that their contributions are recorded.

An example of an instructions sign

'Vote with Your Hands' for Bonnyrigg

Instructions

1 Read over the list of things that already are here or could be at Bonnyrigg in the future.
2 Talk to the helpers about your ideas and they will write them down.
3 Choose a colour from the list.
4 That colour is in one of the paint containers.
5 Put your hand in the paint.
6 Put your hand mark on the cloth to show what's important to you.
7 Wash your hands in the bucket.
8 Please just vote once with your hands so we can count up what's important to people.
9 Print beside your hand what it means – the colour you have chosen. Or the helper can print it for you.
10 Come inside the Youth Centre, enjoy the BBQ and speak out in more detail about your ideas.

Footscray SpeakOut facilitators' instructions

Stall Two: Arts and culture

Objectives:

To facilitate a 'Vote with Your Hands' exercise (a 'finger-painting' exercise) where people indicate their interest in dimensions of arts and culture.

Tools for this session:

- Your stall, which will have relevant prompting questions, photos and background information on display. These are fixed props.
- A large 'Vote with Your Hands' sheet affixed to the wall (organized in colour-coded and labelled categories).
- A set of water soluble finger paints in different colours, each colour corresponding to a category on the sheet.
- Washing up materials (water and towels) for cleaning hands after this exercise.
- A4 maps of Footscray.
- Coloured pens that correspond with the colour categories on the 'Vote with Your Hands' sheet on the wall.

Tasks:

BE FRIENDLY AND WELCOMING!

The question is: 'What should the future Footscray have artistically and culturally?' People will display their interests in a 'Vote with Your Hands' exercise.
Ask each person to look at the 'Vote with Your Hands' categories:

- RED: more opportunity to learn to be an artist or craftsperson
- GREEN: more arts events such as theatre or gallery exhibitions
- BLUE: more arts business and development – studio
- ORANGE: more community festivals and cultural displays
- PURPLE: more public art like sculpture and murals.

COMMUNITY
WORKSHOPS

The process moves surprisingly quickly so it's important to be prepared. You will need to think through every stage of your agenda step by step and predict your requirements. We have found it useful to use the 'worst-case scenario' approach to identify potential problems.

Designing and Managing a Workshop

This chapter, which explores requirements for a community workshop or other participatory event, builds on the material in Chapter 5 and does not repeat basic workshop or venue set-up advice. The following topics are covered in this chapter:

- What is a good workshop?
- Setting up
- The workshop room
- Who is in charge?
- Presentation and display boards
- Managing the workshop
- Workshop props
- Paper props and green sheets
- Other table requirements
- Presentation of work in progress to participants
- Using PowerPoint presentations
- The *Fishbowl*
- The value of a dedicated gofer.

What is a good workshop?

A good workshop is about learning. Good workshops often have these qualities:

- commonly understood goals
- a clear process for reaching those goals
- awareness that people come with personal preoccupations and feelings as well as an interest in the subject
- a sense of involvement in making decisions and subsequent actions, which means that all members should participate.[1]

Setting up

These matters, addressed in Chapter 5, are not repeated in this chapter, as they apply equally to SpeakOuts and community workshops.

The *Outer Circuit*

- Location: selecting a venue
- Room size and shape
- A suitable and comfortable environment
- Layout and acoustics
- Lighting and electrical power supply
- Telephones
- Furniture and other equipment
- Registration desk
- The welcoming process
- Drinks on arrival
- Audio and visual equipment
- A box of essential materials.

The *Inner Circuit*

- Presentation and display boards
- Issues and questions
- Stall essentials
- Ending on time
- People who still want to talk
- Ending, debriefing and socializing phase
- Arrangements for debriefing
- Arrangements for cleaning up.

The workshop room

Ideal size of workshop

A workshop works best if there are fewer than eight people per table, plus the facilitation staff. Fifty people is a reasonable number. Larger workshops, which present challenges related to acoustics, catering, queuing and crowd management, are certainly possible. We've successfully managed workshops for 500 participants.

In Chapter 5, we discussed room size and shape for SpeakOuts and mentioned the implications for community workshops. Figure 9.1 shows the sort of 'cabaret-style' seating we recommend for workshops.[2] When assessing the room for its suitability for a workshop, it's helpful to think through the workshop process step by step, asking questions like: Will the building be large enough to accommodate queues for drinks or meals? Is circulation between tables really possible when the room is full? How will you accommodate an overflow crowd?

The furnished room

To calculate how much space you will need and how furniture will fit, you need to visit the room or space in advance with the furniture supply people (if furniture is not supplied at the venue). We cannot overemphasize the importance of making an accurate scale plan of the room or space. When calculating spaces for tables and chairs, consider adequate space for circulation and access to fire escapes. Ensuring good sightlines to the stage from all seated positions is also essential (although participants can move chairs for plenary sessions).

We recommend ordering more chairs than you will need to accommodate observers. A few extra tables will be invaluable for laying out materials while you are setting up and can be used for briefing and debriefing, while other people are setting up and taking things down.

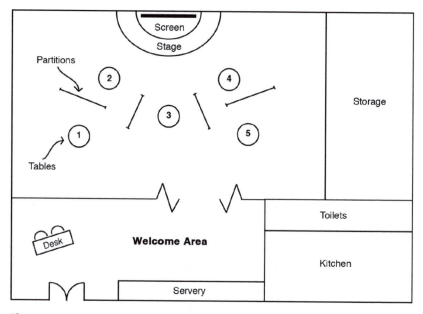

Figure 9.1 A typical workshop layout

Who is in charge?

One person must be in charge of the whole workshop process, including management and facilitation: the workshop Director or Coordinator. We strongly recommend that a second person be in charge of technical details and arrangements: the Event Manager or Producer. If these roles are clearly identified, all helpers will know whom to ask for help. Some logistical matters highlighted in the case studies in Chapter 4 related to inadequate separation of those roles and perhaps a misunderstanding of the Producer or Event Manager's role.

Authority for signing for deliveries

Both the Director or Coordinator and Event Manager or Producer must have 'authority to sign' for deliveries and make undertakings on behalf of the client or organizing body. These arrangements will need to be confirmed in advance. It's good to have a small amount of money for essentials on hand as well.

Electrical and 'handyman' requirements

In our experience, something electrical often goes wrong: fuses blow, power is inadequate and so forth. It is a good idea to have among your helpers an electrician or a handyperson who can fix things in a jiffy. A good set of tools and a ladder always come in handy, especially for high-level mounting of plans and signs.

Presentation and display boards

In community planning and design, one of the objectives of engagement processes is to share information pertaining to the plan or design under consideration. Presentation of information using big and bold letters, as well as images and interactive activities, has proven to be effective. Reports need to be summarized and long words or jargon paraphrased or explained. Use foamboard, cardboard or large sheets of paper on walls to create display boards that can be written or drawn on.

Item/issue	Comments	☐ √
Convert all technical language and jargon into plain words		
Translate key material into local languages		
Use images, clipart and picto-grams wherever possible		
Ask for advice about presenting material in languages other than English		

Managing the workshop

Working in groups and the props required

We set up our workshops in 'cabaret style' and do not use formal seating in rows unless we expect an extended formal 'lecture' component. Working in groups requires that all relevant information and tools be within easy reach. The process moves surprisingly quickly so it's important to be prepared. You will need to think through every stage of your agenda step by step and predict your requirements. We have found it useful to use the 'worst-case scenario' approach to identify potential problems. Depending on how well you know the community and participants, you can predict some problems.

Working in small groups of up to eight people is the most efficient and effective approach. While some people will always favour formal meetings with seating in rows, there is considerable evidence to show that balanced participation is rarely achievable in larger groups, as some people may dominate discussion. With facilitated group work, participants are able to contribute to the table discussion in a balanced and equitable way that fosters empowerment. When facilitators can encourage quieter participants to contribute on an equal level with a more vocal member, it diffuses power within the group. We may start a workshop with nine or ten tables, which are later reduced to fewer tables, as participants leave early and others can be reallocated.

Requirements of table groups

The requirements for each table group will vary from workshop to workshop and depend largely on the issues to be addressed. Wall space is always a problem. We recommend that you critically assess a venue to see if there is enough wall space (or even window space) to display the butcher's paper that emerges from several hours of small group work. The display area needs to be near the table. If not, you may need to hire or acquire sturdy, movable partitions as display areas. The amount and format of information are important considerations. A balance is required between too much and too little, irrespective of how well information is presented. For all visual material, avoid technical jargon and label features in simple language. Replace words such as 'axonometric' with 'bird's-eye view' and clearly annotate drawings, plans and maps with street names and landmarks.

Windows are often the only surface available for affixing butcher's paper. Remember that in the evening, as glass becomes cold, condensation makes affixing difficult and frequently causes paper to fall off.

The following table lists the essentials for a workshop table.

Item/issue	Comments	□ √
Briefed and informed facilitator		
Briefed and attentive recorder with clear printing skills		
Sign-up sheets for participants to record their names and addresses		
Green sheets (sheets for comments or questions copied onto green paper)[3]		
Agenda		
Pens for filling out sign-up and comment sheets		
Butcher's paper or flip chart paper for public recording[4]		
Any other pens necessary for a specific design exercise		
Two partitions or flat wall surfaces for sticking up butcher's paper and plans[5]		
Pins, tape or reusable adhesive for affixing butcher's paper		

Filling out forms at the workshop tables

We recommend that participants register, fill out forms and conduct other formalities at their own tables (rather than the reception desk), assisted by the table facilitator. This reduces congestion at the registration desk and personalizes the arrival and settling-in process. It also helps to focus the participant and allows the participant, facilitator, recorder and other participants to become introduced over a particular task (signing up and becoming familiar with the venue).

Figure 9.2 Facilitators help people understand site constraints and planning principles

Workshop props

Workshop props or materials are the tools that make workshop processes possible. Clear props that are tactile and friendly are essential. When preparing props, consider the needs of the participants. Remember that they may not be as familiar with plans and technical drawing as a design professional. Thus, it is critical that all props be in simple language. Label all plans clearly.

Above all, don't be too precious when designing props. In one design negotiation exercise, the pieces of coloured paper cut to represent land uses fitted together perfectly like a jigsaw puzzle. Participants were reluctant to alter the shapes until the facilitators took to them with scissors. There appeared to be a 'sanctity' associated with the 'perfect' pieces.

Item/issue	Comments	☐ √
Use clear maps or plans of the site. Use 'normal' colours, like green for parks and blue for waterways		
Some contextual information to help participants understand the location of boundaries and orientation of the site		
An extra-large site plan at the front of the room for participants to refer to and talk about[6]		
Lots of enlarged photos and annotated plans at each table and displayed around the room[7]		
Lots of large copies of the agenda for everyone to see. We enlarge ours to metric A1 size and brighten them with crayons		
Greenery (pot plants)		
An elevated platform at the front so that the group facilitator and other speakers can be seen from the floor		
Podium/rostrum		
Slide projector with spare bulb		
Overhead projector with spare bulb		
Data projector		
Projection screen (check if room can be darkened)		

Item/issue	Comments	☐ √
• Large and bold badges to identify: • Staff • Project team members • Facilitators • Recorders • Participants		
Extension cords		
Double adapters		
Tables for all projectors, large enough to hold a pile of overhead transparencies		
Access to photocopier		
Pins for sticking up posters where walls make reusable adhesive and tape unacceptable, e.g., soft partitions		
Green sheets or comment sheets		
Sign-up sheets at each table		

Paper props

At workshop tables, we use a number of 'paper props' to assist the participants and the facilitator. We use sign-up sheets (distributed to tables to reduce congestion at the registration desk), green sheets (comment sheets), briefing notes, take-home versions of plans, maps, summaries of reports, lists of consultants and other people to contact about the project.

We find that small, clear plastic boxes or coloured plastic baskets on workshop tables are useful for keeping these paper props, pens, crayons and so forth from getting buried under papers, handbags and coffee cups.

Green sheets

A feature of the workshop is that all questions are answered in an open format. However, some people have difficulty asking questions, even in small groups. Or they may wish to make a comment or complaint in a more private way. We have designed green sheets for exactly that purpose. Experienced facilitators will readily appreciate their purpose. They enable people to fill out a sheet with a question or comment and the responsible person will respond, either by telephone, by post or in person, as appropriate.

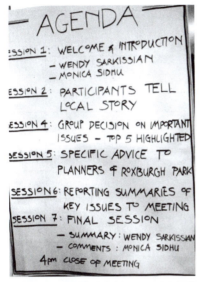

Figure 9.3 A large agenda helps everyone keep abreast of proceedings

PERTH METROPOLITAN FREIGHT STRATEGY

green sheet green sheet green sheet green sheet green sheet green sheet green sheet green sheet
green sheet green sheet green sheet green sheet green sheet green sheet green sheet green sheet

If there are any issues which you feel were not fully addressed at this Search Conference, or any additional comments which you would like to make, please write them on this sheet.

A member of the Study Team will contact you within a week to discuss your concerns.

Thank you.

Comments *(use the back of the sheet as well if you wish)*

CARRYING THE LOAD
AIR
SEA
RAIL

Name: ....

Address: ....

.... Postcode: ....

Telephone Number: ( ) ....

Facsimile Number: ( ) ....

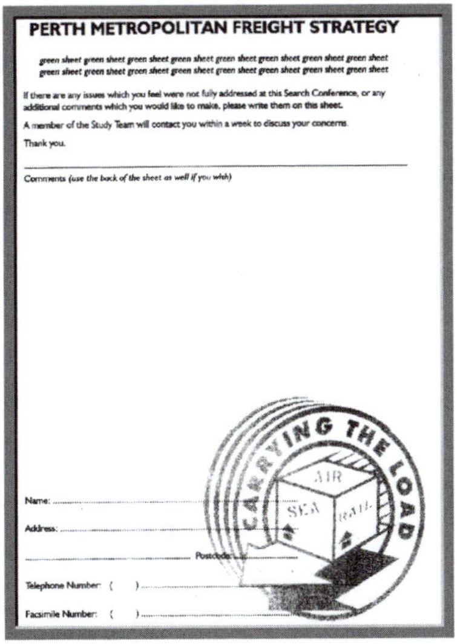

Figure 9.4 A green sheet for a stakeholders' workshop

Other table requirements

Other table requirements will depend on any additional activities participants will undertake. Listed below are some possible requirements. The list will need to be modified for specific exercises.

Item/issue	Comments	☐ √
A small box or basket at each table for equipment and materials. We use transparent plastic boxes		
Reusable adhesive		
Drawing pins		
Velcro dots and strips		
Scissors		
Clear adhesive contact film		
Thick markers (black and colours)		
Pencils/crayons. Bold colours will be easier to reproduce for inclusion in a report or for reporting back at a workshop. Do not use yellow or other pale colours		
Writing material clear enough for photocopying and analysis		
Masking tape		
Gaffer tape for sticking cables to floors and carpets and to reinforce masking tape as required. We recommend the use of bright colours such as yellow for additional safety		
Site plans or maps boldly labelled with non-technical terms		
Glue sticks		
Coloured paper or card for cutting up		
Tracing/detail paper		
Rulers/scales		
Hooks and eyes for hanging materials		
Butcher's paper		

Presentation of work in progress to participants

Displaying work in progress in a community workshop is very important. We believe that all research conducted in a planning or design study should be made accessible to community members. However, the material may need to be summarized, redrawn and rewritten and presented in simple language. We have found that our colleagues are sometimes reluctant to do this, as they feel it's 'unprofessional'. This does not mean 'dumbing-down' but rather providing information that is culturally appropriate and accessible to the workshop participants.

Panels with simple material and clear summaries, displayed prominently, allow participants to familiarize themselves with the study's aims and work to date and empower them to participate effectively.

Item/issue	*Comments*	☐ √
Presentation of work in progress in clear, bold and interesting formats		
Avoid technical jargon and use everyday terms and language understood by your audience		
Consider multilingual presentation of information reflecting the make-up of the participating community		
Mount information on a light material (we use foamcore or lightweight corrugated plastic or foamboards to ensure easy display at the venue)		
Decide how and where information will be presented		
Ensure adequate wall or vertical surface space to display all information		
Carefully consider how mounted material will be affixed to the vertical surface. Test if necessary. Can reusable adhesive be removed without soiling or damaging walls? (Some venues have very strict policies. Check in advance)		

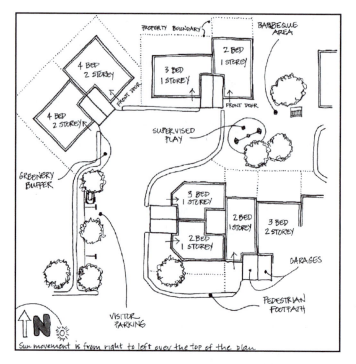

Figure 9.5 Good graphic representation encourages conversation about issues

Verbatim recording

We can't overemphasize the importance of vertical scribing and careful recording – ensuring that the words people speak are recorded, as well as the flavour of their message. This takes time and requires the Recorder (as we explain in Chapter 10) to manage the pace of the workshop so that points do not get missed. When recording is carefully done, verbatim comments give power and authenticity to a report or presentation. The message in Figure 9.6, recorded by an inexperienced recorder, nevertheless communicates what the participant meant to say.

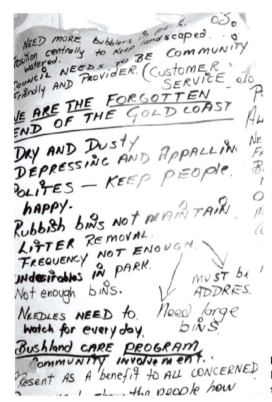

Figure 9.6 Residents reported living in 'the forgotten end of the Gold Coast'

Using PowerPoint presentations

We suggest that if you are using PowerPoint, do not override the recommended font size *unless you are making the font larger*. For example, for a slide with a few major bullet points, PowerPoint suggests 32 point for the text and 44 point for the title. For one with more detail, the recommended point size for the text is still 28 point. We also suggest that you keep the number of words to a limit and use the opportunity provided by the software to make handouts for distribution to workshop participants. That way they can read along and make notes for their own use.

Title - 44 pt

Text - 32 pt

Sub-text - 28 pt

Many excellent books can help ensure that your presentations (and especially those by technical 'experts') are appropriate for workshop and meeting audiences and participants. *Presentations for Dummies* (2004) by Malcolm Kushner[8] is an excellent start, as is *Brilliant Presentation* by Richard Hall (2007).[9] Kushner has a particularly valuable section called 'Avoiding common mistakes with PowerPoint' (pp235–243). Set out below are some important pointers from both of these books.

From *Presentation for Dummies*:

Dos:

- Follow the '4 by 4' rule: no more than four lines and four words to a line.
- At the very most: six words per six lines.
- Make the ending look good.
- Be careful that sounds and transitions don't become annoying.
- Check carefully for misspelled words.
- Be careful to talk about what's on the slide and not something else.

Don'ts:

- Don't use too much text.
- Don't overemphasize your logo.
- Don't mix different types of clipart.

- Don't use too many colours.
- Don't emphasize everything.
- Don't 'prettify' without a purpose.
- Avoid including too much information per slide.
- Avoid too many special effects.
- Don't read slides out word for word.
- Don't forget to practice.

From *Brilliant Presentation*:

Dos:

- Write a contents page to begin with.
- Make a heading for every slide.
- Use Notes pages for your own notes (do not use the PowerPoint as the speaker's notes).
- Consider using no bullets at all.

Don'ts:

- Don't become obsessed with the pictorial side of things.
- Avoid large slabs of text.
- Not more than five bullet points or 30 words total per slide.
- Do not use sub-headings or sub-bullets.
- Avoid animations, transitions and sound without expert back-up.
- Avoid complex charts (best to have more charts than one complex one).
- Don't read your slides to the audience.

As an example, the author of *Brilliant Presentation* provides this example of six PowerPoint slides that meet his criteria:[10]

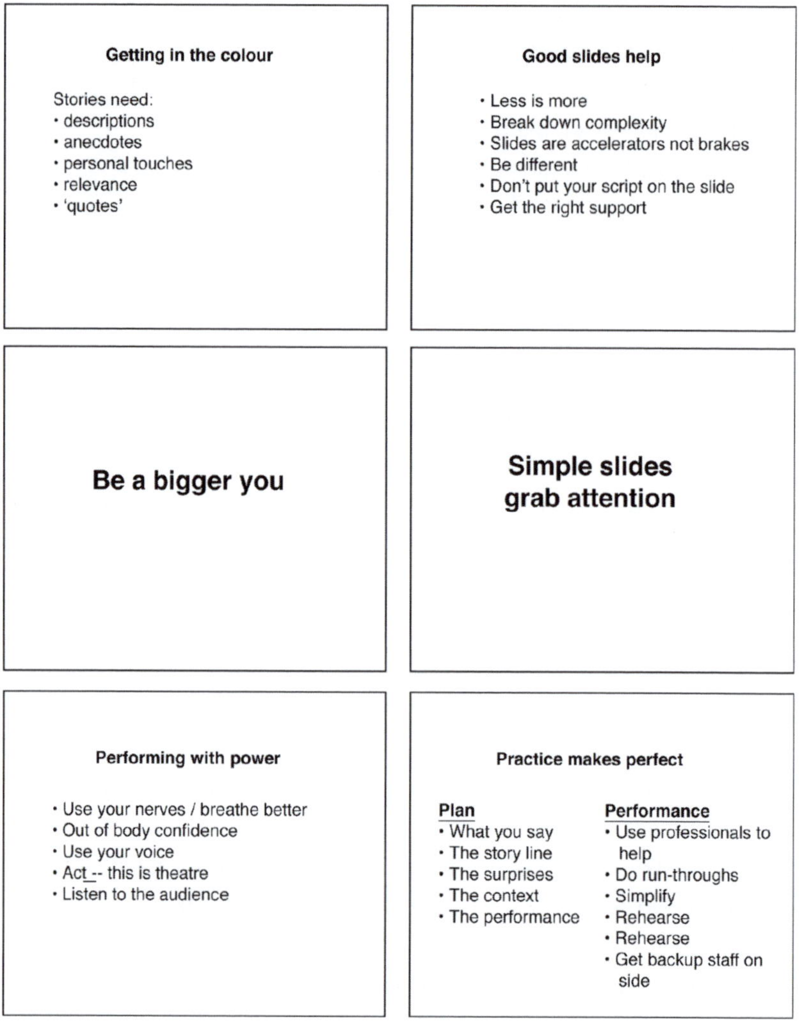

Getting in the colour

Stories need:
• descriptions
• anecdotes
• personal touches
• relevance
• 'quotes'

Good slides help

• Less is more
• Break down complexity
• Slides are accelerators not brakes
• Be different
• Don't put your script on the slide
• Get the right support

Be a bigger you

Simple slides grab attention

Performing with power

• Use your nerves / breathe better
• Out of body confidence
• Use your voice
• Act -- this is theatre
• Listen to the audience

Practice makes perfect

Plan
• What you say
• The story line
• The surprises
• The context
• The performance

Performance
• Use professionals to help
• Do run-throughs
• Simplify
• Rehearse
• Rehearse
• Get backup staff on side

Figure 9.7 An example of appropriate PowerPoint slides

Item/issue	Comments	☐ √
Check all equipment well in advance and avoid use of equipment where not 100% certain it will work properly		
Ensure the PowerPoint features do not detract from the message/content		
Be careful that the presentation doesn't look too polished or finished, particularly if it's draft material		
A data projector PowerPoint presentation can look expensive and may raise concerns in some communities about the costs involved		
If it's not all set up and ready to go, it's boring to wait while someone fiddles with the technology, trying to get it to work		
Use the 'Notes' feature in Power Point to make handouts. Make sure the print size is not too small to read		

The Fishbowl

The *Fishbowl* is a highly effective and innovative workshop approach.[11] It provides an arena where participants can watch other participants or members of a planning team work at a problem common to everyone. It can also be used for dramatic role-play sessions. Elevated seating is an integral part of this technique for those observing the activities 'in the round', as it enables everyone to see and be seen. Thus, everyone can be included in a process that may involve only a small number of participants.

We have used the *Fishbowl* approach at the end of a long and difficult community workshop that aimed to resolve structure-planning problems related to a proposed suburban estate. The planning team sat at a round table in the centre of the participants (seated on raised seating) and discussed how they could resolve the contradictions in the residents' requirements. Three hand-held microphones enabled all comments to be heard. At the same time, comments were recorded in summary on an overhead projector for all to see. Finally, the team's planner reported back to the whole group on a possible solution. The community applauded the openness and flexibility of the team members. And it is important to note that the engineers on the project team suggested this approach!

In another model, 'People from one perspective sit and talk in the middle while all others watch and listen. And then people from another/opposed perspective sit and talk in the middle while everyone else watches and listens. If there are more than two significant perspectives, the process continues until all perspectives have been heard. Then it starts over again, with the conversations now influenced by what they've heard from the other perspectives.' See www.co-intelligence.org/CIPol_ComunityProcesses.html.

For a *Fishbowl* process, using our version, the requirements are set out in the table below.

Item/issue	*Comments*	□ √
Elevated seating around a lower central table and chairs or locate the Fishbowl on a raised platform		
Public recording of discussion		
Overhead or data projector		
Butcher's paper		
Access to a public address system: microphone on table to make discussion of the central group clearly audible for all participants		
Microphones to pass among participants (several hand-held ones are best)		

Item/issue	Comments	☐ √
A person working as a workshop recorder (for written recording)		
Videotaping (Fishbowls can yield exciting video material)		
Carpeted room to minimize acoustic problems		
Screen for overhead projection, located to provide ease of viewing		

Ending a workshop

We suggest that workshop sessions end on time so people are free to go. Team members can then be available to discuss further with those who want to stay. This matter is discussed in Chapter 5. Sometimes when a meeting is particularly energetic and participants want to stay, it's best to call a close to formal proceedings (to avoid embarrassment of those who must leave) and then continue for a while in a more informal vein.

Final comments: The value of a dedicated 'gofer'

The success of the staff and volunteers in carrying out their tasks depends largely on having the essential materials provided and ready to use. A summary checklist of necessary materials has helped us in creating a much smoother event. We present a summary of that checklist in Appendix A. Having a volunteer to help as a 'gofer', who is constantly checking whether facilitators or Recorders need more materials throughout a workshop or SpeakOut, can be a tremendous help.

STAFFING, FACILITATION, ANALYSIS AND EVALUATION

We have lost track of the times that clients have rung our office on a Tuesday morning after an intensive weekend workshop or SpeakOut to ask if the results were ready yet...
Or the times that clients have said something to this effect,
'Don't bother with all that analysis. Honestly, it's not worth it. We just need the broad-brush picture at this stage.'

Staffing, Facilitation and Recording

Introduction: Organization of this chapter

This chapter discusses staffing community engagement processes and then focuses on specific requirements for community workshops and SpeakOuts. There is a wide variety of material available to assist with training and facilitation. For guidance, see the references in the notes for chapter and at the end of the book. The materials in this chapter are drawn from a wide range of source materials, listed in the references. The contents draw heavily on published material on group dynamics, workshop facilitation, communication, search conferences, interpersonal dynamics, creativity, conflict resolution and participation methods.

Staffing a community engagement process

A great deal of effort goes into a successful community workshop. One person (the Chair) is usually in charge, but no one person can do it alone. Adequate resources must be available. When sensitive or controversial local issues are being discussed, the workshop Chair (or Coordinator) will be fully occupied keeping things moving. If project team members and table facilitators fully understand the process, they can be a great support to the Chair.

Many genuine processes cannot survive without the support of client staff. Senior client staff need to be well briefed and available to speak and listen to community representatives. It is imperative that they understand that they are present to work with the community representatives.

Our worst community engagement experiences have been when the client and his senior technical consultants have been chatting loudly at the back of the room while we were trying to bring a contentious community workshop to a satisfactory close. At these times, we do not feel part of a team and certainly do not feel supported. Teamwork is the essence of community workshops. And the more complex they are, the more there will need to be specific attention paid to staffing and teamwork issues.

To do this valuable work effectively requires lots of helpers. Figure 10.1 shows an example of who may be involved.

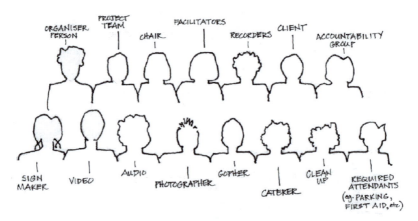

Figure 10.1 Staffing for a community workshop

Core values of facilitation

In a brilliant book, *Facilitator's Guide to Participatory Decision-Making* (1996), Sam Kaner and colleagues suggest that facilitation should abide by four values:

1 *Full participation*: People permitting themselves to state half-formed thoughts that express unconventional perspectives.

2 *Mutual understanding*: Taking time to understand everybody's perspective in order to find the best idea. A sense of acceptance and understanding is what allows people to develop innovative ideas that incorporate everyone's point of view.

3 *Inclusive solutions*: As the Quakers say, 'Everybody has a piece of the truth.' The work is to include everyone who has a stake in the outcome, finding solutions that may not be originally obvious – a process that leads to creative, innovative thinking.

4 *Shared responsibility*: Participants must be willing to implement the proposals they endorse. They should make every effort to give and receive input before final decisions are made. This needs everyone's support to be sustainable. There is a commitment to share responsibility, which is evident throughout the process and is designed into the agenda.[1]

Ground rules for community workshops

Seven basic rules can help make a discussion flow evenly, with the result that the greatest number of ideas is canvassed in the shortest time. They can be summarized as follows:

1 Everyone's contribution is valuable, must be listened to and recorded.

2 Everyone must talk: they have come to make a contribution and must be given the chance to do so, even if it is a small contribution or they are shy.

3   However crazy or improbable a suggestion may seem, give it the chance to influence the picture. This is particularly important in the brainstorming sessions.

4   Work towards the goal of each session. Make sure that people don't start making judgements about what specific outcomes may occur from the workshop.

5   No one is allowed to consume group time with their hobby horse.

6   Conflict is healthy and differences are important. Don't let differences or conflict drift into confrontation. No one is to be bullied into changing their opinion.

7   By merely attending the workshop, people have made the point that they want to be involved in the consultations and are committed to resolving conflicts.

Managing conflict

The process that a group goes through to solve a difficult problem has been well defined and described. It is neither smooth nor sequential and is characterized by confusion and misunderstanding. Further, most people find it hard to tolerate the inherent ambiguity and confusion when people do not have shared frames of reference. A group's most significant breakthroughs are often characterized by a period of struggle. This process, from *divergent* to *convergent* thinking and then to *resolution*, has been called 'the diamond of participatory decision-making'.[2]

The dynamics of conflict in workshops

Dealing with conflict is always an issue in community workshops. It is critical that all views be presented but that nobody is given the chance to dominate proceedings to the detriment of others. Often this is difficult work, especially with outspoken people (particularly politicians) in attendance. Facilitators often find that they must resort to basic conflict-resolution approaches to keep an even balance at their workshop tables. Some of the 11 suggested skills identified by the Conflict Resolution Network may help in managing a workshop discussion group. They are summarized below:

1 *Win/win (or 'all gain') approach*: Take a new look at conflict and cooperation. Seek out possibilities for mutual gain.
2 *The creative response*: See problems as opportunities. Although conflicts are frequently seen as crises, they may also be regarded as an invitation for change.
3 *Empathy*: See the other person's point of view. Recognize the motivations behind the apparently uncaring behaviour of other people.
4 *Appropriate assertiveness*: Know your needs and rights and how to state them clearly.
5 *Cooperative power*: This is the difference between power *over* and power *with* someone else.
6 *Managing emotions*: Learn how to handle your own anger and frustration in tense situations.
7 *Willingness to resolve*: Understand the role that resentment can play in preventing successful negotiation.
8 *Mapping the conflict*: It is useful to draw up a map of the conflict which includes looking at the underlying needs, values, objectives and visions of all participants.
9 *Development of options*: Create a smorgasbord of choices from which conflict participants can choose action more appropriate for both parties.
10 *Negotiation skills*: Make the problem the 'enemy' rather than the person. Handle objections as 'and' not 'but'.
11 *Broadening perspectives*: Recognize your view as one point of view and understand the others' points of view as also valid and necessary as part of the whole.

Inevitable problems

Despite the best preparation, problems will inevitably occur. Pat Materka (1986, p104) summarizes how to deal with 'problem' participants:

- You can't anticipate them. Like a rear-end collision, they will happen to you when you least expect it.
- You can't avoid them.
- You can't change people, especially not in a short workshop, but you can deal with them.
- You can't allow them to steal all the attention at the expense of the rest of the participants.
- You can divert people, cool their tempers and try to channel their energy towards your objectives.

The agenda

The agenda, an important element in the workshop, should be planned beforehand, prominently displayed and show:

- topics to be discussed
- the order in which they will be discussed
- the priority
- a suggestion of the time to be devoted to each topic.

The role of facilitator

Facilitation is basically helping the group deal with information and ideas and, ideally, to come to an agreement. In doing this, the facilitator should maintain equity, recognize each individual and try to balance personal and group needs. While the workshop Chair or Coordinator manages the whole workshop process, table facilitators manage dynamics at tables. Here are some facilitation pointers for those people:

- Have all the necessary equipment ready (pens, paper and any background material).
- If anyone comes in looking lost, make them feel welcome; remember, they have something to offer the workshop.
- The aim of the group is to seek opinions. The facilitator can suggest different ways to proceed (for example, brainstorming).
- Have some questions ready for beginning discussion and restarting discussion if the group bogs down.

Guidance for facilitators and recorders[3]

Good processes don't necessarily guarantee good community workshops. However, a lack of attention to these issues almost certainly guarantees failure. With honest intent and care for the needs of each participant, the opinions of the community should be able to be communicated fairly. Set out in the box below is a summary of the roles required for successful SpeakOuts.

At-a-glance summary of SpeakOut facilitation and recording

Purpose

- Facilitation in a SpeakOut aims to help people share their views openly in a balanced way.
- A well-run SpeakOut is equitable, recognizes each individual and tries to balance personal and group needs, while not letting anyone dominate the discussion.
- With careful facilitation, even the most shy and reticent can be encouraged to speak out.
- All opinions have equal value in a forum and all views are recorded in a form that everyone can see.
- The two roles of listener and recorder are separate. The listener gives their undivided attention to the person who is speaking, while the recorder records participants' comments in a vertical format with a large pen for all to see.
- A workshop facilitator (or manager or organizer) is in charge of the whole SpeakOut.

Continued

Features

- Recording on a vertical surface for all to see
- Listener and recorder work closely together
- Participants can challenge the written record as it is produced
- Has a cooperative flavour
- Shy people feel they can speak out
- Conflict is handled competently and not discouraged
- Is rewarding to individual participants.

Key roles

Listener

- Explains their role
- Summarizes SpeakOut goals
- Demonstrates active listening skills
- Adapts to the participants' communication styles
- Supports and validates participants and their views without bias
- Helps people feel welcome
- Introduces themselves and invites participants to introduce themselves
- Ensures participants' voices are heard fairly by recorder
- Clarifies and paraphrases to assist the recorder
- Manages the time so that the recorder can keep up
- Has the necessary equipment ready
- Has a clear mind, free of distractions and is able to focus on the needs of the people who are speaking out
- Has some questions ready for beginning the listening process and restarting discussion if people are hesitant
- Ensures participants' voices are heard fairly
- Pays close attention to language, style of speech and how the participant is feeling
- Manages silence with new questions to keep the conversation moving
- Demystifies the role of the listener
- Explains why they are doing things
- Ensures that people who come to speak out can accomplish their goals
- Works closely with the recorder to ensure recording accurately represents participants' views.

Continued

Recorder
- Introduces themselves and explains their role
- Stands close to the person who is talking so they can hear easily
- Pays close attention to what is being said
- Has some control over timing: makes sure that the person is not speaking so quickly that a good record cannot be made of the discussion
- Records on a vertical surface so everyone can see as the public record emerges and comment upon and correct recording if it is inaccurate in any way
- Uses verbs and action words to summarize comments
- Avoids paraphrasing if possible
- Seeks clarification from the person speaking where necessary
- Is responsible for getting the paper to the typist for transcription and for labelling all paper from their table.

The qualities of a good facilitator

In a workshop setting, a table group usually has a facilitator, the active participants and a recorder to write down what is being said, when it is said, without interpreting what has been said. The facilitator's role is crucial to the success of any workshop. Being grounded and well organized means that everyone is made to feel as comfortable as possible at the start. Facilitation is done by facilitators, supported by recorders and other helpers.

This process can be helped by ensuring that all materials are ready so that the facilitator can concentrate on the workshop. It is important to arrange the members of the group so that everyone can see everyone else and that they are all on the same level. Above all, make sure that everyone can hear what is being said.

We have found that people from the following groups make the most effective facilitators: counsellors, social workers, community development workers, teachers, child-care workers, therapists, community services staff and, of course, people trained specifically in group work. Few architects or technical specialists make good facilitators, in our experience. We recommend that you select facilitators who have good listening skills. Recorders can also be selected from these groups. Some people in the more technical professions make good recorders if they are good listeners.

The facilitator must be approachable. To demonstrate their accessibility, facilitators need to resist the temptation to congregate with other facilitators. When working in a group, facilitators should consider themselves as equal to a member and realize that they are not indispensable. The facilitator should also be sensitive to timing and the need to move on, as well as being supportive of group members. The facilitator is primarily a listener, with active listening a primary function. One of their group-building functions is to listen for half-stated contributions and question whether the idea has really been considered by everyone or whether it needs elaboration.

We have had great success working with local residents who have been trained as facilitators and recorders. The effectiveness of facilitators can sometimes be impaired if they do not understand the site or the project. They may need to be taken on a site visit beforehand as part of the briefing.

The facilitator's role is to share information, not to set themselves above the group as an 'expert'. This may be achieved by being open to questions and soliciting feedback. In the process they can attain useful insights and valuable information. One need not be labelled 'facilitator' in order to employ facilitation techniques in a group. Any group member can call the group back to the subject of the discussion, interrupt patterns of conflict or misunderstanding between other parties, offer clarifying comments, summarize activities or give evaluative feedback. In some groups, many or all of the members share these responsibilities. Other groups, whose members are less skilful at group process, will expect the facilitator to perform this function alone.

Facilitation and communication

The facilitator's effectiveness depends on his or her ability to communicate well with the group and to help group members communicate well with each other. It's wise to try to adapt to group members as much as possible. Language is very important: avoid technical terms, professional jargon and slang, which may offend some participants.

Believe it or not, dress *is* an important issue. Facilitators are advised to dress neatly, but not too formally. Sometimes professionals feel the need to 'dress down' for community workshops and local people may find that offensive.

Listening

We have found that when you are listening to someone, it's valuable to try not to evaluate immediately what is being said in terms of what it means to you. A more effective way can be to try to understand what it means from the other person's perspective. Asking questions helps us understand better and provides the opportunity for us to give an answer that has meaning to the other, from her or his point of view.

Clarifying roles

Demystifying the facilitator

As workshop participants are sometimes unfamiliar with facilitation as a leadership style, it's necessary to be pretty direct to ensure that all group members understand the facilitator's role. You may find yourself repeating yourself as you explain that you do not have authority and are not 'expert' in any way.

Giving feedback

Asking and providing feedback are key facilitation skills. The group facilitator can help the group by providing feedback, which should focus on:

- the behaviour of the group, not the individual
- actual observations, not inferences
- the description of what has been said, not judgement
- the sharing of ideas, not the giving of advice

- the exploration of alternatives, not the production of solutions
- listen to what has been said, not why it has been said.

Feedback statements are more helpful if they are:

- *Specific rather than general*: 'You bumped my arm', rather than 'You never look where you are going'.
- *Tentative rather than absolute*: 'You seem unconcerned about this problem', rather than 'You do not care about what happens'.
- *Informing rather than commanding*: 'I have not finished yet', rather than 'Stop interrupting me'.
- *Suggesting rather than directing*: 'Have you ever considered talking to Tim about the situation?', rather than 'Go talk to Sally'.
- *Tied to behaviour rather than abstract*: 'You complain frequently', rather than 'You are immature'.

Recording

The role of a recorder

The recorder works closely with the facilitator or listener. Recording, or writing down the content of group discussions, is an essential component of good community workshops and SpeakOuts. In our work, we prefer to separate the roles and have separate, discrete tasks for recorders. It's difficult, tiring and demanding work and we believe it should not be delegated to community members because they will, in effect, be 'gagged' if they choose to volunteer to record. Workshop participants should understand the purpose of this role and how it will be useful to the group. The two drawings below show how the recorder works and their 'dance' relationship with the facilitator.

Figure 10.2 The recorder and lists

Figure 10.3 The dance between the facilitator and the recorder

Recording in small groups: Some basic protocols

One of the essential qualities of a good workshop is that it leads to something – a record can be made and discussed and acted upon later. It is critical that care be taken in all recording and reporting back arrangements to avoid bias – including the sorts of bias that can creep in during the writing up stage. We have found that often there is a temptation on the part of some people with interests in projects to screen out the unfavourable comments or de-emphasize negative views. We are always very careful to show the emphases in all reporting back.

Some of the following suggestions will help to ensure that recording is fair, unbiased and effective:

- Record all workshop comments at tables on a large sheet of paper on a vertical surface so that everyone can see what is being recorded and correct it if they don't agree that it is an accurate transcript.
- Find a location for the recorder close to the table (we often use a free-standing partition) so that they can clearly hear all that is said.
- Never require a facilitator to record; they are two entirely separate jobs.
- Consider using overhead or data projectors in the plenary session so that everyone in a large workshop can read with ease the presentations from each table.
- Avoid tape-recording unless absolutely necessary. It is fraught with problems: it is often subject to technical problems; requires a monitor throughout the proceedings; is a 'secret' method which is not really accessible to the public; is incredibly time-consuming to transcribe and very seldom necessary except in legal cases.

Seven guidelines for workshop recording

1 The recorder does not contribute to the discussions at the table beyond seeking clarification of a particular point.

2 The recorder sets the pace at which the table works and can therefore halt discussion to ensure that a point is recorded or to ask a participant or the facilitator what is meant by their comments.

3 Everything must be written down publicly and clearly. Usually large, separate sheets of butcher's paper are pinned on notice boards for public recording. It is better to record on a vertical surface so everyone can see as the public record emerges and comment upon and correct recording if it is inaccurate in any way. It is difficult to record on the table surface, which is likely to be cluttered with cups and papers. We never use flip charts, as the previous pages are obscured when the page is turned over.

4 Remember that all information recorded will be included in the appendix of a report.

5 To help in the interpretation of recorded notes, it is imperative to use *verbs*, that is, a word that asserts action, occurrence or being. For example to record 'traffic' as an issue is meaningless, but by recording 'traffic is a problem' or 'traffic causes no problems' explains what is meant.

6 Recorders can seek clarification from the group. This can be done by simply asking: 'Is this what you meant by that statement?' or 'I didn't quite get that. Could you repeat it, please?' It's also a good idea to record as much as possible in people's own words.

7 Ensure that each piece of paper with recorded contributions is clearly marked with the table number, the session number from the agenda and the page number. This crucial detail avoids misinterpretation in the analysis stage.

Figure 10.4 Recording as listening, Western Australia, 2003

Techniques and group processes

There are many ways to help people in a workshop group generate ideas, be creative and come to agreement. Careful observation is the key. Here are some cues to watch for:

- *Restlessness*: Are people shifting around a lot? Are they clearing their throats or having side conversations? If so, you are probably losing them.
- *Silences*: Do they seem comfortable or uncomfortable? Silences can be agonizing. People may be bored because you are going too slowly or because the material is too simple; people may be uncomfortable with the topic or may be shy with each other and too self-conscious to talk in front of the group.
- *Do people look at you when you talk*? If so, they probably feel comfortable with you and are intrigued by what you are saying. If they avoid eye contact, something may be wrong.

- *Do people look at each other when they talk?* Again, if they do not avoid one another's gaze, it is a sign that the group is relaxed and at ease. If two or more people will not look at each other or talk to each other, something may be wrong.
- *Posture*: People often lean forward and shift positions when they want to say something. Posture reflects tension or how relaxed a person is, as well as how tired or alert people are.

Some common facilitation methods used in community workshops

Brainstorming approaches

Brainstorming is a method for generating ideas and solving problems. It is a way of tapping into the creativity and knowledge of the community. Brainstorming generates ideas. It is literally a process that encourages 'a storm in the brain' – ideas raging without any particular order. The aim is not to come to a decision. Each person can suggest an idea. It can be crazy, but it is still valuable. The recorder writes down all ideas just as they are said. Questions should be asked to start discussion. The method is not intended to produce *solutions* to each problem, but simply to generate ideas, comments and suggestions. Each comment is to be considered of equal value. It is important to ensure there is no *discussion* about the merit of specific comments. If there are disagreements or strong agreement, record them.

Ten rules for brainstorming

1 The aim is to generate ideas, not to make decisions.
2 Everyone should speak and their opinions should be listened to and respected.
3 Do not debate. Conflicting views are a healthy sign and should be recorded. Do not strive for agreement in the first session.
4 Keep the discussion moving – just toss in ideas.

5   Creative and 'oddball' ideas are also valuable and should be recorded.

6   Stay away from 'it is too hard' and 'it will never work, we have tried that before' – keep the creativity flowing.

7   Do not let anyone dominate the discussion. Give everyone their turn and encourage the more hesitant members to speak out too.

8   Record all ideas, including disagreements.

9   Suspend judgement and criticism just for this session.

10 Every comment has equal value. Not all the people attending the session will have the same degree of experience, but they will still have valuable contributions which should be listened to.

Common problems with brainstorming approaches

Three common problems often arise during this session, so it's wise to be prepared for them:

1   *Problems*: People find it difficult to be creative because they can see the problems in their ideas and will say, 'If ... then we could'. Your job is to get them to stop worrying about the 'if' at this stage.

2   *'Yes, but' and disagreement*: Other people will listen to an idea and say, 'yes but'. Your job is to control this and encourage people to listen to what each other has to say without judgement.

3   *Conflict*: There will be contradictory and conflicting views about what is desirable. Your job is to get them all recorded and see that no one person's view is considered right.

Rounds

Rounds are a technique for getting people to speak in a group. In 'rounds' each person has an equal opportunity to speak and be heard, as each person speaks in turn, encouraged by the facilitator. The facilitator should explain at the beginning of the rounds that statements should be brief and specific. A time limit may be set. Rounds can be either structured – each person speaks in turn – or unstructured – anyone can speak. Just keep moving from one person to the next around the table, asking each to make a contribution. A talking stick can be used to help balance discussion.

Consensus decision making

This process is very different from brainstorming and is sometimes called the 'groan zone' of convergent decision making. The first step is to agree to reach an agreement. Then the facilitator encourages individual participation and ensures that those who are going to be affected make the decisions. These are some of the qualities of consensus decision making:

- agreement to reach agreement
- people have the right to their own beliefs
- know your own limits
- only if you speak, can you be heard
- non-hierarchical process
- value differences
- encourage creative synergy
- value clarity, conciseness and focused discussion
- autonomy with cooperation
- active participation is the responsibility of each person
- if the issue does not directly affect you, leave it to those who are affected by it
- knowing when to listen and when to speak.

Reporting back in a plenary session

Reporting back in a community workshop can be an effective summary of the collective work of the group or the most boring part of the whole event. Try to avoid the situation where table after table presents their 'findings' (all nearly identical) to an exhausted group that has been working on the same topic for hours. We recommend that representatives of later tables highlight only those elements that *differ* from the previous ones.

We also recommend that facilitators do the reporting back from tables, rather than asking community members to do it, for reasons of simple efficiency. The facilitator should then ask group table members if they have anything else to add before the next table reports back.

Debriefing of facilitators and recorders

The facilitator must stay in touch with the mood of the group, sense its energy and try to keep it on track, while ensuring balanced participation. Much of what goes on will be recorded intuitively and subconsciously in the mind of a sensitive facilitator. We find that a session of an hour or less asking the facilitators and recorders (in a workshop or SpeakOut) to discuss all that transpired that was not recorded yields invaluable results. It is also a rich source of information about local politics and interpersonal relations, often issues not reflected in the formal workshop record.

Some final comments

You may be reading this chapter because you have been asked to act as a facilitator, recorder, listener, helper or resource person at a workshop, SpeakOut, search conference, community forum or other community engagement event. Please try not to allow the material in this chapter to intimidate you. People everywhere – and especially in groups – generally respond to clarity of intent and an open heart. Be your natural self. Look people in the eye and stay focused on your task. It is work. It will be demanding. But it should also be rewarding. And it should be fun.

Item/issue	Comments	☐ √
One person needs to be in charge of the workshop set-up. They need to have a clear idea of what is required. They may need written authority to sign for deliveries and make decisions on behalf of the client		
Set-up people need to be available a few hours before the workshop starts to ensure everything is in order		
Briefed and experienced facilitators at each table		
Briefed and experienced Recorders at each table. In addition, one or two roving Recorders can help get an overview of what is going on		
Make certain that the following people are present: and well briefed about the workshop:		
• the project team members		
• Accountability Group members (a community group overviewing the process)		
• representatives of the client, including senior members of the client organization		
• an audio technician or a person who is handy and knowledgeable about 'technical' matters		
• video people (camera people and assistants), as required		
• 'gofers' – people who know where things are and how to get things done quickly. (They will need access to a car)		
• people to look after the registration desk. The gofer may double as the person who watches the registration desk for late arrivals once the workshop has started		
• parking attendants may be required to direct traffic in parking areas if specially provided areas are designated for the event		
• security guard for overnight surveillance of marquees or equipment in insecure venues or neighbourhoods with very high crime rates		
• a photographer		
• sign maker/graphics person to make large, bold, friendly, personal, clear and legible signs		

Analysis of Materials Generated by a SpeakOut or a Workshop

Introduction

This chapter is a reminder that the hours of work by eager participants and committed facilitators, listeners and recorders do not morph magically into a completed report. We have lost track of the times that clients have rung our office on a Tuesday morning after an intensive weekend workshop or SpeakOut to ask if the results were ready yet for the Board or Council meeting on Tuesday night. Or the times that clients have said something to this effect: 'Don't bother with all that analysis. Honestly, it's not worth it. We just need the broad-brush picture at this stage.' Then they say something like this:

> Maybe we will be able to find some money to pay you for analysis later on, but for now just your general thoughts will be fine. We're just after your general impressions of what was said and any problems you identified ...

Any experienced community engagement practitioner will tell you that this problem occurs repeatedly. Thus, we believe that it requires a separate – if short – chapter simply to make the point. There is no value in collecting community comments, opinions and contributions if you are not going to engage in systematic analysis and reporting. It's not ethical and it's a waste of everyone's time and money.

Steps in analysis of SpeakOut and workshop information

1. Transcribe
2. Type
3. Tabulate
4. Sort
5. Analyse
6. Interpret
7. Report writing
8. Draft report
9. Conclusions and recommendations
10. Feedback from community to draft report
11. Revisions
12. Final report
13. Pass on results
14. Manage results up the line
15. Manage politics
16. Final report to community (which modes?)

Figure 11.1 The essential steps

We believe that the road from a SpeakOut or a workshop to analysis and eventual insights – and recommendations – has predictable and identifiable steps. Figure 11.1 shows our best guess at what those steps should comprise.

Making sense of what emerges from a SpeakOut or a community workshop requires careful attention to all of these steps. One of the compelling reasons for this care is to permit participants to 'track' their contributions throughout the reporting process and in the final report. What they originally say will be recorded verbatim in the appendices to the report, which will be an exact transcript of what was recorded (which, hopefully, will be an accurate representation of what was said, depending on the skill and experience of the recorder). Further, as the analysis of the raw material proceeds, participants should be able to identify their contributions and see how they influenced the report and its recommendations. This care is essential if we are to build and maintain community trust in community engagement processes.[1]

The lump-and-split categorization process

Because the amount of information collected during SpeakOuts and community workshops can often be overwhelming, we need a practical process to sort and analyse that information, while at the same time reducing opportunities for bias and ensuring that nothing is lost. Our approach is called 'lump-and-split' analysis. It is useful for analysing information recorded by recorders in a workshop or a SpeakOut.

Figure 11.2 Finalizing brainstorming lists in workshops

The process can be used to categorize the material generated during a brainstorming session within a community workshop (see Chapter 10 for a discussion of forms of brainstorming).

The process can also be used after the recording process is complete by researchers sorting material and summarizing findings from a workshop or a SpeakOut.

Features of this approach

This type of transparent and systematic sorting method is often used to ensure that all the information is sorted into recognizable and discrete categories for later analysis. This approach is suitable for use in all workshops and SpeakOuts whose products are primarily words, rather than drawings. In the case of interactive exercises, other methods must complement the lump-and-split process (for example, mapping, analysis of photographs and preferences).

Costs

This is not a time-consuming or expensive method if information is carefully recorded before it is categorized. If the process is used after a workshop or SpeakOut, there will be transcription and analysis costs. All community engagement processes incur reporting costs.

Costs will be influenced by:

- the level of analysis required
- the quality of the written record
- how much material can be derived from the written record
- the ability of the workshop organizer and facilitator to supervise the quality of the work produced
- how well table groups managed to pursue session objectives and understood workshop proceedings.

The step-by-step process explained (for a community workshop)

This is a simple method of content analysis. It begins with compiling lists following a brainstorming stage or collected throughout a SpeakOut session and then lumping or combining each point with other similar points. The splitting occurs after the lumping to allocate notional headings to the grouped material. Where the process is used *at a workshop table*, one of the benefits is that the participants collectively make two important decisions: (1) which items to group together and (2) the titles to allocate to each group of issues. This reduces bias and eliminates errors of interpretation.

The steps in this process (in a community workshop) are described below. Methods for analysing SpeakOut records are discussed later in this chapter. The diagram in Figure 11.3 summarizes the process.

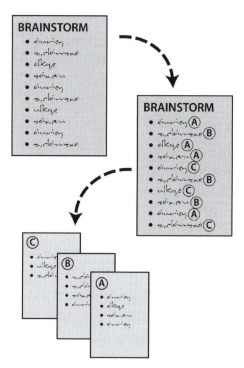

Figure 11.3 Diagram of the lump-and-split process

Brainstorming stage

- Issues are brainstormed at workshop tables and recorded by a recorder.
- Issues are recorded by a recorder during a SpeakOut process.
- All recording is 'vertical scribing', that is, recorded publicly in large letters on sheets of paper attached to a board or backing so that all participants can see the emerging record and correct it if the recorder makes an error or mis-hears a participant's contribution.
- Use active words like these:
  - *remove* the seating by the fence
  - *upgrade* the train station lighting
  - *cut down* vegetation beside the path to the train station
  - *install* seating for supervising adults next to the small playground
  - *build* more toilets in the amenities block
  - *put up* some signs to show the location of the western car park.

Review stage

- The group reviews the record of their previous session, displayed on a wall or partition.
- The material is the written record of a brainstorming session, recorded on a vertical surface by the group's recorder (see Figure 11.5).
- The recorder and facilitator work together to help the group sort material into discrete categories, to which everyone agrees.

Lumping stage

- The recorder reads aloud the brainstorming notes, starting at the top of the list.

- The recorder marks the first idea with the letter **A** (see Figure 11.6). It is important not to use numerals, as this may give a false sense that rankings or priorities are being allocated.
- The recorder marks each subsequent idea that is similar to the first idea with the same letter (**A**), advised by group members, working collectively. The issues need only be 'similar' and not exactly the same. Sub-categorizing is also possible at a later stage if a category contains too many dissimilar items.

Splitting stage

- When the list has been exhausted, the recorder returns to the top of the first page of notes and allocates the letter **B** to the next item.
- The process then continues, with the recorder allocating a **B** to all related items, advised by the group members.
- When the list has been exhausted, the recorder returns to the top of the first page of notes and allocates the letter **C** to the next item.
- The process then continues, allocating a **C** to all related items.
- The process of allocating letters continues until all recorded material has been marked with a letter. This generally generates about eight to ten categories.
- The letters are then transferred by the recorder to a separate large sheet.
- Working from the top (letter **A**), the group decides on the name of each heading (see Figure 11.7).
- Alternatively, material under the first major category headings could be further categorized into more detailed categories, depending on the specifications for the project and/or the final report.
- Finally, all the original points are recorded under the new headings (see Figure 11.8).

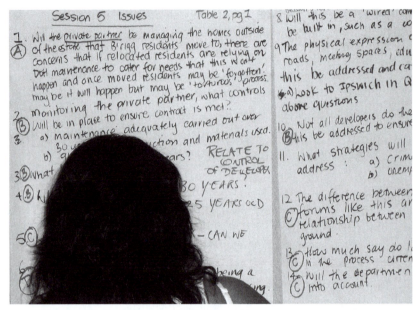

Figure 11.4 Allocating letters to a brainstormed list

An example from a SpeakOut

The objective of this community workshop was to gauge support and elicit suggestions for proposed improvements to a central business district (CBD) and a development plan for a small rural city. This list of categories could then be further prioritized and actions identified for different stages. Alternatively, the material under category headings could be further subdivided into more detailed categories, depending on reporting requirements.

Categorizing a record back at the office

While the lump-and-split process works well in workshops, it's also valuable for sorting SpeakOut findings after the event. Using the basic 'table/sort' function in Microsoft Word, this can be achieved quite easily once the material has been typed into a Word document. The simple steps are set out below.

- *Suitable Access from Station Square into the heart of CBD.*
- *Central theme to market CBD and to create a character for the CBD*
- *Exploring incentives to get businesses into the town.*
- *CBD Beautification and undergrounding power lines.*
- *Shade structures, all weather covering over roads – Ellena, Lennox and Adelaide Streets.*
- *Encourage owners of businesses in CBD to bring their shopfront awnings up to a good standard.*
- *Need clearways for when traffic congestion is at its worst.*
- *Regulating size of vehicles accessing CBD.*
- *Encouraging outdoor dining: CBD.*
- *Left-hand turn into and out of Ellena Street to Lennox Street.*

Figure 11.5 Brainstorming stage: butcher's paper transcript from a brainstorming session

The list

- Step 1: Type all points by issue stall as bullet points in a Word document.

Lumping: List 1

- Step 2: Type an **A** beside the first item. To make electronic sorting easier, we have found that typing **AAA** and **BBB** etc., works best.
- Step 3: Put an **A** beside similar items on all the lists until they are all exhausted.
- Step 4: Go back to the top of the list. Type a **B** beside the second item.
- Step 5: Type a **B** beside all similar items on all lists.
- Step 6: Continue until all items have a letter beside them.

> A Suitable Access from Station Square into the heart of CBD.
> B Central theme to market CBD and to create a character for the CBD
> B Exploring incentives to get businesses into the town.
> A CBD Beautification and undergrounding power lines.
> A Shade structures, all weather covering over roads – Ellena, Lennox and
>   Adelaide Streets.
> B Encourage owners of businesses in CBD to bring their shopfront
>   awnings up to a good standard.
> C Need clearways for when traffic congestion is at its worst.
> C Regulating size of vehicles accessing CBD.
> B Encouraging outdoor dining: CBD.
> C Left-hand turn into and out of Ellena Street to Lennox Street.

Figure 11.6 Lumping stage: issues lumped and assigned letters

Splitting: List 2

- Step 7: Look at all the **A**s. Find a generic title that fits them.
- Step 8: Type in a separate list (List 2).
- Steps 9 onwards: Do the same for all the other letters.
- Final Step: Cut and paste all **A** issues from the bullet points under the **A** heading. Do the same for all letters.

One of the great benefits of using the lump-and-split process in a *community workshop* is that it builds participant understanding and ownership of the emerging findings and the public record. It also reinforces the commitment of the workshop facilitators and managers that they will not 'mess with the record'. The participants decide on the grouping and give their own titles to the category headings. Whereas a social planner may use a term such as 'social infrastructure', community participants may be much happier with a heading like 'local facilities'.

A Beautification,
B Marketing and promotion,
C Traffic and parking,
Etc.

Figure 11.7 Splitting stage 1: a new list of category headings

Category A: Beautification
A CBD beautification and undergrounding powerlines
A Shade structures, all weather covering over roads: Ellena, Lennox and Adelaide Streets
A Suitable access from Station Square into the heart of CBD

Category B: Marketing and promotion
B Central theme to market CBD and to create a character for the CBD
B Exploring incentives to get businesses into the town
B Encourage owners of businesses in CBD to bring their shopfront awnings up to a good standard
B Encouraging outdoor dining: CBD

Category C: Traffic and parking
C Need clearways for when traffic congestion is at its worse
C Regulating size of vehicles accessing CBD
C Left-hand turn in and out of Ellena Street to Lennox Street

Figure 11.8 Splitting stage 2: original issues sorted under new category headings

5

OTHER CONSIDERATIONS
AND EVALUATION

One of the great benefits of a systematic debriefing is that it allows workers to report on the affective qualities of their interactions and raise issues of trust, enthusiasm, cynicism, perceived energy levels of participants and other matters that would not have been part of the information collected at their issue stalls.

Other Considerations

This chapter reminds us about the many building blocks of a successful workshop or SpeakOut, in addition to basic set-up and furnishing requirements. Some of these can operate as drawcards, while others contribute to hospitality, welcoming and participant comfort.

Drawcards

Community engagement processes such as SpeakOuts and community workshops require organizers to operate in 'hospitality mode', where it is best to imagine that you are having people over to your house. Recalling Karl's despairing plea in Chapter 2, how would you behave? What's necessary for you to be confident that participants will feel welcome, received and comfortable? Because it is a drop-in event, dependent on drawing people from 'outside', a SpeakOut places particular emphasis on drawcards. Different communities respond to different types of attractions, such as food, entertainment, presence of interpreters and other socially or culturally appropriate features.

Communication: Technology, signs and badges

With modern information technology, providing information to potential participants now involves more than letterboxing, good signs and distributed information. You can establish a noticeboard or a blog on the web, set up a project email address for comments and questions or set up a project webpage and link it to the agency's or proponent's home page. You can even establish discussion groups on the Internet. In some communities, these approaches will work brilliantly. However, it's important not to assume that everyone is connected through a computer. In many communities, you will still need to rely on non-electronic communication to reach a diversity of community members.

Good signs

The 'welcoming' process is made infinitely easier with good signs: from the car park to the registration desk, identifying the location of children's activities, restrooms and so on. You can never have too many signs for a workshop. Even with ample signage, some participants still get lost. We recommend that you label everything and make sure signs point in the right direction. Signage can never be too bold. Make certain that your outdoor signs are waterproof and that they can't blow away. Lightweight corrugated plastic or foam board is good for outdoor signs, as it is waterproof and durable so signs can be reused. It is light and can be attached with reusable adhesive or Velcro. Ensure that paints used outdoors are also waterproof. And remember that a little dampness can destroy the appearance of a sign printed on an inkjet printer. A laminator for small signs that need to be made at the last minute is a relatively inexpensive and invaluable addition to any stationery cupboard.

Remember, you may need to get permission to display signs.

Figure 12.1 A good sign of the commitment of the sponsoring body

---

Some signs that might be required are:

Workshop/meeting this way

Welcome

Sign indicating name or title of workshop and sponsor or organizing body

Car parking (if specially provided)

Access for people with disabilities

Entry

Registration

Toilets

Exits

Help yourself to tea and coffee

Children's activities this way

Please place questionnaires here

Telephone

Message board

Table numbers (best hung from the ceiling above each table or erected on tall boards attached to tables to ensure visibility)

Signs explaining displays of previous research and other materials for participants to look at before the workshop begins

Extra foam board, paper, pens and adhesives for unexpected sign requests (e.g., 'this toilet out of order')

'People signs' (or badges) identifying coordinators, clients, facilitators, recorders and other staff members and their roles.

Bold badges for all staff

Extra arrows to add to signs

Audio and visual recording

Audio and video recording of workshops is one way to ensure an accurate and complete record. It is not always appropriate at SpeakOuts. We recommend taking notes during plenary sessions in workshops, as transcribing from the audio recording is very time-consuming. An audio recording is valuable, however, for checking records for issues in dispute or for highly legalistic or political processes.

Photography

Taking photographs is also a great and relatively inexpensive way of recording the process and the product as it emerges. Photographs make a great addition to any report. It's always necessary to ask participants' permission before taking photographs or videotaping. In a workshop, as opposed to a SpeakOut, the issue of photography and videotaping should be raised from the front of the room before any small group sessions begin. It is often best to wait until people have been introduced and gained some trust and confidence before asking if they agree to have the workshop videotaped or photographed. In our experience, if you ask too early, you are more likely to get a negative response.

In most places, photography will require signed permission forms. One general way of handling the 'permission' issue in a workshop is to advise participants that they can change their minds about being photographed during the workshop or that individuals can request that they not be photographed directly. If participants object, simply switch off the cameras. Generally, however, participants are less likely to show concern if they are asked politely and if the purpose of the photographs is explained (for example, illustrations for reports, presentations and books).

In some cases, you may need written permission to use video material and photographs in a publication. In some countries and some public spaces, there are laws dictating the use of photography, especially photographing children. These must be obeyed. In Australia, for example, legislation does not permit photography of children without signed permission from a legal guardian.

Item/issue	Comments	☐ √
Always ask participants' permission first		
Avoid using a flash, as they are intrusive. Be wary of automatic cameras unless you can control the flash mechanism. If you do use a flash, know how to engage 'red-eye' function		
Check lighting at the venue, as various lights give different tints to the photograph. Fluorescent lights, for example, give a green tinge to photographs		
Set camera resolution according to the requirements for eventual use of the photographs. (It's best to shoot at high resolution and downsize for website or PowerPoints later)		
Ensure you have adequate camera memory sticks or cards		
If camera batteries are rechargeable, bring the charger and an extra set of batteries. If you are using non-rechargeable batteries, bring enough to change them at least twice during a workshop or SpeakOut		
Find a lockable secure place for camera storage and battery charger during the event		

'More is more'

With respect to photography and video recording, our motto is 'more is more'. We have learned to brief our video camera operators in great detail and regard every workshop as a 'photo opportunity'. Clients and proponents often seek photos and videotapes after the event (for annual reports, a film about the city, a training videotape) and are disappointed if you can't comply, even though they did not think of it at the time of the workshop.[1] We celebrate the advent of digital cameras as a great help in this work and mourn the demise of the old, reliable Polaroid camera, which was an invaluable tool for community engage-ment practice. A new Polaroid camera is about to arrive, we are told.

If participants request that photographs should not be taken, you must honour their request. However, it is usually possible right at the end of the workshop to ask to take a few 'record shots' to show how the room was set up. After the event ends, you can also take photographs of props, signs, plans and materials provided by other groups.

Audio recording

It's important to ask whether it's really necessary to audio-record the workshop session. We rarely make audio recordings, having found that they are more trouble than they are worth, for our purposes. If you do proceed, remember that the acoustic quality of the venue will be a consideration affecting the type and quality of audio equipment required. The venue may have a public address system. If it does, it's wise to speak to someone who knows its cap-abilities and how it works. Remember to test and double-check every piece of equipment before you use it. We have an adage that has proved to be true: 'For want of a double adapter, the workshop can be lost.' It's valuable to get into the habit of thinking through 'worst-case' scenarios when electronic equipment is concerned.

Audio recording of a large workshop requires many microphones, a full-time mixer/technician and lacks the flexibility required to be used in small groups at an interactive workshop. Our advice is that you tape-record those parts of the workshop that are easy to record (such as role plays, speeches and whole-group plenary sessions). Record the rest using a typist at a laptop or a roving reporter. The records prepared by recorders at workshop tables or issue stalls will, of course, be your main record.

You will need one roving microphone for every 20 participants or the ques-tioner may finish before the microphone even reaches them. Towards the end of an intensive workshop, tired recorders may miss important points. You may consider engaging relief recorders at this stage.

Item/issue	Comments	☐ √
Public address system[2]		
Check sound levels ahead of time[3]		
A person stationed at the back of the room to report on sound levels once the workshop begins		
Recording facility, equipment and tapes and/or disks		
Fixed microphone for on stage. Make sure it works, know how to use it and what to do when/if it 'squeals'		
Roving microphones for audience communication (ideally, one for every 20 participants)[4]		
Determine the quality necessary when recording – for video transfer[5]		
Check sensitivity of microphone and podium (can be noisy)		
Ensure one knowledgeable person is in charge		
Decide who will record and change tapes and/or disks		
Audiotapes or disks for digital audio recording		
Check batteries for all battery-operated equipment and carry spare batteries, including microphone batteries, as appropriate		
During a break, test the quality of recording so far		

Video recording

Video recording is a fantastic way of recording and reporting. A video becomes an important document reporting on an event and short clips can easily be inserted into PowerPoint and other presentations. Even video with poor sound quality can be used with a voice-over. Consider the quality of the video. Who is the potential audience? Will the video need to be of broadcast quality?

With careful briefing, your video operator or crew can operate unobtrusively. In our experience, if this is done well, participants come to ignore a video crew and get on with the business of the workshop or the SpeakOut. The greatest problem is often the hand-held microphone. It's good to be able to encourage the crew to keep it out of people's faces while they are working. A careful balance needs to be struck between capturing high-quality material and being intrusive.

Be aware of the heat and intrusive nature of lighting for videotaping. This may cause ventilation and cooling problems in indoor settings on hot days.

Figure 12.2 Video is a good way to record a SpeakOut, Chinatown, Hawai'i, 2006

Item/issue	Comments	☐ √
Consider whether you require a professional or an amateur crew		
If you are using a professional crew, try to make sure that you will get value for money		
Fully brief people who will shoot the footage. Inform them of the issues, the types of shots required and the qualities of the workshop or SpeakOut you expect them to capture		
A 'shot list' is necessary to assist both amateur and professional video personnel so that they can focus on issues that are important		
Hired equipment: check whether it has adequate audio recording or if a separate microphone will be required. Use a separate microphone if possible		
Is lighting adequate, but not intrusive? What will be the effect of fluorescent lighting? Can it be turned off?		
Prepare a detailed running sheet for the camera crew (explaining where, when and what you wish to emphasize)		
Gaffer (duct) tape to tape down cables to the floor (yellow is best)		
Extra videotapes or disks		
Extra batteries for all equipment (microphone, audio and video recording equipment)		
Ensure that you can provide security for all equipment. Perhaps a locked room or a space that is constantly supervised		
Test batteries and all connections before use		
Make sure that all instruction books are included		

A warning

We've blown our share of fuses over the years. It's wise to be aware that in some older or run-down community and church buildings, the electricity demands of lighting and other equipment necessary to support videotaping may overwhelm the wiring.

Models and aerial photographs

An effective way to communicate what is going on in a proposed development or on a site is by locating a large aerial photograph (orthophoto map) or scale model in the centre of a SpeakOut or workshop. Depending on the project, you can make the model user-friendly by designing it so that components can be lifted out. We have tried many versions of the model in a SpeakOut setting and confirm that simple is best. The sorts of elaborate models that some architects produce (with purple grass and trees made out of steel wool or paper clips) rarely resonate with community participants. Our most effective models have been home-made, of recycled materials, prepared with small budgets.

Figure 12.3 This is *not* the sort of model that will be helpful in a workshop or SpeakOut

Figure 12.4 A simple model helps all participants understand options

Similar advice applies to aerial photographs. A high-quality orthophoto map with all major streets and landmarks and features clearly labelled will generate lots of discussion. Most people cannot read maps or plans so this alternative works well for them. A facilitator (who has good local geographical knowledge and can help people find their homes and other features) to staff the model or map is essential in both a SpeakOut and workshop setting.

'Greening' your workshop and SpeakOut

We are all concerned that our work will not impose further burdens on our fragile ecosystems. And many of the processes that communities will be engaged in in the future will be about sustainability and protecting life on Earth. Ecological consciousness can change the way we work with communities and can raise many provocative questions about workshop design and management. As communities everywhere begin to engage with the planetary crisis that now confronts us all, participants will be increasingly sensitive to environmental considerations. These considerations will inevitably extend to your workshop or SpeakOut processes. A comprehensive discussion of practical approaches to community engagement with sustainability can be found in *Kitchen Table Sustainability* (Sarkissian et al, 2008).

Item/issue	Comments	☐ √
Ensure that the workshop venue is easily accessible by public transport and that your proposed start and finish times suit the public transport timetables		
Provide free bus or train tickets to participants (this was a highly successful feature of a transport workshop we attended in outer suburban Perth)		
Consider providing a bus to collect participants from key transport interchanges		
Try to select a venue that does not entirely depend on air conditioning in summer		
Paper use: use recycled paper for all printed materials, print on both sides, reduce where possible to get more than one page per side (but be careful that older eyes can still read the print) and recycle leftover workshop paper		
Produce reports on recycled paper printed on both sides		
Arrange timetabling to encourage staff and participants to share cars		
Hire crockery and utensils rather than using disposable plates and plastic cups and cutlery[6]		
Employ local caterers and staff who do not have to travel long distances to the workshop		
Use xylene-free pens or markers for butcher's paper and for any displays		
Ensure that all equipment purchased for your 'stationery cupboard' is as ecologically responsible as possible		
Try to ensure that all presentation material and signs can be reused throughout the community engagement process		

The most important thing you can do to work for a more sustainable environment is to put Nature on the agenda: to design a programme that encourages people to ask questions about planning and design that go beyond strictly human-centred and utilitarian approaches. Some people find this very unsettling. In terms of workshop design and management, how you do your work reflects your values. 'Greening' your workshop means paying attention to the ecological impacts of all the choices you make in workshop location, timing, design, materials and operation. Some of the suggestions we have found helpful are given in the table on the previous page.

Insurance

We are living in an increasingly litigious era where everyone is concerned about 'risk minimization'. Management of risk, a major concern of government authorities, often means that they will not provide insurance cover for community workshops. While we favour 'care maximization' over risk minimization, we recognize that risk factors are important considerations for many. Consultants and community groups may need to take responsibility for the provision of their own public liability insurance.

Issues of liability and insurance are not pleasant but they must be addressed. Be clear about who is responsible in the event that something goes wrong or someone is injured. Always ensure that any community workshop or SpeakOut is covered by adequate public liability insurance. It is also wise to cover the equipment in the event that it is stolen, lost or damaged. If equipment is being hired, ask the 'what if' questions regarding accidental damage, loss, theft and acts of God.

Many government agencies may be able to include staff and participants in their 'umbrella' insurance but this must be checked and confirmed in writing beforehand. Some departments hold no public liability cover whatsoever, however. It's important to check that all workers are covered by workers' compensation insurance. Remember to get competitive quotes and above all, confirmations in writing. If you are employing employees of a consulting firm in your event, ensure that they are registered and eligible for workers' compensation in case of accidents. Ensure that all volunteers are also covered.

Child and infant care

Some children will not wish to participate in a workshop or will be too young to be part of planning or design exercises. To ensure that adults, other young people and children are able to participate comfortably without distractions, it is important to provide infant and child care. Parents are very particular about this matter and thus the caregivers must be experienced and qualified. It will be necessary to check local regulations and requirements for registration and insurance. We recommend that you check with the local council regarding statutory requirements. The number of caregivers will depend on the number of children and this will also dictate the size of the room being used.

One good source for child-care workers for community engagement events is the local child-care centre. Staff members are often willing to work at a community workshop as it provides them with extra income. It's generally not fair or a good idea to expect professionals to work as volunteers in this context.

Insurance issues associated with child care are frequently complex. Sometimes your existing public liability insurance cannot be extended to cover those functions. If this becomes an insurmountable problem (and it often is, in our experience), you may find the simplest solution is to pay for people's usual babysitting arrangements. Although we always offer to provide child care for workshops and SpeakOuts, our offer is rarely taken up.

Ensure that all spaces used for child care have access to toilets and places to change infants. In winter, ensure that rooms are adequately heated.

Some basic child-care requirements

Item/issue	Comments	☐ √
Portable heater if room is not heated		
Small carpet if room is not carpeted		
Video and television (check power points, extension leads, double adapter requirements)		
Tape recorder and tapes or CD player and discs to play music		
Toys and games appropriate for ages of children		
A quiet place for infants to sleep. Sheets, blankets and small foam mattresses		
Basic kit of nappies (diapers), tissues, etc. for changing infants		
Basic drawing materials		
Access to toilets		
Access to kitchen, for heating bottles and other food		

Food and catering

In most societies, community activities are accompanied by the sharing of food. It's an integral part of the process of community decision making, celebration and renewal. Somehow, that is often forgotten and local people are expected to come to workshops to share their wisdom in uncomfortable circumstances without even the offer of a cup of coffee. Food supports process. It's as simple as that. Not only does it provide the energy to keep people going, it allows congeniality to be developed. It helps people to relax, to become acquainted and to converse informally.

Catering is one aspect of community engagement that is often seen as excessive or superfluous. Remember Karl's sad tale about the project manager in

Chapter 2. And remember that you may be inviting people to participate in a long and often tiring process. Workshops are often held in the evening and participants arrive straight from work. They simply cannot be expected to engage and provide valuable information on a few biscuits and a cup of instant coffee. Do not forget that your workers will also need to be fed. If they come in the morning for a workshop that starts after lunch, you will need to provide them with lunch. Refreshments will enable them to remain focused. If they are being briefed in the morning, you may need to provide food for them *before* the workshop begins. It is always good practice to have tea, coffee and juice available to participants on arrival. We believe it is better to order too much food than to run out. The Salvation Army never rejects our leftover cakes and sandwiches.

This is not to say that lavish and heavy meals should accompany participatory processes or that food and drink should be used to 'buy' people's compliance. The type of catering will depend on local circumstances. Arrangements must be culturally appropriate. We recommend that you use local organizations (such as a school parents' organization or a church auxiliary) to do the catering for the workshop, however simple it may be. In some cases, for example, a local council may feel that evidence of extravagance would be inappropriate. (Is there an election coming up?) In another case, in a small country town in Australia, it might be an insult to local people if the Country Women's Association were not asked to provide the refreshments (with an appropriate donation from the project budget, of course) and the local Garden Club to provide the flowers.

It is important to resist the temptation to have 'the absolute minimum' in terms of food and drink. People do get very tired in these workshops, facilitators and participants alike. High-quality food not only provides energy, but the 'hospitality' experience of sharing food, prepared with care and attention, also makes them feel welcome and valued. An important function of the workshop or a SpeakOut is that it is an exercise in hospitality.

Almost certainly, your caterers (unless they are professional caterers) will require extra assistance when they arrive. It is a good idea to delegate the job of helping them set up to a member of your workshop or meeting team.

Item/issue	Comments	☐ √
Check your numbers carefully and make sure that you have ordered enough food and check the size of servings provided by the caterer		
Food for support staff during set-up and briefing session: • high-energy food to support process • low in sugar • low in fat • high protein • complex carbohydrates • lots of raw food		
Special food for children's activities		
Check food preferences and allergies in advance		
Vegetarian option, depending on local circumstances		
Culturally appropriate food (it is best to avoid bacon and pork)		
Warm food		
Cold food		
Finger food to ensure ease of eating		
Confirm exactly what the caterer will provide		
Tea/coffee/milk: • decaffeinated • herbal • soy milk • low fat/skim milk (Note most children/young people don't drink tea/coffee – they prefer hot chocolate, juice or cordial)		
Fruit juice		

Item/issue	Comments	☐ √
No foam cups and preferably no paper plates (hire crockery if necessary)		
Adequate bench space, microwave oven, fridge, stovetop or convection oven to meet caterer's requirements		
Crockery		
Cutlery		
Cups and glasses		
Urn (do you need an extension cord?)		
Rubbish bins		
Rubbish bags		
Paper napkins		
A clean bucket or large jug (to fill the urn)		
Decide where and when the food is to be served		
Place to wash up		

Entertainment

Providing entertainment during a SpeakOut (or other types of workshops) can be a tricky business, as entertainment can be both a drawcard and a distraction. Aim to select the type of entertainment that suits the local culture, the venue type and that will support the event. In some communities, singing, dancing, playing music or storytelling are forms of cultural celebration that bring people together. Tapping into community groups can help with deciding the most appropriate type of entertainment. This approach enables organizers to be culturally sensitive and gain local support.

Logistically, it is important to be aware of the sound level of any potential performance. Entertainment that is too loud can drown out discussion at the issue stalls and work against the aims of the SpeakOut. Adjusting the location of the entertainment within the venue (in terms of visibility and/or sound level) can help determine its effectiveness. If speakers and a sound system are used, be sure that the sound does not blast in the direction of the issue stalls. On other occasions, when entertainment is included in the agenda (for example as a blessing or opening chant), the performance should take centre stage.

Item/issue	Comments	☐ √
Determine the type of entertainment that is appropriate		
Find the most suitable location for the entertainment group		
Determine if they are for hire or are a local group (part of the community) which does not expect to be paid		
Make careful arrangements about the sound system and speakers if they are to be used		
Is a stage needed?		
Confirm when and where the entertainment group should report upon their arrival		

Interpreters

Successful SpeakOuts have been held in communities with large numbers of non-English speakers. Traditionally, these people tend to be excluded from engagement processes because of language and cultural barriers. One practical way to include these groups in workshops and SpeakOuts is by ensuring that interpreters are present. To involve interpreters, identify the most prominent community languages before approaching local ethnic groups that may be able to help with interpreters. Having interpreters not only helps break through the language barrier, but can also increase enthusiasm about the SpeakOut process. They can help attract participants to the event. We have found that if the interpreters wear appropriate labels and simply wait by the registration desk, they can easily be identified by members of their communities and then accompany them around the SpeakOut circuit.

Item/issue	Comments	☐ √
Identify the languages spoken in the community		
Identify any local ethnic-based groups or associations		
Decide how many interpreters will be needed per language		
Identify and invite interpreters and make arrangements for their payment		
Send all briefing materials to interpreters, including material about the project, as well as training materials for listeners and recorders		
Arrange a briefing for the interpreters, preferably separate from the briefing for listeners and recorders		
Involve interpreters fully in the briefing for interpreters and recorders and welcome their suggestions and comments		
Involve the interpreters fully in the debriefing session		

Involving senior management from the start

We cannot overemphasize the importance of involving senior people from the hosting agency or the proponent from the start and making sure that they attend all processes. Technical experts (such as engineers, architects and planners) can wear badges or labels that proclaim: 'Ask me. I know what's going on.'

When things go 'feral'

Organizing a community planning workshop or a SpeakOut is like organizing any community gathering. There are always moments when things go 'feral'. Despite all the planning, things happen that require brilliant, on-the-spot teamwork and outcome-focused responses. Based on our experiences, below are some examples of (big) things that may go wrong and some suggestions about what to do if they do occur in your processes.

1 Inclement weather, high wind, pelting rain …

Kelvin reminds us that we've had all sorts of shocking experiences in our SpeakOut and workshop planning careers. The most awesome was attempting to hold a workshop on a hill in a suburban greenfield site when a massive storm downed four marquees with a 110km/h wind. Wendy and Kelvin are still recovering 20 years later![7]

Making sure that you have a secure and appropriate venue should always be a priority when planning a SpeakOut or community workshop. Be prepared with an alternative if things really go wrong or there is a sudden change in the weather, particularly if your venue is outdoors. We recommend that you seriously consider an alternative venue and equipment to allow the event to continue. If possible, look for another venue in the same general locality.

2 Power outages

We have laboured this point and here it is again: the next important thing to pay attention to is power availability and reliability. At unpredictable times, the power may go out. That's when you really need back-up plans. When the venue chosen is indoors (a community centre, warehouse or the like), unless there is a way to get the power authority to bring the power back up, it is probably best to find a power generator or to reschedule. However, when the venue is outdoors, we recommend renting a power generator (a quiet, modern one), as it is often wasteful and risky to cancel and reschedule.

3 Computer/laptop incompatibilities

An infuriating problem occurs when the projector cannot communicate with the laptop and vice versa. These sorts of problems can be predicted and resolved beforehand. Having an experienced and dedicated gofer and technical person for resolving these sorts of problems is essential. Our estimate is that these problems occur about 50 per cent of the time!

4 When one voice tries to stop it all

In a memorable workshop in Melbourne in 1989, Wendy and Kelvin were confronted by a coup in the community organization which meant that the activist they had been negotiating with for several months had been thrown out by other members of the organization. The deposed President made one last stand in the facilitator training session, demanding that Wendy step down as workshop Chair on the basis of a procedural technicality. This was about two hours before proceedings were to commence. Five hundred people had registered for the workshop. Wendy effectively called the man's bluff and he was last seen being escorted out of the marquee by two female members of the new leadership. But it was a tense and destabilizing time. Our reconnaissance was not very effective: we should have known that that was coming. A lot was at stake and all our arrangements for a huge workshop almost collapsed in that moment.

Conclusions

We don't want to conclude this chapter on a negative note. Please be reassured that things do not *always* go wrong. We have been the recipients of marvellous and unexpected acts of generosity and helpfulness as we have planned and managed community workshops and SpeakOuts. We have witnessed teamwork miracles. We've felt loved and supported by our colleagues and communities. We've witnessed inspired facilitation, listening and recording. We've heard brilliant ideas from community participants – adults, children and young people. These are the times when we know this work is worthwhile.

Our attention to the fine details of organizing community events simply aims to remove concerns about *arrangements* so that people can get down to the community business – the business of giving advice, making decisions, working in partnership and being empowered. We support an engaged citizenry. That, ultimately, is why we do this work and why we encourage others to do it.

Evaluation

The importance of evaluation

Formal evaluation of a SpeakOut (as well as a community workshop) can be undertaken as a way of testing the effectiveness of the model for eliciting information required, involving the community and building community capacity. Several approaches can be used:

1　Record participant numbers with the utmost care. Careful attention to sign-up sheets at the reception desk and at each issue stall is necessary to ensure accurate numbers of participants (this is essential for benefit–cost analyses to ensure that the process provides value for money). Make sure that the reception desk is staffed at all times.

2　Comprehensive debriefing of all Listeners, Recorders and other staff will give a clear indication of the effectiveness of the SpeakOut and the flavour of participant responses.

3　Evaluation questionnaires or questionnaires designed to elicit information on specific matters can be completed by participants before leaving.

4　Systematic analysis of the comments recorded at issue stalls can yield a clear idea of the emphasis of community issues and the strength of community opinions.

5   Publicizing a report on the SpeakOut and distributing it to community organizations for comment can contribute to another level of analysis. Because SpeakOuts are often held to provide information for a planning or design process related to a specific site, evaluation is vital as it can prompt specific action.

6   Where questionnaire surveys are conducted, great care is necessary to ensure that bias does not creep into the research design.

7   Tailor-made processes are necessary for evaluating the effectiveness of a SpeakOut for children and young people.

Evaluations of SpeakOuts and their outcomes are generally issue-based and are used to prioritize community comments and suggestions about those issues. Evaluations need to include recommendations for further work (including, for example, membership and terms of reference for Accountability Groups or other continuing participatory processes).

Asking participants to assess a SpeakOut

It's often helpful to ask participants themselves to assess the quality of the work by listeners and recorders. Although time is always an issue, a simple questionnaire could address some of these questions.[1]

The Listener

- Did the listener clearly explain her or his role to each participant?
- Was the listener effective in getting participants to focus on the task at hand?
- Was the listener effective in getting participants to use one method or interactive activity at a time?
- Was the listener able to keep the flow of participants moving along smoothly from stall to stall?
- Did the listener talk too much?
- Did all participants who visited or passed by this stall have a chance to participate?

- Was the listener respectful of participants and their ideas?
- How well did the listener handle disruptive behaviour of participants (if any)?
- Was the listener able to remain neutral and not get involved?
- Did the listener become defensive when criticized?
- Was the listener effective in bringing a discussion with a participant to closure, especially if others were waiting to speak?
- Did the listener effectively support the recorder?

The recorder

- Did the recorder define her or his role to each participant?
- Was the recording of participants' comments and results of interactive exercises legible?
- Were separate options easily identifiable and carefully recorded?
- Did the recorder capture the basic ideas of participants' contributions?
- Did the recorder make corrections without getting defensive?
- Did the recorder slow down to ensure a clear record of what the participant was saying?
- Did the recorder effectively support the Listener?

SpeakOut space

- Was the SpeakOut room or space of the appropriate size and shape for the number of participants involved?
- Were displays and furniture arranged and oriented effectively for this type of SpeakOut?
- Was the atmosphere of the SpeakOut appropriate for the occasion (not too formal or too relaxed)?
- Were levels of light, heat, ventilation and noise suitable?
- Were the required materials and equipment available and properly designed to facilitate comment?

Issues identification

- Were issues clearly defined?
- Did the division of issues by issue stall appear to be logical to participants?
- Were these issues relevant to the needs and interests of participants?
- Did participants feel that they had enough information or expertise to analyse and solve the problems presented at stalls?
- Did the SpeakOut process encourage participants to examine a wide enough range of alternatives or options?
- Did participants feel they had to rush prematurely to wrap up their activities at any stall?
- Was relevant material reproduced in appropriate local languages?
- Were interpreters available to assist participants for whom English is not the first language?

Visual displays

- Was the material presented in an accessible and legible form?
- Were visual prompts used to reduce reliance on reading ability?
- Did displays clearly explain the purpose of the material?
- Was display material well organized and well presented?

Interactive exercises

- Was the choice of material for interactive exercises appropriate (i.e., issues that could be worked through in a short exercise with little assistance)?
- Was the interactive display material presented in an accessible and legible form?
- Were maps and plans of appropriate size, adequately labelled and easy to read?
- Did instructions for the exercises clearly explain the purpose of the material?

The value of systematic debriefing

In Chapter 5, we discussed the exceptional benefits of systematic debriefing after a SpeakOut. A well prepared facilitator and note-taker (preferably not someone who has already done this all day) can help workers assess the effectiveness of the whole process, as well as that of their own stall. Notes from the debriefing session can form part of the SpeakOut record, as well as the evaluation. One of the great benefits of a systematic debriefing is that it allows workers to report on the *affective* qualities of their interactions and raise issues of trust, enthusiasm, cynicism, perceived energy levels of participants and other matters that would not have been part of the information collected at their issue stalls. The same applies, of course, to a community workshop.

Staff on the reception desk will also have valuable advice about how the whole experience was received by participants.

Glossary

Action research

Research oriented towards bringing about change, often involving respondents in the process of investigation, with the researchers being aware of their influence on the research process by being a part of the environment they study.

Animateur

A person with specific skills employed to assist in organizing and enlivening a community process, such as children's participatory design activities. Generally used in community cultural development projects and working with children and young people. This person may also be a community artist.

Appreciative Inquiry (AI)

A form of asset-based community development where the focus is on finding the best in people and situations and helping people list and amplify those assets or qualities in a community. The focus is on innovation and unexplored potential, rather than lists of weaknesses and deficiencies. It can lead to visions of values and possible futures.

Asset-Based Community Development (ABCD)

Challenges the traditional approach to solving urban problems by focusing service providers and funding agencies on the needs and deficiencies of neighbourhoods. It has been demonstrated that community assets are key building blocks in sustainable urban and rural community revitalization efforts. These community assets include: the skills of local residents, the power of local associations, the resources of public, private and non-profit institutions, and the physical and economic resources of local places.

Brainstorming

Vigorous discussion to generate ideas in which all possibilities are considered. Widely used first step in generating solutions to problems (Wates, 2000).

Brainwriting

Ask each of the group members to respond in silence with four written suggestions to a defined problem; individually at completion, group members exchange papers with each other and add suggestions to the 'new' paper, those notes are then compared and discussed.

Capacity building

The development of awareness, knowledge, skills and operational capability by certain actors, normally the community, to achieve their purpose (Wates, 2000).

Citizens' jury

An opportunity for a randomly selected group of the public (usually about 15 to 20 people) to deliberate about an issue for between one and five days. A professional facilitator helps them understand a range of viewpoints and search for common ground. Expert witnesses are called on a variety of issues and are questioned by the jurors. The findings are presented to decision makers.

Civil society

The arena of organized citizen activity outside of the state and market sectors. People coming together to define, articulate and act on their concerns through various forms of organization and expression.

Community

Used in many ways. Usually refers to those living within a small, loosely defined geographical area. Yet any group of individuals who share interests may also be described as a community. Also sometimes used to describe a physical area rather than a group of people (Wates, 2000).

Community engagement

Community engagement, as used in this manual, refers to engagement processes and practices in which a wide range of people work together to achieve a shared goal guided by a commitment to a common set of values, principles and criteria.

Community indicators

Measures devised and used by communities for understanding and drawing attention to important issues and trends. Useful for building an agenda for education and action (Wates, 2000).

Community planning

A process whereby an authority or organization works with others to plan, provide and promote the well-being of communities with the active involvement of communities in the decisions that affect people's lives. In Australia, this is often called social planning.

Consensus

Consensus has two common meanings: (1) a general agreement among the members of a given group or community, each of which exercises some discretion in decision making and follow-up action and (2) the theory and practice of getting such agreements. Consensus requires respect for group members' opinions. Once a decision is made, it is important to trust in members' discretion in follow-up action.

Consensus forum

A large number of stakeholders deliberate for between one and three days with the goal of reaching common ground on broad and complex issues and influencing decision making. They are selected to be representative of the community, as well as by invitation and are overseen by a Guidance Team. Trained table facilitators assist and a forum report is prepared for comment.

Coordinator or Chair/Head facilitator

The person in charge of the meeting or workshop, who manages the entire process, directs the flow of SpeakOut information, monitors effectiveness of work at workshop tables and keeps the proceedings to the agenda and on time.

Co-production

Implies shared responsibility between citizens and public officials (and more established shared legitimacy of interest and involvement), in producing services and managing development processes. Purpose: to work together constructively through inevitable tensions and conflicts, negotiating outcomes with recognized power and responsibility sharing. Term used widely in Europe to mean community engagement.

Cultural diversity

Cultural diversity encompasses the cultural differences that exist between people, such as language, dress and traditions, and the way societies organize themselves, their conception of morality and religion, and the way they interact with the environment.

Cultural planning

The strategic and integral use of cultural resources in urban and community development.

Deliberative poll/survey

A representative, random sample of the population (150 to 400 people) is surveyed before and after listening to and questioning competing experts and taking part in dialogue with peers over one to four days. Care is taken to provide a briefing document and facilitation to assist participants. A final report informs policy.

Design charrette or charrette

Intensive design session, often including an 'all-nighter', originally just for architecture students but more recently including the public and professionals. The term originated at the Paris Ecole des Beaux-Arts at the turn of the century. Projects were collected at designated times on a cart (*charrette*), where students would be found putting finishing touches to their schemes. The term *charrette* is often used without the word 'design'. Similar to a 'design workshop' (Wates, 2000).

Designing for Real

Term used to describe the use of adaptable models to develop detailed design proposals for a building or site. Participants explore options by moving parts of the model around, e.g., parts of a building or whole buildings. Similar concept to *Planning for Real* but on a smaller scale (Wates, 2000).

Enquiry-by-design consensus forum

An interactive process held over one to four days involving a representative group of people (stakeholders, random sample and self-nominations) who learn about issues, deliberate with each other and search for common ground. Multidisciplinary technical teams brief participants. Participants agree on definition of triple bottom line criteria, advantages and disadvantages of options and prioritize options. A follow-up report is prepared later.

Event Manager or Producer

The person who organizes all the logistical details and planning for a SpeakOut and manages the event on the day.

Facilitation

Bringing people together to decide what they wish to do and to work together to decide how to do it.

Facilitator

A person with group process skills responsible for the balanced flow of information at a workshop table group of approximately six to ten people. This person often reports back on behalf of their group to plenary sessions. They and the table recorder receive their briefing instructions from the Chair or Head facilitator.

Fishbowl

An innovative workshop approach, where some participants sit in the centre of a large group (in the 'round') and participate in a process that the others observe. It can be used in role plays within workshops or in community meetings or workshops as a way of highlighting the role of the professional planner in resolving community issues. Workshop technique where participants sit round and observe a planning team working on a problem without taking part themselves.

Future search conference

Highly structured two and a half day process allowing a community or organization to create a shared vision for its future. Ideally, 64 people take part: eight tables of eight (Wates, 2000).

Green sheet

Feedback forms (usually printed on green paper) for workshop participants to fill in if they wish for further information, want to be contacted after the event or feel that issues they wish to raise were not addressed fully during the workshop. The workshop Chair or other representative of the client should respond to all green sheets in writing or by telephone as soon as possible after the workshop.

Listener

A facilitator at an issue stall in a SpeakOut.

Mock-up

Full-size representation of a change or development, usually on its proposed site, prior to finalizing the design, used to test the proposed design (Wates, 2000).

Open day

Process conducted for all or part of a day, when a project or organization encourages people to come and find out what it is doing via displays and provides opportunities to make comments. Often used to generate interest and momentum. Similar to a *SpeakOut,* only without the intensive facilitation of that model (Wates, 2000).

Open House event

Event designed to allow those promoting development initiatives to present them to a wider public and secure reactions in an informal manner. Displays and experts to explain plans and drawings are the usual way this event is organized. Sometimes a small discussion group is also held for an hour or less. Halfway between an exhibition and a workshop.

Open Space Technology (OST)

Framework developed by Harrison Owen in the 1980s to allow for maximum participant involvement in a conference or workshop. There are no keynote speakers, agendas, pre-announced workshops or panel discussions. Rather, participants create their own conference, becoming facilitators, leaders and participants (Wates, 2000).

Open Space workshop

Workshop processes that last from half a day to three days for between 20 and 1000 participants. It is a process for generating commitment to action in communities or organizations. Features include starting without an agenda, with the issues to be discussed formulated by the participants themselves, who then arrange for them to be discussed.

Participatory democracy

A process that involves people directly in decision making that affects them, rather than through formally elected representatives such as councillors or MPs, as in representative democracy (Wates, 2000).

Participatory design

Design processes that involve the users of the item or places being designed.

Planning for Real

Eye-catching, hands-on participatory design method using three-dimensional models of a neighbourhood or structure plan. Registered brand name for a UK-based method of community involvement in planning and development focusing on the construction of flexible cardboard models and suggestion and priority cards. Community priorities and a profile of community needs and desires are the outcomes.

Post-it™ note

Or simply 'Post-it'. Registered brand name for a sheet of paper with a sticky edge. Come in pads. Great technical aid to collective working as, unlike cards, they can be stuck on vertical surfaces and moved around to create groups. Come in 'super-sticky' form, which are most useful.

Public meeting or forum

May range in size from 20 to several hundred people, usually attending because of wide advertising such as letterboxing or newspaper advertising. Participants may be the general public or nominated by groups and organizations. Format may involve contributions by a speaker or panel followed by questions and discussion. Advertised, open-access event at which issues are presented and commented on and at which decisions may be made. Term is normally used to refer to fairly formal events with the audience sitting in rows facing a speaker or panel of speakers with a chairperson who controls the proceedings.

Recorder

A person assigned to a group table to record, in a format all can read, the ideas and decisions of group members. Ideally, this person is paid and is not a volunteer community member, as it is demanding work. Community members, trained and paid, can make excellent recorders.

Risk assessment

Examination of risks from disasters existing in any community. The basis for risk reduction. Comprises three components: hazard analysis; vulnerability analysis; resource assessment (Wates, 2000).

Role play

Adopting the role of others and acting out scenarios. Used to help people understand the views and aspirations of others.

Scoping

Preliminary exploration of a subject or project.

Search conference

A structured meeting of between 30 and 50 invited participants selected to be heterogeneous but sharing identifiable interests; often conducted early in a project to identify a broad cross-section of views; lasting from half a day to several days.

Conference or workshop for key interested parties organized as a first stage in a community engagement process on a project. May include briefings, role play, reconnaissance, interactive displays, workshops and plenary sessions. Similar to planning day or community planning forum.

Social capital

Ability of social structures and institutions to provide a supportive framework for individuals; includes firms, trade unions, families, communities, voluntary organizations, legal/political systems, educational institutions, health services, financial institutions and systems of property rights.

Social marketing

Seen as a strategy for changing behaviour, one that combines the best elements of the traditional approaches to social change in an integrated planning and action framework. Importantly, this approach uses advances in communication technology and marketing skills.

SpeakOut

An interactive event a bit like an Open House, but intensively staffed with facilitators and recorders. Participants drop in and visit a number of issue stalls set up with interpretative material about the community or planning issues under consideration. A staffed exhibition with lots of interesting things to read. It provides an informal and interactive 'public meeting' environment where a wide range of people have a chance to participate. One feature is that it encourages casual, 'drop-in' participation at people's convenience. At the SpeakOut, people find issues about which they wish to 'speak out' and have their say, with comments clearly recorded by a recorder. A listener pays close attention and asks questions.

Stakeholder

An individual, organization, group, agency or business with an interest in the future of the project and/or the community.

Sticky wall

A rectangular sheet of parachute silk sprayed with repositional adhesive. Useful for affinity diagram exercises because notes do not require adhesive backing.

Sustainable community

Community that lives in harmony with its local and global environment and does not cause damage to distant environments or other human or non-human communities – now or in the future. Quality of life and the interest of future generations are valued above immediate material consumption and economic growth (see Wates, 2000).

Sustainable development

Development that meets the needs of the present without compromising the ability of future generations to meet their own needs (Brundtland Report definition) (Wates, 2000).

Table group

Within a workshop, a group of six to ten people under the guidance of a facilitator and assisted by a recorder, usually working through a structured agenda and reporting back to the full workshop group in plenary sessions.

21st century town meeting/dialogue

A method involving very large numbers of community, industry and government representatives (100 to 5000 or more) in a forum of one or two days. Participants engage in formed deliberation in small groups, connected through networked computers. They work from pre-designed questions, entering their individual team consensus, as well as priority ratings and rankings. The goal is to find common ground and priorities on broad and complex issues. This is a multi-step process with intensive facilitation and includes trained facilitators and theme teams, as well as volunteer scribes.

Vision, visioning, guided visualization and guided imagery

An image of how things may be in the future. May be in words or pictures. Provides a useful guide for developing project and programme priorities. Having 'vision' implies being imaginative. Creative visualization and visioning exercises can be used as the first stage of a participatory planning process (Wates, 2000). A vision gives a community direction and an overall philosophy. Working through a vision builds consensus and provides a shared picture of the future. It also generates community energy and commitment to take the necessary actions to achieve it.

Week with a Camera

Participatory design exercise usually used with school children aged about 11 or 12, where children are given a disposable camera and asked to take photographs relevant to the subject of the study. A facilitated collage-making workshop is then held and children make representations of the issues that interest and concern them. Adult facilitation is required but need not be by highly specialized people.

Workshop

A dynamic meeting, lasting from half a day to two days, usually consisting of table groups of six to ten people, invited on the basis of skills or specialized interests, or a particular target group. Public workshops can also be held for the general public. Structured sessions are aimed at producing proposals for solutions and are usually aided by a facilitator who explores issues, develops ideas and makes decisions. It is a less formal and more creative counterpart to a public meeting or committee and is structured for the active involvement of participants. A *topic workshop* focuses on specific issues. A *design workshop* includes the use of participatory design techniques.

World Café

A non-confrontational and creative structured process to help large numbers of people engage in interactive conversations and build mutual understanding and collective learning about important issues by working in small groups. The process culminates in a whole-group conversation.

Appendix A:
A Quick-and-Easy Checklist

Many different SpeakOuts and community workshops have been organized in various venues in many different places in the past 19 years. Depending on the design of each SpeakOut, the organizers have come up with some kind of action checklist to help with the hundreds of details that need to be taken care of.

Below is a generic SpeakOut checklist taken from (and inspired by) the existing checklists that have been useful in the past. You can create your own format of checklist that works for you and the type of SpeakOut you want to organize. Please refer back to the content of this book for more detailed information.

Time	Activity/ session	Details	Who?
Pre-workshop	Venue set-up	• Accessible, highly visible location in the area • Big enough room for the number of participants expected (or use adaptable venue, like tent) • Determine points of entry (create them if there are no natural ones) that are easily identifiable • Design circulation flow of the crowd between and in issue stalls	

Time	Activity/ session	Details	Who?
		• Extra rooms or stalls for storage, children's activities, catering, briefing and debriefing sessions and a safe place to store valuables • Sufficient lighting (natural or electrical) • Control the temperature (or make sure to provide enough shade if venue is outdoors) • Enough cover (or anticipate bad weather if venue is outdoors) • Kitchen or catering facilities (or access to water supply) near the workshop or SpeakOut location (but not too close so as to avoid distraction) • Accessible washrooms • Available parking and proximity to public transport • Accessible for wheelchairs • Access to power outlets • Obtain permit and take care of insurance	
	Catering	• Determine type of food (breakfast, lunch, dinner, or a series of finger foods) • Assign caterer (or hire professionals) • Provide enough utensils • Waste bins and recycle bins	
	Entertainment	• Contact entertainers (local groups or community-oriented professionals) • Town crier or clowns to attract and draw people in • Face-painters • Borrow or rent audio sound system	

Time	Activity/ session	Details	Who?
	Equipment	• Tables and chairs (rent if need to) • Foam boards (pin boards?) • Decoration materials • Laptop and portable printer • TV/video or screen	
	Supplies	• Agendas with process description • Green sheets for comments or questions • Cardboard or plastic box at each stall to hold material • Butcher's paper • Thick marker pens • Pins • Masking tape • Pens • Reusable adhesive • Scissors • Hook-and-loop fasteners, such as Velcro dots or Velcro strips • Paper for extra signs • Extension cords • Double adaptors • Non-permanent markers and white board duster or cloth	
	Signs	• SpeakOut or workshop 'name' and logo • Site 'map' with stalls, activities and facilities labelled	

Time	Activity/ session	Details	Who?
		• Stall name and numbers • Large signs identifying activities • Large signs identifying facilities (food, toilet, registration, parking lot) • Large signs identifying main entry and summary of SpeakOut or workshop	
	Registration desk	• Locate the desk to facilitate queuing and reduce congestion • Ensure that it is sheltered and that it is placed in a transition/welcoming zone that feels quite separate from the main SpeakOut or workshop • Registration sheets • Sign explaining the timetable of events • Sign explaining the SpeakOut or workshop • Welcome and 'Register Here' sign • 'Ask Me' badges for project team members, facilitators and recorders • 'Where do you live?' sign • Large aerial map of the area for 'Where do you live?' • Coloured sticky dots	
	Advertising/ invitation	• Send invitations to entire list of stakeholders • Advertise in local paper • Advertise in the area newsletter (liaise with schools, churches and other groups in the area) • Place invitation and background material on website	
	Information on display	• Design and set up the issue stalls	

Time	Activity/ session	Details	Who?
		• Consider how and where the information will be presented • Label everything! If previous workshop information can be used – clarify it and use it • Redraw the material and present in simple language • Display work in progress using clear summaries • Avoid technical jargon and use everyday terms and language that is easily understood • Translate information reflecting the participating community • Mount information on foamcore or foam board • Prepare photos (print on heavy glossy paper or laminate)	
	Facilitators and other staff	• Appoint Coordinator and Producer • Contact details for facilitators circulated • Email confirmation of facilitators attending • Facilitator agenda drafted • Facilitator notes circulated • Stalls and roles allocated, including registration table • Allocate a place and time to brief and debrief the facilitators and recorders • Make sure the Accountability Group members are overviewing the process (invite them to help in the preparation of the SpeakOut) • Interpreters (from community) confirmed • Set-up and tear-down staff organized	

Time	Activity/ session	Details	Who?
On the day	Facilitator and recorder briefing	• Ensure facilitators and recorders attend • Facilitator and recorder agenda • Staff for registration desk • Run through process with staff at registration desk	
	Registration	• Large aerial map for 'Where do you live?' • 'Where do you live?' sign • Instructions for 'Where do you live?' • SpeakOut instructions • Tickets or 'passport' for food • Instructions for children's area, including directions • Process description for the main project and description of consultation conducted to date (if any)	
Post-workshop	Facilitator and recorder debriefing Clean up	• Ensure all attend • Nominate a note-taker • Copies of pay sheet pro formas and the statutory declarations for payment • Ensure hire people are organized to pick up gear at the end of event • Ensure tent or marquee people are organized to pick up tents at the end of event • Ensure all attend until one hour after the end of event to help with pack-down	

Appendix B:
Footscray SpeakOut Stall
Prompts and Instructions

Time	Activity/ Session	Details
9:00am – 10:00am	Facilitator Briefing	Please, please, please be on time. We will start the briefing at 9:00am sharp! Tasks: • Briefing for the events of the day • Allocation of set-up responsibilities
10:00am – 12:00pm	SpeakOut Set Up	All hands are required for setting up the SpeakOut stalls and activities. Facilitators will be responsible for setting up their own stall and, in general terms, the following people will oversee the following tasks: Andrea Cook: Reception Desk and General Display Set Up Wendy Sarkissian: Stall set up Steph Walton: Shopfront set up (Kids' Activities) Lily Rattray: Entertainment and Food set up Tasks: • Set up the displays at each of the six 'issue' stalls • Set up reception and general displays • Organize entertainment, food and children's consultation activities • Be prepared for early arrivals (from 11:00am)

Time	Activity/ Session	Details
12:00pm – 6:00pm	The Speak- Out	The SpeakOut is a drop-in format and so during this time everybody will work at their stall according to the tasks laid out for each (see the attached pages).

The stalls/activities during the day include:
- Reception (all day)
- Stall 1: Getting Around (all day)
- Stall 2: Arts and Culture (all day)
- Stall 3: Retail/Shops (all day)
- Stall 4: Housing (all day)
- Stall 5: Learning in Footscray (all day)
- Stall 6: Having Fun in Footscray (all day)
- Children's Consultation (4:00pm to 6:00pm)
- Free Sausage Sizzle and Local Food (1:00pm to 4:30pm)
- Western Bulldogs Footy Clinic (mid-afternoon)
- Entertainment (all day)

NEVER leave your stall unattended! Two facilitator/ recorders are assigned to each stall. Wendy, Steph, Andrea and Lily will act as 'relief' facilitators to allow you a break for lunch, toilet, etc.

Tasks:
- Undertake the exercise/s described for your stall in the attached briefings
- Carefully record (according to the directions in the attached) the information given to you by people participating at your stall
- Seek clarification/support from a lead facilitator (Andrea Cook or Wendy Sarkissian) if you are having any difficulties at your stall

Time	Activity/ Session	Details
6:00pm – 7:00pm	Speak Out Pack Up and Facilitator Debriefing	The material from the SpeakOut will only be useful if it is organized well at the pack-up stage. Please be careful in the pack-up to make sure that things are neat and labelled. Please plan to attend the debriefing as this is an important aspect of the process evaluation. **Tasks:** • Ensure the recorded material (all the material that will go into the SpeakOut analysis) from your stall is packed up neatly and LABELLED with your stall number/issue area • Display material needs to be separately packed up for return to the Council

Reception Desk

Objectives:

To welcome people, orient them to the SpeakOut, describe activities on hand and provide them with the materials they need to participate and enjoy the SpeakOut.

Tools for this session:

- a SpeakOut 'Agenda' describing the event and the activities – one for each person/group attending
- sign-up sheets – make sure people sign up so we have a complete record of participants
- green sheets (SpeakOut evaluation) – make sure each person has a green sheet to fill in over the day
- a 'where are you from' map – an arrival activity to help people get acquainted with the maps we are using by locating their home and putting a red dot on that spot
- tickets for people to give to food vendors for their free sausage or vegetarian/halal food.

Tasks:

BE FRIENDLY AND WELCOMING! You are the first face people will see at the SpeakOut and so you are an 'ambassador'.

Make people feel welcome.

Ask people to sign the sign-in sheet.

Describe the SpeakOut process (using the display panels at the Reception area) and point out where the various activities are on the map. Give each person the following:

1 a copy of the agenda
2 a green sheet
3 a ticket for their free food (they give the ticket to the vendor of the food option (sausage sizzle or vegetarian/halal).

Ask people to put a dot where their house is on the large aerial photo. Help them put their dots on the map if necessary.

Answer questions if asked. Find a lead facilitator (Andrea Cook or Wendy Sarkissian) if you are unable to answer the question.

Stall 1: Getting Around

Objectives:

To facilitate two activities, one regarding 'cars, trucks and parking' and the other regarding 'public and pedestrian transport'.

Tools for this session:

- your stall which will have relevant prompting questions, photos and background information on display – these are fixed props

Cars, Trucks and Parking Exercise

- pre-numbered coloured dots
- a large transport map of Footscray with wide margins for recording comments
- butcher's paper for additional comments if you run out of room on the margins

Pedestrian and Public Transport Exercise

- A4 transport maps of Footscray
- a number of pens in two colours – red to be used (CONSISTENTLY) for the pedestrian roaming range and blue to be used (CONSISTENTLY) for public transport roaming range.

Tasks:

BE FRIENDLY AND WELCOMING!

Cars and Trucks and Parking (One resource person facilitating and recording)

The question for this exercise is 'What is the single worst place for you in your car in Footscray' and is meant to be a question that will 'bound' people's responses about traffic and parking (as this can be an emotive and contentious issue).

Ask each person to apply a pre-numbered dot to the large displayed transport map.

Then record their comments about why that spot is bad to the side of the map, matching the scribed comment to the dot number.

Public and Pedestrian Transport (One resource person facilitating and participants self-recording)

Ask people to mark on the A4 map their pedestrian roaming range using the *red pens* (where they regularly travel as a pedestrian).

Do the same (on the same map but with the *blue pens*) for people's public transport use (e.g., what public transport routes and facilities they regularly use).

Encourage them to 'annotate' their map where they can with details about their regular pedestrian and public transport issues (e.g., where they enjoy walking, where they have difficulty getting around by public transport, etc.).

When they are finished, display their maps on the marquee wall.

Stall 2: Arts and Culture

Objectives:

To facilitate a 'Vote with Your Hands' exercise (which is a 'finger painting' exercise) in which people will indicate their interest in dimensions of arts and culture.

Tools for this session:

- your stall which will have relevant prompting questions, photos and background information on display – these are fixed props
- a large 'Vote with Your Hands' sheet affixed to the wall (organized in colour-coded and labelled categories)
- a set of water soluble finger paints in different colours, each colour corresponding to a category on the sheet
- washing up materials – water and towels – for cleaning hands after this exercise
- A4 maps of Footscray
- coloured pens that correspond with the colour categories on the 'Vote with Your Hands' sheet on the wall.

Tasks:

BE FRIENDLY AND WELCOMING!

The question for this exercise is 'What should the future Footscray have artistically and culturally?' and people will display their interests in a 'Vote with Your Hands' exercise.

Ask each person to look at the categories for 'Vote with Your Hands':

- RED: more opportunity to learn to be an artist or craftsperson
- GREEN: more arts events such as theatre or gallery exhibitions
- BLUE: more arts business and development – studio
- ORANGE: more community festivals and cultural displays
- PURPLE: more public art like sculpture and murals.

When they are finished, display their maps on the marquee wall.

Stall 3: Retail/shops

Objectives:

To facilitate an exercise where a laminated map is used as a base map for people to mark out retail 'precincts' they would like to see in the future Footscray. Each participant will map this out, a photograph will be taken of each completed retail map and then the base map will be wiped clean for the next participant.

Tools for this session:

- your stall which will have relevant prompting questions, photos and background information on display – these are fixed props
- a large laminated map of Footscray on the wall
- a white board wiper
- a selection of coloured non-permanent markers
- a digital camera (shared with Stall Four).

Tasks:

BE FRIENDLY AND WELCOMING!

The question for this exercise is 'In the future, should there be different styles of shopping experience within the Footscray business area, or just one central retail area?'

People may need to be given some key prompts like 'Do you see a distinct Asian shopping area here now? Is that good? Should it be promoted that way?' You can also use other prompts such as 'African shops and restaurants', 'market or fresh food shopping', 'ethnic restaurants', 'niche market shopping', etc.

Ask people to mark on the map the way they would like to see the different kinds of shopping experience organized in the future (as 'precincts').

As you are talking, map the precincts they describe on the map using a different colour pen for each precinct. Carefully label each precinct.

When they have finished their retail precinct map, take a photo of the map using the digital camera.

During quiet times at your stall, Andrea will download the photos you have taken and print out the photo for display at your stall.

Stall 4: Housing

Objectives:

To facilitate a three-dimensional construction from each participant which will reflect their preferences regarding built form and density in the Footscray study area. This will be a 'density/form' building block exercise where people will build up Footscray's density to their liking. Each model will be photographed and the photo displayed before the next person starts fresh with their model.

Tools for this session:

- your stall which will have relevant prompting questions, photos and background information on display – these are fixed props
- a large aerial map of the Footscray central area secured to the table
- a set of Lego blocks in pre-arranged 'heights'
- luggage tag labels
- Blu tack to affix labels to the model
- a digital camera (shared with Stall Three).

Tasks:

BE FRIENDLY AND WELCOMING!

The question for this exercise is 'In the future, what height should housing and other buildings in Footscray be?'

This exercise will be done with individuals or small groups who want to work together. Each person/group will build a model. This will be labelled and then photographed before the next person/group starts a fresh model on the same base map.

First, familiarize people with the aerial map and get them oriented (i.e., work together to find key landmarks such as the train station, the Nicholson Street Mall where they are, etc.).

Ask about existing housing and whether they can show, with the different size blocks, where low-rise housing (one to two storeys) is, where medium-rise housing (three to six storeys) is and where higher-rise housing (more than six storeys) is.

Ask them to build up the areas where they could imagine higher-rise housing and other buildings.

If people are stuck, show them prompting material and ask they questions from the display (e.g., 'Can you imagine this kind of housing in Footscray' while pointing to different photos and then asking 'Where can you imagine this kind of housing?').

As they are building their model, use the luggage tag labels to label their 'buildings' and annotate their model (e.g., '12-storey existing building' or 'A 15-storey block of flats could go here' or 'nothing higher than 6 storeys here').

When the model is completed and annotated/labelled, take a photograph of the model with the digital camera.

During quiet times at your stall, Andrea will download the photos you have taken and print out the photos for display at your stall.

Stall 5: Learning in Footscray

Objectives:

To facilitate a community 'skills audit' regarding what people are skilled at and what they would be interested in learning – to be passed to community education providers.

Tools for this session:

- your stall which will have relevant prompting questions, photos and background information on display – these are fixed props
- a large 'skills audit' panel displayed on the wall
- coloured dots
- blank butcher's paper for comments
- large site map of Footscray.

Tasks:

BE FRIENDLY AND WELCOMING!

The question for this exercise is 'What are YOU skilled at? What would you like to learn?'

Ask people to put a coloured dot beside all the skills they have EXPERIENCE in. This can be work experience or as an interest/hobby they have done over time.

Then ask people to put a coloured dot beside those skills they would like to develop or learn how to do.

The completed panels will show all the skills that this community has and those they are interested in acquiring.

Comments to supplement the skills audit can be written on the blank butcher's paper provided.

Finally, ask people to locate important learning facilities on the map. These facilities can be schools but they can also be less formal – small community projects, etc. Label all contributions with the name of the facility and the type of learning they provide.

Stall 6: Having Fun in Footscray

Objectives:

To facilitate a graphing exercise where people will build up sections of a large 'bar graph' with symbols reflective of how they enjoy Footscray (by category). Each person will be given a symbol with a space to write comments that will be added to the 'bar graph' according to the category, giving us an indication of preferred ways of 'having fun in Footscray'.

Tools for this session:
- your stall which will have relevant prompting questions, photos and background information on display – these are fixed props
- a large display panel with several categories regarding how/where people spend their leisure time across the bottom – sprayed with REPOSITIONAL SPRAY so that things stick to it and can be moved around
- a set of different coloured symbols (which correspond to the categories) with spaces to write on them that will be affixed to the base panel to build a 'graph'
- a display map on which people's comments regarding where they'd like to 'have fun in Footscray' can be recorded.

Tasks:

BE FRIENDLY AND WELCOMING!

The question for this session will be 'What is or would be fun to do in Footscray?'

First, show people the graph on display and show them the categories:
- TEAM SPORT
- INDIVIDUAL SPORT
- ENJOYING NATURE
- RESTAURANTS AND CAFES
- PUBS AND CLUBS
- ATTENDING ORGANIZED EVENTS
- 'HANGING OUT'
- OTHER ... ?

Ask them to think about what they enjoy doing. It can be something they do in Footscray or something they would like to be able to do in Footscray.

When they have thought of their favourite pastime, they will take a symbol that matches (e.g., if they like playing soccer, they will take a RED 'Team Sport' symbol and write the detail of this favourite pastime in the blank centre.

Then ask them to affix their symbol to the chart, building each category up as people respond so that it resembles a bar chart when completed.

People may fill out more than one 'Fun in Footscray' symbol if they wish.

The facilitator will also ask questions about where they enjoying doing this activity and mark it on the map as the discussion unfolds.

If the person can't do the activity in Footscray, ask if they have suggestions as to where a good place might be to develop that activity (e.g., a good place for a soccer field or a new café or theatre...).

Notes

Chapter 2

1   See Stewart (1994), pp163–178

2   'Talk Any Kine: Deepening the SpeakOut model with community-led collaboration and an arts-based approach to community engagement in a low-income community in Honolulu', April 2007. The thesis explores the potential of the SpeakOut model of community engagement that integrates arts and culture in a culturally and socially diverse community. In the low-income, immigrant community of Chinatown, Honolulu, the SpeakOut model (developed initially in Australia in 1990), was redesigned to deepen the level of engagement by the local community and to add a celebratory component both to empower local people and to attract them to attend and engage

Chapter 3

1   A somewhat less dynamic approach to the SpeakOut is found in the Open House model developed by Canadian participation specialist, Desmond Connor and perhaps in some of the Action Planning approaches in the UK (see Wates, 2000). See also Connor (1997b). Australian facilitation specialist and consultant Carla Rogers of Evolve Facilitation and Coaching developed a similar model some years ago, originally calling it the iForum. It is now called the Meeting Marketplace™. In this model, stations rather than stalls are used, but many of the concepts are similar. See www.evolves.com.au for the Meeting Marketplace ™ Toolkit (Evolve Facilitation and Coaching, 2008). A series of 'stations' allows people to engage in different ways. Stations differ in terms of their purpose, communication and learning styles. In this model, somewhat similar to the SpeakOut model, there are at least five stations, with each station offering a different way to participate. An essential part of the model is the orientation station, as well as a

café and a 'group think-tank' (from the *iForum™ Short Guide* by Carla Rogers)

2   The model can be used for a discussion of non-spatial policy issues but it works best when the topics under discussion can be categorized into between seven and nine easily distinguishable components and showcased at stalls dedicated to those individual issues

3   See Sarkissian et al (2008), pp58–61

4   For information about the False Creek North *Have Your Say!* Day, see Chapter 4.5. See also www.pricetags.ca/pricetags/pricetags104.pdf (Price, 2008)

Chapter 4.1

1   See Coates et al (2008). All material describing the engagement processes described in this chapter is exclusively taken from published reports, which were distributed widely in the Bonnyrigg community in 2005

2   For confidentiality reasons, detailed representation of the children's collages was not possible. However, a full analysis of their ideas, collected through the 'Week with a Camera' exercise is included in the report on that process. See van Ruth and Shore (2005)

3   See Murray et al (2005), Shore and Sarkissian (2005) and Coates et al (2008)

Chapter 4.2

1   Established in 1968, EAH Housing was founded to address the needs of low-income families and elders living in Marin County, California. Originally named the Ecumenical Association for Housing, EAH was organized from grass-roots efforts in response to the death of Dr Martin Luther King, Jr. See http://eahhousing.org

2   Operation Weed and Seed is a US Department of Justice initiative designed to reclaim, restore and rebuild neighbourhoods by 'weeding' out the criminal element, then 'seeding' the community with services that support neighbourhood revitalization. Currently, there are over 300 sites throughout the United States

Chapter 4.3

1   Aerial photographs (high-quality orthophoto maps) always work better than maps for these sorts of exercises and, in fact, for almost all community engagement processes

2   Throughout Canada and the US, 211 is a toll-free number to phone for information and resources relating to health and government-type programmes and services. The number 211 is used for non-emergency situations, whereas 911 is for emergency situations when immediate help is needed

Chapter 4.4

1   Plan C (2007b), *Townsville Family Charter SpeakOut Festival: Project Evaluation*, p10
2   See Sarkissian et al (2008), pp15–37
3   After dozens of SpeakOuts in three countries, we believe that a whole day is much too long for a freestanding SpeakOut. Three to four hours is more than enough, partly because of the set-up and break-down time that is required

Chapter 4.5

1   Statistics Canada (2006)
2   For a more detailed history of the False Creek North site, see Price (2008)
3   The areas for improvement recognized by the City were taken from a lecture by Larry Beasley to the students in the Post-Occupancy Evaluation course, School of Community and Regional Planning, 12 January 2007
4   See Brown (2005) and the World Café website, www.theworldcafe.com
5   For details of the 'Week with a Camera' exercise, see Sarkissian et al (1997), pp77–79 and Sarkissian (2008)
6   The indoor venue limited the use of paint that would have been used for the 'Vote with Your Hands' activity explained in Chapter 8
7   The role of the sketcher is an important component of the innovative and highly effective community engagement Minnesota Block Exercise. See Sarkissian et al (2008), pp61–70

Chapter 5

1   Consult public transit timetables when setting the times for the beginning and conclusion of a meeting. Adjust these times in response to the public transit timetable. You may also consider putting on a special bus to pick up and return participants to a local public transit interchange
2   Where possible, select a venue that does *not* have a separate entrance for people with a disability
3   Ensure that information generated will be able to be reproduced. By using bold colours, the information produced is easier to reproduce for inclusion in a report or for reporting back to the community. We remove yellow or other pale colours from crayon boxes

Chapter 6

1   Much of the material in this chapter is indebted to the work of Nick Wates, particularly *The Community Planning Handbook* (2000). We are deeply grateful to Nick for his visionary and helpful work. His book was designed to guide the

work of practitioners and we believe that, through our use of it over many years, we have proved that it was worthwhile. Among the relevant parts of Nick's book which have informed these interactive processes in the SpeakOut model are the following: gaming, pp68–69; interactive displays, pp72–73, including visual likes and dislikes, comments on proposals and sticky dot displays; mapping, pp76–77, including activity maps, mental maps and mind mapping; models, pp82–83; photo surveys, pp94–95; prioritizing, pp104–105, including the fence method, p105; simulation, pp116–117; table scheme displays, pp120–121, including voting on likes and dislikes with sticky dots; skills surveys, p198 and definition and checklist, p175; storytelling, p199 and the timeline exercise, p20

2   See, for example, the following three books about Appreciative Inquiry: Cooperrider et al (2003); Reed (2006); Whitney and Trosten-Bloom (2003)

3   These exercises are a low-budget attempt to undertake the sort of community engagement with density issues that has characterized the innovative work of the Minneapolis Design Center and the Center for Neighborhoods in Minneapolis through the Corridor Housing Initiative and the Minnesota Block Exercise. We discuss this model at length in Sarkissian et al (2008), pp61–70. See also Center for Neighborhoods (2008c) 'Minnesota Block Exercise'

Chapter 7

1   'Biophilia', a term coined by S.R. Kellert and E.O. Wilson in 1984, literally means 'love of life'. See Kellert (2005), pp3–4. In this context, it means the study of the relationship between humans and Nature. The *biophilia hypothesis* argues that humans have an innate preference for natural landscapes and respond positively to both viewing and being in Nature. *Biophilic design* is design of the built environment that fosters people's interactions with Nature

2   See Baron-Cohen and Harrison (1997), p14

3   Plan C (2007a) *An Inclusive Community Engagement Process Developing the Children's Garden For the Gold Coast Regional Botanic Gardens: Rosser Park, Volume One – Engagement Outcomes Report*

Chapter 9

1   For a discussion of the role of community education and capacity building in community engagement, see an earlier book in this Earthscan Community Planning suite: Sarkissian et al (2008), pp39–71

2   For a comprehensive discussion of the merits of different seating arrangements for workshops, see Chambers (2002), pp87–95

3   These are very useful for additional comments. We ask participants to fill them out if they feel any issue has not received adequate attention. Concerns or questions on these sheets must be carefully and promptly followed up after the workshop. It's important to determine in advance who will be responsible

4   Labelling of the butcher's paper is important as it facilitates efficient reporting of the recorded information and avoids confusion in the typing-up stage. (Pre-label each sheet with table number, session number and page numbers)

5   Partitions or other surfaces need to be sturdy enough for a Recorder to press against firmly while recording. Flimsy or unstable display partitions are not suitable

6   This site plan needs to be large enough to be seen from each table and bold enough to be read and understood easily

7   Annotations need to be carefully considered to provoke discussion. This is relatively inexpensive as photos can be photocopied or enlarged using a colour copier or printer

8   See Kushner (2004), pp197–243

9   See Hall (2007), pp69–75

10   Hall (2007), p89

11   The *Fishbowl* method is used by facilitators in many other ways in other contexts. This is our distinctive approach. Others use it as '[a] technique used to increase participation and understanding of issues. The fishbowl represents an inner group of participants in a roundtable format involved in a decision-making process that is "witnessed" by a larger group who have the opportunity for input and questioning (see also Expert Panels, Samoan Circles). The fishbowl can be adapted with the use of role-playing techniques to highlight conflicts and alliances, the patterns that connect different points of view and the previously unrecognized linkages between different aspects of issues or problems. The fish bowl process can be modified to allow participants from the wider audience to join the roundtable.' See Victorian Government Department of Sustainability and Environment (2005c), Effective Engagement: Toolkit: www.dse.vic.gov.au/DSE/wcmn203.

Chapter 10

1   See Kaner et al (1996), p24

2   Kaner et al (1996), p21

3   Based on Sarkissian et al (1986). See also Auvine et al (1994). This chapter has drawn heavily on material, reprinted with permission, from Auvine et al (1978) *A Manual for Group Facilitators,* published by the Center for Conflict Resolution. The complete manual is available from the Center. Extracts from the following pages have been selected for this chapter: 2, 3, 15–19, 23–31. This chapter draws on published material on group dynamics, workshop format, communication, search conferences, interpersonal dynamics, creativity, conflict resolution and participation methods. The following classic sources have been used:

Auvine et al (1978)
Avery et al (1981)
Bradford (1976)
Cragon and Wright (1980)
Hart (1981)

Lakey (n.d.)
Materka (1986)
See also Sarkissian et al (1986) and Sibbet (1980)

Chapter 11

1 Maintaining trust in community engagement is a major concern, especially when technical and scientific material is being discussed. For a full discussion of this issue, see Sarkissian et al (2008), pp159–185

Chapter 12

1 For some ideas about the value of video in community engagement, see Sarkissian (2007), pp98–102

2 It's wise not to rely on the one provided without checking. Be familiar with its capabilities and the possibility of linking it to recording equipment.

3 Consider doing a test an hour or so before the meeting gets under way so that there is adequate time to sort out any technical problems.

4 With respect to microphones, it's good to ask: How many are needed and how will they rove? Who will be there to help? Check their range and the quality of the sound.

5 It's wise to check with someone who knows and not to assume that this can be sorted out later.

6 For small workshops or if you are operating a storefront, it's probably wise to invest in a set of mugs and inexpensive cutlery.

7 For the rest of that story, see Sarkissian with Walsh (1994c), pp33–50

Chapter 13

1 Adapted from Doyle and Straus (1993)

References

Abbott, J. (1995) 'Community participation and its relationship to community development', *Community Development Journal*, vol 30, no 2, pp158–168

Arnstein, S. R. (1969) 'A ladder of citizen participation', *Journal of the American Institute of Planners*, vol 35, no 4, pp216–224

Aslin, H. J. and Brown, V. A. (2004) *Towards Whole of Community Engagement: A Practical Toolkit*, Murray-Darling Basin Commission, Canberra

Australian Capital Territory (ACT) Office of Multicultural and Community Affairs, Chief Minister's Department (2000) *Consultation Protocol 2000*, Chief Minister's Department, Canberra

Australian Capital Territory (ACT) Office of Multicultural and Community Affairs, Chief Minister's Department (2001) *Consultation Manual*, Chief Minister's Department, Canberra

Auvine, B., Extrom, M., Poole, S. and Shanklin, M. (1978) *A Manual for Group Facilitators*, Center for Conflict Resolution, Madison, WI

Auvine, B., Densmore, B., Extrom, M., Poole, S. and Shanklin, M. (1994) 'Facilitating meetings', in W. Sarkissian and D. Perlgut (eds) (1994) *The Community Participation Handbook: Resources for Public Involvement in the Planning Process*, second edition, Institute for Sustainability and Technology Policy, Murdoch University, Perth

Avery, M., Auvine, B., Streibel, B. and Weiss, L. (1981) *Building United Judgment: A Handbook for Consensus Decision Making*, Center for Conflict Resolution, Madison, WI

Ayre, D., Clough, G. and Norris, T. (2000) *Facilitating Community Change*, Community Initiatives Inc, San Francisco

Bannick, N., Cheever, S. and Cheever D. (2005) *A Close Call: Saving Honolulu's Chinatown*, Little Percent Press, Honolulu

Baron-Cohen, S. and Harrison, J. E. (1997) *Synaesthesia: Classic and Contemporary Readings*, Blackwell, Oxford

Behrendt, L. (1997) 'Indigenous people and consultation: Exploring issues of equality, effective representative government and democracy', in Open Government Network, *Reaching Common Ground: Open Government, Community Consultation and Public Participation*, Proceedings of the Reaching Common Ground Conference, 23–24 October 1996, Open Government Network, Sydney, pp103–111

Bellman, G. (undated) *Handbook of Structured Experiences for Human Relations Training*, Volume V , Pfeiffer and Company, San Diego

Blomeley, N. (1996) 'Talking with Indigenous Australians', in R. Menere and J. Bird (eds) *Health and Australian Indigenous Peoples: Study Guide,* Southern Cross University, Lismore, Australia

Borrup, T. (2006) *Creative Community Builder's Handbook: How to Transform Communities Using Local Assets, Arts, and Culture*, Fieldstone Alliance, Saint Paul, MN

Bradford, L. P. (1976) *Making Meetings Work: A Guide for Leaders and Group Members*, Pfeiffer and Company, Vol V, San Francisco, CA

Brock, K. and Pettit, J. (eds) (2007) *Springs of Participation: Creating and Evolving Methods for Participatory Development*, Practical Action, Rugby

Brown, J. and Isaacs, D. (2005) *The World Café: Shaping Our Futures through Conversations that Matter*, Berrett-Koehler, San Francisco. See also www.theworldcafe.com

Bunjamin-Mau, W. (2007) *'Talk Any Kine*: Deepening the SpeakOut model with community-led collaboration and an arts-based approach to community engagement in a low-income community in Honolulu', unpublished Masters of Urban and Regional Planning Area of Concentration, Department of Urban and Regional Planning, University of Hawaii at Manoa, Honolulu

Burkholder, S. H., Chupp, M. and Star, P. (2003) *Principles of Neighborhood Planning for Community Development*, Center for Neighborhood Development, Cleveland, OH

Cameron, E. (2001) *Facilitation Made Easy: Practical Tips to Improve Meetings and Workshops*, Kogan Page, London

Cameron, J. (2003) 'Collaborating with communities: An assets-based approach to community and economic development', Paper presented to the Planning Institute of Australia, National Planning Congress 2003, Adelaide

Carman, K. and Keith, K. (1994) *Community Consultation Techniques: Purposes, Processes and Pitfalls: A Guide for Planners and Facilitators*, Department of Primary Industries, Information Series QI 94030, Brisbane, Queensland

Carson, L. (1997) 'When community consultation hits the wall', in Open Government Network, *Reaching Common Ground: Open Government, Community Consultation and Public Participation*, Proceedings of the Reaching Common Ground Conference, 23–24 October 1996, Open Government Network, Sydney

Carson, L. and Gelber, K. (2001) *Ideas for Community Consultation: A Discussion on Principles and Procedures for Making Consultation Work*, New South Wales Department of Urban Affairs and Planning, Sydney

Chambers, R. (2002) *Participatory Workshops: A Sourcebook of 21 Sets of Ideas and Activities*, Earthscan, London

Chess, C. and Purcell, K. (1999) 'Public participation and the environment: Do we know what works?', *Environmental Science and Technology*, vol 33, no 16, pp2685–2692

City of Adelaide (1999) *Communication and Consultation Model: Manual*. Prepared by A. Hazebroek (Hassell) and W. Sarkissian (Sarkissian Associates Planners), City of Adelaide, Adelaide, South Australia

City of Vancouver (1993a) *CityPlan Ideas Fair: The Check Book Responses*, City of Vancouver, Vancouver, 28 May

City of Vancouver (1993b) *CityPlan Ideas Fair: The Check Book*, City of Vancouver, Vancouver, May

City of Vancouver (1993c) *CityPlan Ideas Illustrated*, City of Vancouver, Vancouver, July

City of Vancouver (1993d) *CityPlan Newsletter*, City of Vancouver, Vancouver, January, February, April, May/June

City of Vancouver (1993e) *CityPlan Tool Kit, Various issues*, City of Vancouver, Vancouver

City of Vancouver (1993f) *CityPlan: Making Choices Workbook*, City of Vancouver, Vancouver

City of Vancouver (1994a) *CityPlan Making Choices Workbook: Preliminary Results*, City of Vancouver, Vancouver

City of Vancouver (1994b) *CityPlan Newsletter*, City of Vancouver, Vancouver, March

City of Vancouver (1994c) *CityPlan: A Program for Vancouver CityPlan, Take Part, Make a Difference*, City of Vancouver, Vancouver, 14 October

City of Vancouver (1994d) *The Future is in Your Hands: A Message from the City of Vancouver*, City of Vancouver, Vancouver

City of Vancouver (1994e) *Who Decides Vancouver's Future: A Guide to the Vancouver CityPlan*, City of Vancouver, Vancouver

City of Vancouver (1997) *Community Visions Programme,* Newsletter No 2, City of Vancouver, Vancouver, October

Clarke, H. (1994) 'Public participation in Alexandria', in W. Sarkissian and D. Perlgut (eds) (1994) *Community Participation in Practice: Handbook,* second edition, Murdoch University, Institute for Sustainability and Technology Policy, Perth

Coakes, S. (1999) *Consulting Communities: A Policy Maker's Guide to Consulting with Communities and Interest Groups,* Social Sciences Centre, Bureau of Rural Sciences, Agriculture, Fisheries and Forestry-Australia (AFFA), Canberra, June

Community Disability Alliance Incorporated (undated) *Checklist for Planning Events that Are Accessible to People with Disabilities,* Community Disability Alliance Inc, Brisbane

Connor, D. M. (1990) *How to Prevent and Resolve Public Controversy* (25-minute instructional video with 194-page video guide), Connor Development Services Ltd, Victoria, BC

Connor, D. M. (1993a) 'A generic design for public involvement programs: Part 1', *Constructive Citizen Participation,* vol 21, no 1

Connor, D. M. (1993b) 'A generic design for public involvement programs: Part 2', *Constructive Citizen Participation,* vol 21, no 2

Connor, D. M. (1994a) 'Editorial: When representatives don't . . .', *Constructive Citizen Participation,* vol 21, no 4, p1

Connor, D. M. (1994b) 'Ten lessons learned in 22 public participation programs for waste management projects, 1975–93', *Constructive Citizen Participation,* vol 21, no 4

Connor, D. M. (1994c) 'Computer networks and public participation', *Constructive Citizen Participation,* vol 22, no 1

Connor, D. M. (1994d) 'Editorial: Aboriginal involvement', *Constructive Citizen Participation,* vol 22, no 2, p1

Connor, D. M. (1994e) 'Preventing and resolving public controversy', conference paper for 'Public Affairs and Forest Management', Canadian Pulp & Paper Association, Toronto, 25–27 March 1985 (Revised 1994), www. connor.bc.ca/preventing.html, accessed 2 June 2008

Connor, D. M. (1995a) 'Generic public involvement principles', *Constructive Citizen Participation,* vol 22, no 4, pp3, 6

Connor, D. M. (1995b) 'Public information/relations/participation?', *Constructive Citizen Participation,* vol 22, no 4, pp4–5

Connor, D. M. (1997a) *Constructive Citizen Participation: A Resource Book,* sixth edition, Connor Development Services, Victoria, BC

Connor, D. M. (1997b) *Public Participation: A Manual,* Development Press, Victoria, BC

Connor, D. M. and Orenstein, S. G. (1995) *The Bridges of Winnipeg: Combining Conflict Resolution and Public Participation for Challenging Cases,* Connor Development Services, Victoria, BC, www.islandnet.com/~connor/winnipeg.html, reprinted from *Consensus*, October 1995, accessed 18 August 2008

Cooperrider, D. L., Whitney, D. and Stavros, J. M. (2003) *Appreciative Inquiry Handbook: The First in a Series of AI Workbooks for Leaders of Change*, Berrett-Koehler, San Francisco

Cornwall, A. and Pratt, G. (eds) (2003) *Pathways to Participation: Reflections on Participatory Rural Appraisal*, Intermediate Technology Development Group Publishing, London

Cragon, F. J. and Wright, D. W. (1980) *Communication in Small Group Discussions: A Case Study Approach*, West Publishing Company, St Paul, MN

Davidson, S. (1998) 'Spinning the wheel of empowerment', *Planning*, vol 1262, 3 April, pp14–15

Delgado, M. (2005) *Designs and Methods for Youth-Led Research*, Sage, Thousand Oaks, CA

Denzin, N. and Lincoln, Y. S. (eds) (2007) *Strategies of Qualitative Inquiry*, Sage, Thousand Oaks, CA

Doyle, M. and Strauss, D. (1993) *How to Make Meetings Work*, Berkley Books, New York

Driskell, D. with the Growing up in Cities Project (2002) 'Participation Toolkit' in *Creating Better Cities with Children and Youth: A Manual for Participation,* Earthscan, UNESCO Publishing and MOST, London

Dugdale, M. (1997) 'Managing large scale multiple issue public consultations', in Open Government Network, *Reaching Common Ground: Open Government, Community Consultation and Public Participation,* Proceedings of the Reaching Common Ground Conference, 23–24 October 1996, The Open Government Network, Sydney

Dunstan, G., Sarkissian, W. and Ward, R. (1994) 'Goonawarra: Core story as methodology in interpreting a community study', in W. Sarkissian and K. Walsh (eds) (1994) *Community Participation in Practice: Casebook*, Institute for Technology Policy, Murdoch University, Perth

Elton Consulting (2003) *Community Engagement in the NSW Planning System*, Planning NSW, Sydney

Emery, M. (ed) (1993) *Participative Design for Participatory Democracy*, second edition, Centre for Continuing Education, Australian National University, Canberra

Emery, M. (1997) 'Participative strategic planning: The search conference', in Open Government Network, *Reaching Common Ground: Open Government, Community Consultation and Public Participation*, Proceedings of the Reaching Common Ground Conference, 23–24 October 1996, The Open Government Network, Sydney

Emery, M. and Purser, R. E. (1996) *The Search Conference: A Powerful Method for Planning Organizational Change and Community Action*, Jossey-Bass, San Francisco

Fiorina, M. P. (1999) 'Extreme voices: The dark side of civic engagement', in T. Skocpol and M. P. Fiorina (eds) *Civic Engagement in American Democracy*, Brookings Institution Press, Washington, DC

Forester, J. (1999) *The Deliberative Practitioner: Encouraging Participatory Planning Processes*, MIT Press, Cambridge, MA

Forseyth, M. (1996) 'The Charrette – is it an effective consultation tool?', Paper presented to the 1996 Open Government, Community Consultation and Participation Conference, Sydney, 23–24 October. Reprinted in Open Government Network (1997) *Reaching Common Ground: Open Government, Community Consultation and Public Participation*, Proceedings of the Reaching Common Ground Conference, 23–24 October 1996, Open Government Network, Sydney

Forsyth, A. (2000) *The YouthPower Guide: How to Make Your Community Better: A Manual Based on the Work of the YouthPower Project Of El Arco Iris Youth and Community Arts Center*, a Program of Nueva Esperanza, Inc, Holyoke, Massachusetts, Urban Places Project, University of Massachusetts, Amherst, MA

Forsyth, A., Lu, H. and McGirr, P. (1999) 'College students and youth collaborating in design: Research in the design studio', *Landscape Review*, vol 5, no 2, pp26–42

Gastil, J. (1993) *Democracy in Small Groups: Participation, Decision Making, and Communication*, New Society, Philadelphia

Gibson, C. and Homan, S. (2004) 'Urban redevelopment, live music and public space', *International Journal of Cultural Policy*, vol 10, no 1, pp67–84

Grogan, D. and Mercer, C. with Engwicht, D. (1995) *The Cultural Planning Handbook: An Essential Australian Guide*, Allen & Unwin, Sydney

Gurwitt, R. (1992) 'Governments that listen', *Governing*, vol 6, no 3

Haeberle, S. H. (1989) *Planting the Grassroots: Structuring Citizen Participation*, Praeger, New York

Hall, R. (2007) *Brilliant Presentation: What the Best Presenters Know, Say and Do*, Pearson Education, Harlow, UK

Hart, L. B. (1981) *Learning from Conflict: A Handbook for Trainers and Group Leaders*, Addison-Wesley, Reading, MA

Hart, R. A. (1997) *Children's Participation: The Theory and Practice of Involving Young Citizens in Community Development and Environmental Care*, Earthscan, London

Hawai'i Arts Alliance (2004) Grant Report to the Ford Foundation, unpublished report to the Ford Foundation, Honolulu

Hawai'i Arts Alliance (2005) Grant Report to the Ford Foundation, unpublished report to the Ford Foundation, Honolulu

Hawai'i Arts Alliance (2006) Grant Report to the Ford Foundation, unpublished report to the Ford Foundation, Honolulu

Hawkes, J. (2001) *The Fourth Pillar of Sustainability: Culture's Essential Role in Public Planning*, Common Ground Publishing Pty Ltd in association with the Cultural Development Network (Victoria), Melbourne

Heron, J. (1999) *The Complete Facilitator's Handbook*, Kogan Page, London

Hogan, C. (2000) *Facilitating Empowerment: A Handbook for Facilitators, Trainers and Individuals*, Kogan Page, London

Hogan, C. (2003) *Practical Facilitating: A Toolkit of Techniques*, Kogan Page, London

Innes, J. E. and Booher, D. E. (2004) 'Reframing public participation: Strategies for the 21st century', *Planning Theory and Practice*, vol 5, no 4, pp419–436

Julian, D. A., Reischl, T. M., Carrick, R. V. and Katrenich, C. (1997) 'Citizen participation: Lessons from a local united way planning process', *Journal of the American Planning Association*, vol 63, no 3, pp345–355

Justice, T. and Jamieson, D. (2006) *The Facilitators Fieldbook: Step-by-Step Procedures, Checklists and Guidelines, Samples and Templates*, second edition, AMACOM Division American Management Association, New York

Kaner, S. with Lenny, L., Toldi, C., Fisk, S. and Berger, D. (1996) *Facilitator's Guide to Participatory Decision-Making*, New Society Publishers, Gabriola Island, BC

Keating, C. (2003) *Facilitation Toolkit: A Practical Guide for Working More Effectively with People and Groups*, Department of Environmental Protection Water and Rivers Commission Department of Conservation and Land Management, Perth

Kellert, S. R. (2005) Building for Life: *Designing and Understanding the Human–Nature Connection*, first edition, Island Press, Washington, DC

Kins, A. and Peddie, B. (1996) *Planning a Complete Community: A Cultural Planning Guide for Local Government*, Community Arts Network, Perth

Kohler-Koch, B. (2008) 'Does participatory governance hold its promises?', conference presentation, CONNEX Final Conference: Efficient and Democratic Governance in a Multi-Level Europe, Mannheim, 6–8 March

Kretzmann, J. P. and McKnight, J. L. (1993) *Building Communities from the Inside Out: A Path towards Finding and Mobilizing a Community's Assets*, Acta Publications, Chicago, IL

Krueger, R. A. and Casey, M. A. (2000) *Focus Groups: A Practical Guide for Allied Research,* third edition, Sage, San Francisco, CA

Kushner, M. (2004) 'Mastering the power of PowerPoint', in *Presentation for Dummies*, Wiley, New York

Lakey, B. (undated) *Meeting Facilitation: The No Magic Method*, New Society Publishers, Gabriola Island, BC

Law, N. and Hartig, J. H. (1993) 'Public participation in the Great Lakes Remedial Action Plans', *Plan Canada*, vol 36, no 2, pp31–35

Local Government Association of Queensland (1996) *Social Planning Guidelines for Queensland Local Government*, Local Government Association of Queensland (LGAQ), Fortitude Valley, Queensland

Local Government Association of Queensland (1998) *Getting Started: A Consultation Guide for Queensland Local Government*, LGAQ, Brisbane

Local Government Association of Queensland (2003) *Community Consultation Guide for Queensland Local Government,* LGAQ, Fortitude Valley, Queensland

Lowry, K., Adler, P. and Milner, N. (1997) 'Participating the public', *Journal of Planning Education and Research*, vol 16, pp177–187

MacGillivray, A., Weston, C., Unsworth, C. and the New Economics Foundation (1998) *Communities Count!: A Step by Step Guide to Community Sustainability Indicators*, New Economics Foundation, London

Malone, K. and Hasluck, L. (1998) 'Geographies of exclusion: Young people's perceptions and use of public space', *Family Matters*, vol 49, Autumn, pp20–26

Martin, B. (ed) (1999) *Technology and Public Participation*, Science and Technology Studies, University of Wollongong, Wollongong, Australia

Materka, P. R. (1986) *Workshops and Seminars,* Prentice Hall, Englewood Cliffs, NJ

Matthews, M. H. (1992) *Making Sense of Place: Children's Understandings of Large-Scale Environments*, Barnes and Noble, Lanham, Maryland, MD

Mayo, M. (2000) *Cultures, Communities, Identities: Cultural Strategies for Participation and Empowerment*, Palgrave Macmillan, New York

McArdle, J. (1994) Resource Manual for Facilitators in Community Development, Employ Publishing Group, Melbourne

McCafferty, G. (1997) 'Pioneering public participation: The creation of the Precinct Committee System in North Sydney', in Open Government Network, *Reaching Common Ground: Open Government, Community Consultation and Public Participation*, Proceedings of the Reaching Common Ground Conference, 23–24 October 1996, Open Government Network, Sydney

McRae-Williams, P. (2006) *Community Consultation Toolkit: A Good Practice Guide for Victorian Explorers and Miners,* Minerals Council of Australia, Victorian Division, Melbourne

Memmot, P. (1997) 'Housing consultation in remote Aboriginal communities', *National Housing Action*, vol 12, no 3, pp23–30

Michelson, W. and Michelson, E. (eds) (1980) *Managing Urban Space in the Interest of Children,* MAB Committee, Toronto

Miesen, R. (1997) 'The Villawood Charrette from a consultation perspective', in Open Government Network, *Reaching Common Ground: Open Government, Community Consultation and Public Participation*, Proceedings of the Reaching Common Ground Conference, 23–24 October 1996, Open Government Network, Sydney

Milne, F. G. K. and Havyatt, L. (eds) (1994) *Consulting the Multicultural Way*, Office of Multicultural Affairs, AGPS, Canberra

Minichiello, V., Aroni, R., Timewell, E., and Alexander, L. (1995) *In-Depth Interviewing: Principles, Techniques, Analysis*, second edition, Longman, Melbourne

Mohanty, R. and Tandon, R. (eds) (2006) *Participatory Citizenship: Identity, Exclusion, Inclusion,* Sage, Thousand Oaks, CA

Moughtin, J. C. and Gibson, T. (1994) 'Grass-roots planning', in W. Sarkissian, D. Perlgut and E. Ballard (eds) *The Community Participation Handbook: Resources for Public Involvement in the Planning Process,* Institute for Sustainability and Technology Policy, Murdoch University, Perth

Munro-Clark, M. (ed) (1990) *Citizen Participation in Government*, Hale and Iremonger in association with the Ian Buchan Fell Research Centre, University of Sydney, Sydney

Murray, J. and Sarkissian, W. (1998) 'Learning through the soles of our feet: A participatory design workshop for youth in Airds, New South Wales', unpublished paper, Sarkissian Associates Planners, Sydney

Murray, J. with Sarkissian, W. and Shore, Y. (2005) Bonnyrigg Living Communities Project, Summary of Phase 1 Community Consultation Outcomes from Community Consultation Processes: 13 December 2004 to June 2005, Draft Report, Sarkissian Associates Planners, Brisbane, July

New Economics Foundation (1998) *Participation Works! 21 Techniques of Community Participation for the 21st Century*, NEF, London

New Economics Foundation (1999) *How to Design a Community Vision*, Central Briefing, Edition 1.1 January, Centre for Participation, NEF, London

New South Wales Department of Community Services (1994) *Community Consultation: NSW Department of Community Services Consultation Protocol*, NSW Department of Community Services, Sydney, November

New South Wales Department of Housing (1993) *New South Wales Aboriginal Housing: Issues for Consultation*, New South Wales Department of Housing, Sydney

New South Wales Department of Local Government (2002) *Draft Social/Community Planning and Reporting Guidelines and Manual: Cultural Planning Guidelines*, Circular to Councils, NSW Department of Local Government, Sydney, June

New South Wales Department of Planning (2003) *Community Engagement in the NSW Planning System,* New South Wales Department of Planning, Sydney

New South Wales Government (1993) *How We Will Consult: Report of the Consultation Protocol Working Party,* NSW Government, Sydney

Ng, K. S. L. (1996) 'Community participation and how it influences urban form', unpublished Master of Urban Design dissertation, University of Sydney, Urban Design Program, Faculty of Architecture, Sydney

O'Brien, J. (1999) 'Community engagement: A necessary condition for self-determination and individual funding', Paper based on a meeting of the Community Engagement Working Group held in Pickering, Ontario, 25 March 1999

O'Neill, N. and Colebatch, H. K. (1989) *Public Participation in Local Government,* Hawkesbury City Council, Sydney

Open Government Network (1997) *Reaching Common Ground: Open Government, Community Consultation and Public Participation,* Proceedings of the Reaching Common Ground Conference, 23–24 October 1996, Open Government Network, Sydney

Oppenheim, A. N. (1992) *Questionnaire Design, Interviewing, and Attitude Measurement,* Continuum International Publishing Group, New York

Owen, H. (1997) *Open Space Technology: A User's Guide,* second edition, Berrett-Koehler Publishers, San Francisco

Painter, M. (1992) 'Participation and power', in M. Munro-Clark (ed) *Citizen Participation in Government,* Hale and Iremonger in association with the Ian Buchan Fell Research Centre, Sydney

Parker, F. (1997) 'Consulting with minority groups', in Open Government Network, *Reaching Common Ground: Open Government, Community Consultation and Public Participation,* Proceedings of the Reaching Common Ground Conference, 23–24 October 1996, Open Government Network, Sydney

Percy, S. L. and Baker, P. C. (1981) *Citizen Coproduction of Public Services: An Annotated Bibliography,* Council of Planning Librarians Bibliography 49, Council of Planning Librarians, Chicago, IL

Peterman, W. (2000) *Neighborhood Planning and Community-Based Development: The Potential and Limits of Grassroots Action,* Sage, Thousand Oaks, CA

Pfeiffer, J. W. and Jones, J. E. (1974) *A Handbook of Structured Experiences for Human Relations Training,* University Associates, San Diego, CA

Pike, M. (2003) *Can Do Citizens: Re-building Marginalised Communities,* The Scarman Trust, London

Plan C (2007a) *An Inclusive Community Engagement Process Developing the Children's Garden for the Gold Coast Regional Botanic Gardens: Rosser Park,* Volume

One: Engagement Outcomes Report, prepared for Gold Coast City Council, Plan C, Brisbane

Plan C (2007b) Townsville Family Charter SpeakOut Festival: Project Evaluation, Plan C, Brisbane

Preiser, W. F. E. and Vischer, J. C. (2005) *Assessing Building Performance*, Butterworth-Heinemann, Oxford

Pretty, J., Gujit, I., Scoones, I. and Thompson, J. (1995) *A Trainer's Guide for Participatory Learning and Action*, International Institute for Environment and Development, London

Queensland Government, Department of Families, Youth and Community Care (1994) *Consulting with Older People*, Department of Families, Youth and Community Care, Brisbane

Queensland Government, Department of Families, Youth and Community Care (1999) *Public Consultation Strategy Project: Profile on Consultation Activities in the Department of Families*, Department of Families, Youth and Community Care, Brisbane

Queensland Government, Department of Main Roads and Queensland Transport (1996) *Public Consultation Policy and Guidelines*, draft report, Department of Main Roads and Queensland Transport, Brisbane

Queensland Government, Department of Main Roads and Queensland Transport (1997a) *Public Consultation: The Way to Better Decisions: Policy, Standards and Guidelines* (brochure), Department of Main Roads and Queensland Transport, Brisbane

Queensland Government, Department of Main Roads and Queensland Transport (1997b) *Public Consultation: The Way to Better Decisions: How to Gain Broader Participation in Consultation*, Department of Main Roads and Queensland Transport, Brisbane

Queensland Government, Department of Main Roads and Queensland Transport (2005a) *Community Engagement: Policy, Principles, Standards and Guidelines*, Department of Main Roads and Queensland Transport, Brisbane

Queensland Government, Department of Main Roads and Queensland Transport (2005b) *Community Engagement: Toolbox*, Department of Main Roads and Queensland Transport, Brisbane

Queensland Government, Department of Main Roads and Queensland Transport (2005c) *Community Engagement: Planner*, Department of Main Roads and Queensland Transport, Brisbane

Queensland Government, Department of Main Roads and Queensland Transport (undated) *Public Consultation Policy: Standards and Guidelines*, Department of Main Roads and Queensland Transport, Brisbane

Queensland Government, Office of Ageing (1994) *Consulting with Older People: A 'How to' Kit,* Department of Family Services and Aboriginal and Islander Affairs, Brisbane, November

Queensland Government, Office of the Cabinet (1993) *Consultation: A Resource Document for the Queensland Public Sector,* Office of the Cabinet, Brisbane

Rafferty, S. (1997) 'Giving children a voice: What next? A study from one primary school', *Spotlights 65,* University of Glasgow, Scottish Council for Research in Education, Edinburgh

Rao, S. S. (1994) 'Welcome to open space', *Training,* April, pp52–56

Red Road Consulting (2006) *Braybrook Community Visioning Plan: Final Report and Addendum,* Report prepared for the City of Maribyrnong, Red Road Consulting, Melbourne

Red Road Consulting (2007a) *Emerald District Strategy Review Stage One Consultation Report and Addendum,* Report prepared for the Shire of Cardinia, Red Road Consulting, Melbourne

Red Road Consulting (2007b) *Fitzroy Street Taskforce Summary Reporting and Transcript,* Report prepared for the City of Port Phillip, Red Road Consulting, Melbourne

Red Road Consulting (2007c) *Melton Small Township Strategy Community Engagement and Consultation Activities: Report on Findings,* Report prepared for the Shire of Melton, Red Road Consulting, Melbourne

Red Road Consulting (2007d) *Oakleigh Pool Redevelopment Community Engagement and Consultation Activities: Final Report on Consultations,* Report prepared for the City of Monash, Red Road Consulting, Melbourne

Red Road Consulting and Sarkissian Associates Planners (2005) *(re)Visioning Footscray Final Report,* Report prepared for the City of Maribyrnong, Red Road Consulting, Melbourne, www.maribyrnong.vic.gov.au, accessed 20 July 2008

Reed, J. (2006) *Appreciative Inquiry: Research for Change,* Sage, Thousand Oaks, CA

Renn, O., Webler, T. and Weidemann, P. (eds) (1995) *Fairness and Competence in Citizen Participation: Evaluating Models for Environmental Discourse,* Kluwer Academic Publishers, Dordrecht, The Netherlands

Rietz, H. L. and Manning, M. (1994) *The One-Stop Guide to Workshops,* Irwin Professional Publishing, Burr Ridge, IL and New York

Rollison, D. (1997) 'The Charrette as a consultation tool', in Open Government Network, *Reaching Common Ground: Open Government, Community Consultation and Public Participation,* Proceedings of the Reaching Common Ground Conference, 23–24 October 1996, Open Government Network, Sydney

Ruth, S. van and Shore, Y. (2005) Living Communities Project for Bonnyrigg, From a Child's Perspective, Draft Report on Children's Consultation, Sarkissian Associates Planners, Brisbane, June

Sanoff, H. (2000) *Community Participation Methods in Design and Planning*, John Wiley and Sons, New York

Sarkissian Associates Planners Pty Ltd (2000) *The Evergreen Report: Growing a Sustainable Future for Brisbane's Older People*, Sarkissian Associates Planners, Brisbane

Sarkissian Associates Planners with Aldbourne Associates and Kevin Taylor (1990) *City Living Country Style: The Goonawarra Story, A Report on an Evaluation of the Goonawarra Community*, Urban Land Authority, Melbourne

Sarkissian, W. (1994) 'Introduction: Community participation in theory and practice', in W. Sarkissian and K. Walsh (eds) *Community Participation in Practice: Casebook*, Murdoch University, Institute for Sustainability and Technology Policy, Perth, pp1–32

Sarkissian, W. (1996) 'With a whole heart: Nurturing an ethic of caring for nature in the education of Australian planners', PhD thesis, Murdoch University, Perth

Sarkissian, W. (1999) Commentary on Lyn Carson, 'The telephone as a participatory mechanism at a local government level', in B. Martin (ed) *Technology and Public Participation*, Science and Technology Studies, University of Wollongong, Wollongong, pp30–31

Sarkissian, W. (2005) 'Stories in a park: Giving voice to the voiceless in Eagleby, Australia', *Planning Theory and Practice,* vol 6, no 1, pp103–117

Sarkissian, W. (2007) 'Video as a tool in community engagement', *Planning Theory and Practice,* vol 8, no 1, pp98–102

Sarkissian, W. (2008) *Engaging 21st Century Communities: The First Australian Handbook for the Development, Construction and Infrastructure Industries*, Urban Development Research Institute, Brisbane

Sarkissian, W. and Cook, A. (2002) 'Savvy cities: Helping our kids out of the bubble wrap', Keynote address, International CPTED Association, Calgary, Alberta, October

Sarkissian, W., Cook, A. and Walsh, K. (1994a) 'Recent developments in participatory planning', in *Community Participation in Practice: A Practical Guide*, Institute for Sustainability and Technology Policy, Murdoch University, Perth

Sarkissian, W., Cook, A. and Walsh, K. (1994b) *Community Participation in Practice: A Practical Guide*, Institute for Sustainability and Technology Policy, Murdoch University, Perth

Sarkissian, W., Cook, A. and Walsh, K. (1997) 'Core practices of community participation in practice', in *Community Participation in Practice: A Practical Guide*, Institute for Sustainability and Technology Policy, Murdoch University, Perth

Sarkissian, W., Cook, A. and Walsh, K. (2000) *Community Participation in Practice: Workshop Checklist*, second edition, Institute for Sustainability and Technology Policy, Murdoch University, Perth, pp51–53 and 146–147

Sarkissian, W. with Cross, A. and Dunstan, G. (1994) 'The conference of the birds: A role play within a workshop', in W. Sarkissian and K. Walsh (eds) *Community Participation in Practice: Casebook,* Institute for Sustainability and Technology Policy, Murdoch University, Perth

Sarkissian, W. with Dunstan, G. (2003) 'Stories in a park: Reducing crime and stigma through community storytelling', *Urban Design Forum Quarterly,* vol 64, published online, www.udf.org.au/archives/2004/02/stories_in_a_pa.php, accessed 7 June 2008

Sarkissian, W. with Dunstan, G. and Walsh, K. (1994) "The Gods must be crazy": A role play simulation within a search conference', in W. Sarkissian and K. Walsh (eds) *Community Participation in Practice: Casebook,* Institute for Sustainability and Technology Policy, Murdoch University, Perth

Sarkissian, W., Hirst, A. and Stenberg, B. (2003a) *Community Participation in Practice: New Directions,* Institute for Sustainability and Technology Policy, Murdoch University, Perth

Sarkissian, W., Hirst, A. and Stenberg, B. (2003b) 'Reconceptualising community participation', in *Community Participation in Practice: New Directions,* Institute for Sustainability and Technology Policy, Murdoch University, Perth

Sarkissian, W., Hofer, N., Shore, Y., Vajda, S. and Wilkinson, C. (2008) *Kitchen Table Sustainability: Practical Recipes for Community Engagement with Sustainability,* Earthscan, London

Sarkissian, W. and Hurford, D. with Wenman, C. (forthcoming 2009) *Creative Community Planning: Transformative Engagement Methods for Working at the Edge,* Earthscan, London

Sarkissian, W., Perlgut, D. and Clark, H. (1986) 'Running successful meetings: Notes for facilitators', in W. Sarkissian and D. Perlgut (eds) (1994) *The Community Participation Handbook: Resources for Public Involvement in the Planning Process,* second edition, Institute for Sustainability and Technology Policy, Murdoch University, Perth

Sarkissian, W. and Perlgut, D. (eds) with Walsh, K. (1994) *The Community Participation Handbook,* second edition, Murdoch University, Institute for Sustainability and Technology Policy, Perth

Sarkissian, W. with Taylor, K. (1991) *Welcome Home Workshops, A Manual for Workshop Planners and Facilitators,* Victorian Urban Land Authority, Melbourne

Sarkissian, W. and Walsh, K. (eds) (1994a) *Community Participation in Practice: Casebook,* Institute for Sustainability and Technology Policy, Murdoch University, Perth

Sarkissian, W. and Walsh, K. (eds) (1994b) 'The Williamstown Rifle Range: A design negotiation exercise with 500 participants', *Community Participation in Practice: Casebook,* Murdoch University, Institute for Sustainability and Technology Policy, Perth

Sarkissian, W. with Walsh, K. (1994c) 'Teamwork and collaborative planning for a new suburban development in Melbourne: The case of Roxburgh Park', in W. Sarkissian and

K. Walsh (eds) *Community Participation in Practice: Casebook*, Institute for Sustainability and Technology Policy, Murdoch University, Perth, pp51–75

Sarkissian, W., Walsh, K. and Campbell, A. (2001) Improving Community Participation in the City of Port Phillip: A Toolbook of Participatory Techniques CD-ROM, City of Port Phillip, St Kilda, Melbourne

Sarkissian, W., Walsh, K., Shore, Y., Lindstad, A., Roberts, S. with LaRocca, S. and Fasche, M. (2002) *Kidscape: Guidelines for Designing Sustainable Residential Environments for Children'*, for the Urban and Regional Land Corporation, Melbourne, Sarkissian Associates Planners, Brisbane

Schwarz, R., Davidson, A., Carlson, M. and McKinney, S. (2005) *The Skilled Facilitator Fieldbook: Tips, Tools, and Tested Methods for Consultants, Facilitators, Managers, Trainers, and Coaches*, Jossey-Bass, San Francisco

Scott, G. G. (1990) *Resolving Conflict with Others and within Yourself*, New Harbinger Publications, Oakland, CA

Shields, K. (2000) 'Support and accountability groups', in *In the Tiger's Mouth: An Empowerment Guide for Social Action*, 2000 edition, Katrina Shields, The Channon, NSW

Shore, Y. with Sarkissian, W. (2005) *Living Communities Project for Bonnyrigg: SpeakOut Draft Report, 2 April 2005*, Sarkissian Associates Planners, Brisbane, July

Sibbet, D. (1980) *A Workbook Guide to Graphic Facilitation of Groups*, The Grove Consultants International, San Francisco, CA

Sibbet, D. (2002a) *Best Practices for Facilitation*, The Grove Consultants International, San Francisco, CA

Sibbet, D. (2002b) *Principles of Facilitation: The Purpose and Potential of Leading Group Process*, The Grove Consultants International, San Francisco, CA

Sidhu, M. (1994) 'Timbarra: Five years on', in W. Sarkissian and K. Walsh (eds) *Community Participation in Practice: Casebook*, Institute for Sustainability and Technology Policy, Murdoch University, Perth

Social Impact Unit, Western Australia (1991) *Working with Communities: A Guide for Proponents*, SIU, Perth

Social Impact Unit, Western Australia (1992) *Public Involvement in Tourism Development*, SIU, Perth

Steinwachs, B. (1992) 'How to facilitate a debriefing' (part of a special issue on Debriefing), *Simulation and Gaming*, vol 23, no 2, pp186–195

Stewart, K. (1994) 'Speaking out for a suburban town centre: The Salisbury experience', in W. Sarkissian and K. Walsh (eds) *Community Participation in Practice: Casebook*, Institute for Sustainability and Technology Policy, Murdoch University, Perth, pp163–178

Stewart, K. with Forsyth, A., Sarkissian, W. and Coates, B. (1994) 'The 1992 Northern Territory Housing Plan', in W. Sarkissian and K. Walsh (eds) *Community Participation in Practice: Casebook*, Institute for Sustainability and Technology Policy, Murdoch University, Perth

Stoecker, R. (2005) *Research Methods for Community Change: A Project-Based Approach*, Sage, Thousand Oaks, CA

Strachan, D. (2006) *Making Questions Work: A Guide to How and What to Ask for Facilitators, Consultants, Managers, Coaches, and Educators*, Jossey-Bass, San Francisco

Street, P. (1997) 'Scenario workshops', *Future*, vol 29, no 2

Stringer, E. (1996) *Action Research: A Handbook for Practitioners*, Sage, Thousand Oaks, CA

Susskind, L. and Elliott, M. (1983) *Paternalism, Conflict and Co-production: Learning from Citizen Action and Citizen Participation in Western Europe*, Plenum, New York

Syme, G. J. and Sadler, B. S. (1994) 'Evaluation of public involvement in water resources planning: A researcher–practitioner dialogue', *Evaluation Review*, vol 18, no 5, pp523–542

Taylor, P. (2001) *Involving Communities: A Handbook of Policy and Practice*, prepared for 'Working together: Learning together', Scottish Community Development Centre, Glasgow

Templeton, J. F. (1996) *The Focus Group: A Strategic Guide to Organizing, Conducting and Analyzing the Focus Group Interview*, second edition, Probus Publishing and McGraw Hill, Chicago

Thomas, J. C. (1995) *Public Participation in Public Decisions: New Skills and Strategies for Public Managers*, Jossey-Bass, San Francisco

Thompson, S. (1997) 'Empowering research methodologies: Developing greater sensitivity and other ways of understanding in urban planning inquiry', in Open Government Network, *Reaching Common Ground: Open Government, Community Consultation and Public Participation*. Proceedings of the Reaching Common Ground Conference, 23–24 October, 1996, Open Government Network, Sydney

Thorne, R. and Purcell, T. (1992) 'Participation and non-participation: Public meetings and surveys', in M. Munro-Clark (ed) *Citizen Participation in Government*, Hale and Iremonger in association with the Ian Buchan Fell Research Centre, Sydney

Thornton, A. (1996) 'Does Internet create democracy?', Master of Arts in Journalism thesis, University of Technology, Sydney, updated 26 March, 2000. Originally created October 1996

Troxel, J. P. (ed) (1993) *Participation Works: Business Cases from Around the World: An Anthology of Readings on Participation in Private Companies*, Miles River Press, Alexandria, VA

Umemoto, K. (2003) 'Walking in another's shoes: Epistemological challenges in participatory planning', *Journal of Planning Education and Research,* vol 21, no 1, pp17–31

United Kingdom Cabinet Office (2000) *How to Consult Your Users: An Introductory Guide,* HMSO, London

United Kingdom Local Government Association (2000) *Let's Talk about It: Principles for Consultation on Local Governance,* LGA, London

Ury, W. (1991) *Getting Past No: Negotiating with Difficult People,* Random Century Business, Sydney

VeneKlasen, L. with Miller, V. (2007) *A New Weave of Power, People, and Politics: The Action Guide for Advocacy and Citizen Participation,* World Neighbors, Oklahoma City

Victorian Government Department of Sustainability and Environment (2005a) *Effective Engagement: Building Relationships with Community and Other Stakeholders, Book 1: An Introduction to Engagement,* Community Engagement Network, Resource and Regional Services Division, Victorian Government Department of Sustainability and Environment, Melbourne

Victorian Government Department of Sustainability and Environment (2005b) *Effective Engagement: Building Relationships with Community and Other Stakeholders, Book 2: The Engagement Planning Workbook,* Community Engagement Network, Resource and Regional Services Division, Victorian Government Department of Sustainability and Environment, Melbourne

Victorian Government Department of Sustainability and Environment (2005c) *Effective Engagement: Building Relationships with Community and other Stakeholders, Book 3: The Engagement Toolkit,* Community Engagement Network, Resource and Regional Services Division, Victorian Government Department of Sustainability and Environment, Melbourne

Victorian Roads Corporation (1997) *Community Participation: Strategies and Guidelines,* VicRoads, Melbourne

Walsh, K. with Cook, A. (1994) 'The beginning of something: The Timbarra "Welcome Home" workshops', in W. Sarkissian and K. Walsh (eds) *Community Participation in Practice: Casebook,* Institute for Sustainability and Technology Policy, Murdoch University, Perth

Walsh, K. with Sarkissian, W., Dunstan, G. and Cook, A. (1990) 'A report on the Timbarra "Welcome Home" Workshop, Sunday 24 June 1990', prepared for the Urban Land Authority by Sarkissian Associates Planners, Pty Ltd, Melbourne

Ward, J. (1993a) *Facilitative and Effective Management Skills for Local Government: Development Resource Book,* Partnership Press, Oakleigh, Victoria

Ward, J. (1993b) *How to Research Community Issues: The Grounded Community Development Research Method,* Partnership Press, Oakleigh, Victoria

Wates, N. (2000) *The Community Planning Handbook: How People Can Shape their Cities, Towns and Villages in Any Part of the World*, Earthscan, London

Wates, N. (2008) *The Community Planning Event Manual: How to Use Collaborative Planning and Urban Design Events to Improve Your Environment*, Earthscan, London

Webber, J. and Willis, K. (1990) 'Partners in planning – principles to involve the community in road planning', *Australasian Transport Research Forum*, vol 15, no 1, pp55–71

Webne-Behrman, H. (1998) *The Practice of Facilitation: Managing Group Process and Solving Problems*, Quorum Books, Westport, CT

Weil, M. (ed) (2005) *The Handbook of Community Practice*, Sage, Thousand Oaks, CA

Weisbord, M. R. (ed) (1992) *Discovering Common Ground*, Berrett-Koehler, San Francisco, CA

Wencour, S. (1991) Review of S. H. Haeberle (1989) 'Planting the grassroots: Structuring citizen participation', *Journal of the American Planning Association*, vol 57, no 4, pp497–501

Westley, F., Zimmerman, B. and Patton, M. Q. (2007) *Getting to Maybe: How the World Has Changed*, Vintage Canada, Toronto

White, R. (1998) *Public Spaces for Young People: A Guide to Creative Projects and Positive Strategies*, Australian Youth Foundation in partnership with the National Campaign against Violence and Crime, Canberra

Whitney, D. and Trosten-Bloom, A. (2003) *The Power of Appreciative Inquiry: A Practical Guide to Positive Change*, Berrett Koehler, San Francisco

Whyte, W. F. (ed) (1991) *Participatory Action Research*, Sage, Thousand Oaks, CA

Wills, J. (2001) *Just, Vibrant and Sustainable Communities: A Framework for Progressing and Measuring Community Wellbeing*, Local Government Community Services of Australia, Townsville, Queensland

Wilson, F. (2007) *A Compilation of Concerns and Ideas for Building a Safe Fort William Neighbourhood*, Neighbourhood Planning Division, City of Thunder Bay, Thunder Bay, Canada. See www.thunderbay.ca

Internet Bibliography

Adelaide Central Community Health Service (2003) 'The Little Purple Book of Community Rep-ing', www.participateinhealth.org.au/clearinghouse/docs/HandBook.pdf, accessed 25 August 2008

Aimers, J. (1999) 'Using participatory action research in a local government setting', in I. Hughes (ed) *Action Research Electronic Reader* (online), The University of Sydney, www.scu.edu.au/schools/gcm/ar/arr/arow/aimers.html, accessed 2 July 2008

Bedrock Brand Consultants (2006) 'Rediscovering Chinatown Honolulu: A commitment to partnership', developed and prepared for the City and County of Honolulu, Department of Planning and Permitting, www.honoluludpp.org/Planning/Chinatown/ExecutiveSummary.pdf, accessed 8 June 2008

Carson, L. and Gelber, K. (2001) 'Ideas for community consultation: A discussion on principles and procedures for making consultation work', New South Wales Department of Urban Affairs and Planning, Sydney, February, www.communitybuilders.nsw.gov.au/builder/participation/icc_pp.html, accessed 2 August 2008

Center for Neighborhoods (2008a) 'Corridor Housing Initiative: Green space and yards', www.housinginitiative.org/greenspace.html, accessed 7 June 2008

Center for Neighborhoods (2008b) 'Corridor Housing Initiative: Nicollet Avenue in Kingfield', www.housinginitiative.org/kingfield.html, accessed 7 June 2008

Center for Neighborhoods (2008c) 'Minnesota Block Exercise', www.housinginitiative.org/blockexercise.html, accessed 19 June 2008

Center for Neighborhoods (2008d) 'Corridor Housing Initiative', www.housinginitiative.org, accessed 12 June 2008

Centers for Disease Control and Prevention (1997) 'Principles of community engagement', CDC/ATSR Committee on Community Engagement, www.cdc.gov/phppo/pce/, accessed 4 August 2008

Child Care Aware (undated) www.childcareaware.org/en/subscriptions/dailyparent/volume.php?id=50, accessed 29 August 2008

City of Minneapolis (2007) 'Corridor Housing strategy wins national "grassroots initiative" award', www.ci.minneapolis.mn.us/cped/corridor_apa_award_2007.asp, accessed 7 June 2008

City of Vancouver (1998) 'Vancouver City Plan', www.city.vancouver.bc.ca/commsvcs/planning, accessed 4 August 2008

City of Vancouver (undated) 'False Creek North Official Development Plan', www.city.vancouver.bc.ca/commsvcs/BYLAWS/odp/odp.htm, accessed 6 September 2008

Coates, B., Kavanagh, D., Judd, B. and Unsworth, L. (2008) *Housing NSW,*

Bonnyrigg Living Communities Project: Telling the Story: Community Engagement in Bonnyrigg, prepared in consultation with the Living Communities Consultative Committee, Housing NSW, Sydney, January, www.housing.nsw.gov.au/NR/rdonlyres/657761B8-B1CD-401E-A914-45D7534AE747/0/Coates_Paper_NHC2008.pdf, accessed 29 August 2008

Community Arts Network Western Australia (2000) 'CAN WA's Programs', www.canwa.com.au/programs/, accessed 4 August 2008

Connor, D. M. and Orenstein, S. G. (1995) 'The bridges of Winnipeg: Combining conflict resolution and public participation for challenging cases', Connor Development Services, Victoria, Canada, www.islandnet.com/~connor/winnipeg.html, accessed 6 July 2008. Reprinted from *Consensus*, October

Corrigan, C. (undated) 'Open space resources', www.chriscorrigan.com/openspace, accessed 17 July 2008

Department of the Premier and Cabinet (2001) 'Queensland Government priorities', www.thepremier.qld.gov.au/priorities/index.shtm, accessed 16 July 2008

Earthscan Publications (undated) www.earthscan.co.uk, accessed 2 June 2008

Elton Consulting (2003) 'Community engagement in the NSW planning system', Planning New South Wales, Sydney, 203.147.162.100/pia/engagement/index.htm, accessed 19 August 2008

Evolve Facilitation and Coaching (undated) www.evolves.com.au, accessed 12 September 2008

Griffith University (2008) 'URP toolbox', www3.secure.griffith.edu.au/03/toolbox, accessed 12 June 2008

Hannemann, M. (2005) 'Mayor's Chinatown Summit: Report', www.honolulu.gov/mayor/chinatownsummit_mr.htm, accessed 2 July 2008

Hashagen, S. (2002) 'Models for community engagement', Scottish Community Development Centre, Glasgow, leap.scdc.org.uk/uploads/modelsofcommunityengagement.pdf, accessed 19 August 2008

Industry Canada (undated) 'Best practice community engagement: Smart communities toolkit', 198.103.246.211/toolkit/toolkit_e.asp?toolType=982314675251, accessed 3 July 2008

Institute for Development Studies (undated) 'Participation team', www.ids.ac.uk/ids/particip, accessed 12 August 2008

International Association for Public Participation (IAP2) (2006) 'IAP2's public participation toolbox', www.iap2.org/associations/4748/files/06Dec_Toolbox.pdf, accessed 8 July 2008

International Association for Public Participation (IAP2) (2007) 'IAP2 spectrum of public participation', www.iap2.org/associations/4748/files/IAP2%20Spectrum_vertical.pdf, accessed 8 July 2008

International Association for Public Participation (IAP2) (undated) www.iap2.org, accessed 7 June 2008

Kitchen Table Sustainability: Practical recipes for community engagement with sustainability (2008) 'The Book', www.kitchentablesustainability.com, accessed 19 June 2008

London, S. (1995) 'Collaboration and community', www.scottlondon.com/reports/ppcc.html, accessed 16 August 2008

McCoy, K. L., Krumpe, E. E. and Cowles, P. D. (1998) 'The principles and processes of public involvement', www.icbemp.gov/science/mccoy.pdf, accessed 15 August 2008

Metropolitan Design Center (2005) 'The Corridor Housing Initiative in brief', Metropolitan Design Center, University of Minnesota, Minneapolis, 21 July, www.housinginitiative.org/pdfs/CHIinBrief_072605.pdf, accessed 19 June 2008

New Economics Foundation (1998) 'Participation works! 21 techniques of community participation for the 21st century', www.neweconomics.org/gen/uploads/doc_1910200062310_PWA4.doc, accessed 8 July 2008

New South Wales Government (1999) 'Government information: Key initiatives', Community Builders: Working Together to Strengthen Communities, Sydney, www.communitybuilders.nsw.gov.au/site/govinfo/#KeyInitiatives, accessed 7 July 2008

New South Wales Government (2003) 'Community engagement in the NSW system', Planning New South Wales, Sydney, 203.147.162.100/pia/engagement/index.htm, accessed 17 July 2008

New South Wales Government (undated) 'Capacity building in health promotion', Department of Health, Sydney, www.health.nsw.gov.au/public-health/health-promotion/capacity-building/index.html, accessed 19 July 2008

New South Wales Government, Youth Consultation Research Project (1999) 'Youth consultation checklist', NSW Department of Local Government, Sydney, May, www.dlg.nsw.gov.au/Files/Information/check.pdf, accessed 5 July 2008

Nick Wates Associates (2006) 'Glossary', www.communityplanning.net/glossary/glossary.htm, accessed 12 June 2008

Oregon's Citizen Involvement Advisory Committee (CIAC) (2008) 'Putting the people in planning – A primer on public participation in planning', third edition, www.oregon.gov/LCD/docs/publications/putting_the_people_in_planning.pdf, accessed 19 July 2008

Organisation for Economic Co-operation and Development (OECD) (2001) 'Citizens as partners: Information, consultation and public participation in policy-making', OECD, Paris, 213.253.134.43/oecd/pdfs/browseit/4201131E.PDF, accessed 23 August 2008

Owen, H. (2002) 'Opening space for emerging order', www.openspaceworld.com/brief_history.htm, accessed 3 August 2008

Phillips, S. D. and Orsini, M. (2002) 'Mapping the links: Citizen involvement in policy processes', Canadian Policy Research Networks, Ottawa, www.cprn.org/doc.cfm?doc=169&l=en, accessed 18 August 2008

Price, G. (2008) 'Price Tags (30 June 2008): False Creek North', Issue 104, www.price-tags.ca/pricetags/pricetags104.pdf, accessed 18 August 2008

Queensland Government (1997) 'Integrated Planning Act', www.ipa.qld.gov.au, accessed 12 August 2008

Roberts and Kay Inc (1999) 'Best practices: Open space technology', www.robert-sandkay.com/newsletters/open_space.html, accessed 5 August 2008

Rogers, C. (2008) 'Evolve Facilitation and Coaching', www.evolves.com.au, accessed 6 July 2008

Salvaris, M. (1997) 'Citizenship and progress', www.anewnz.org.nz/attachments/docs/spre-ms-citizenship-progress.doc, accessed 19 August 2008

Salvaris, M. (2000) 'Community and social indicators: How citizens can measure progress', www.anewnz.org.nz/attachments/docs/spre-ms-community-social-indicators-citizens-m-2.pdf, accessed 19 August 2008

Salvaris, M., Bourke, T., Pidgeon, J. and Kelman, S. (2000) 'Measuring Victoria's progress', www.anewnz.org.nz/attachments/docs/spre-ms-measuring-victorias-progress-2001.pdf, accessed 18 July 2008

Sarkissian, W. (2005) 'The artistry of community consultation', keynote address, Community Arts Network, Western Australia, www.sarkissian.com.au/downloads/keynotes/Artistry%20of%20consultation%20keynote,%202005.pdf, accessed 4 July 2008

Scotland's Community Planning (2002) 'Focusing on citizens: A guide to approaches and methods', April, www.improvementservice.org.uk/community-planning/component/option,com_docman/Itemid,356/task,cat_view/gid,138/dir,DESC/order,date/limit,5/limitstart,40/, accessed 9 August 2008

Scottish Executive Central Research Unit (undated) 'Effective engagement: A guide to principles and practice', January 2002, www.scotland.gov.uk/Resource/Doc/158647/0043039.pdf, accessed 4 July 2008

Silverman, G., Market Navigation, Inc (undated) 'How to get beneath the surface in focus groups', www.mnav.com/bensurf.htm, accessed 3 August 2008

SkyMark Corporation (undated) 'Affinity diagram exercises', www.skymark.com/resources/tools/affinity_diagram.asp, accessed 20 August 2008

Statistics Canada, 2006. Census tract profile, census tract number 9330059.03, available online at Statistics Canada: www12.statcan.ca/english/census06/data/profiles/ct/CTdata.cfm?CTuid=9330059.03&Lang=E Census data

Treasury Board of Canada Secretariat (1994) 'Consultation guidelines for managers in the Federal public service', December, www.tbs-sct.gc.ca/ri-qr/ra-ar/default.asp@language=e&page=publications&doc=consultationguidelines_2fconsultationguidelines_e.htm, accessed 3 July 2008

UNESCO-MOST (undated) 'Growing up in cities', www.unesco.org/most/guic/guicmain.htm, accessed 4 July 2008

US Census Bureau (2000) 'Census 2000', www.census.gov/main/www/cen2000.html, accessed 28 June 2008

Vancouver Community Network (undated) 'The citizen's handbook: A guide to building community', www.vcn.bc.ca/citizenshandbook/Welcome.html, accessed 7 July 2008

Victoria Government, Department of Human Services (1999) 'Building capacity for effective health promotion in the Eastern Metropolitan Region', www.dhs.vic.gov.au/phd/9907059, accessed 7 July 2008

Victoria Government, Department of Human Services (2006) 'A guide to community consultation in rural and regional communities', Victorian Government Health Information, Victoria, www.health.vic.gov.au/ruralhealth/consult/index.htm, accessed 7 July 2008

Victoria, Department of Premier and Cabinet (2001) 'Growing Victoria together: A vision for Victoria to 2010 and beyond', www.dpc.vic.gov.au/CA256D8000265E1A/page/Growing+Victoria+Together!OpenDocument&1=30-Growing+Victoria+Together~&2=~&3=~, accessed 7 July 2008

Walker Art Center (2005) 'Art and civic engagement: Mapping the connections', learn.walkerart.org/civic.wac, accessed 28 June 2008

Warringah Council (NSW) (undated) 'Community consultation matrix and community consultation toolkit', www.warringah.nsw.gov.au/council_now/com_consult.aspx, accessed 3 August 2008

Wenman, C., Hofer, N., Lancaster, J., Sarkissian, W. and Beasley, L. (2008) 'Living in False Creek North: From the Residents' Perspective. Summary of Findings and Recommendations from the False Creek North Post Occupancy Evaluation', www.sfu.ca/city/PDFs/POEBrochure_FINALFORINTERNET_June17.pdf, accessed 6 September 2008

Western Australia (2003) 'Consulting citizens: Planning for success', Citizens and Civics Unit, Policy Office, Department of the Premier and Cabinet, Perth, June, www.citizenscape.wa.gov.au/documents/ccu_plan_success.pdf, accessed 3 July 2008

Western Australia, Department of the Premier and Cabinet (2002) 'Consulting citizens: A resource guide', Citizens and Civics Unit, Policy Office, Department of the Premier and Cabinet, Perth, April, www.citizenscape.wa.gov.au/documents/guidecolour.pdf, accessed 3 July 2008

Wilcox, D. (1994) 'The guide to effective participation', www.partnerships.org.uk/guide/index.htm, accessed 4 August 2008

Youth Affairs Council of Victoria Inc (2004) 'Taking young people seriously. Consulting young people about their ideas and opinions. A handbook for organisations working with young people', Youth Affairs Council of Victoria Inc, Melbourne, www.yacvic.org.au/pages/policy/participation.htm, accessed 20 August 2008

About the Authors

Wendy Sarkissian PhD, FPIA

Wendy Sarkissian is committed to finding spirited ways to nurture and support an engaged citizenry in the pursuit of sustainable futures. A qualified teacher, she holds a Master of Arts in literature, a Master of Town Planning and a PhD in environmental ethics and has taught in schools of planning, landscape architecture and architecture in Australia and overseas.

As a consultant, she has pioneered innovative planning and development approaches in an astonishing variety of contexts and this work has earned her 40 professional awards. Dr Sarkissian is co-author of the award-winning *Housing as if People Mattered: Illustrated Site Design Guidelines for Medium-Density Family Housing* (1986) and the award-winning suite of five books, *Community Participation in Practice* (1994–2003).

Her doctorate from Murdoch University explored ways of nurturing an ethic of caring for Nature in the education of town planners. This approach – focusing on the caring instinct – is a hallmark of her writing and speaking. Wendy's successful career as consultant and academic has provided first-hand knowledge of many contexts, from developers' boardrooms to low-income housing estates. She has worked with senior managers and advisers to local municipalities, government departments and private enterprise, primarily in the urban, community, housing and development sectors. She is a Fellow of the Planning Institute of Australia. She is co-author of *Kitchen Table Sustainability: Practical Recipes for Community Engagement with Sustainability* (Earthscan, 2008).

Wiwik Bunjamin-Mau, MURP

Wiwik Bunjamin-Mau is a qualified planner with several years of community planning experience in rural and urban settings in Hawai'i. Her last position as the Community Facilitator/Organizer for The ARTS at Marks Garage (*Marks*), a community project of the Hawai'i Arts Alliance, led her to deeper community engagement work in the predominantly immigrant community of Chinatown, Honolulu, Hawai'i. During her tenure at *Marks,* Wiwik was introduced to the SpeakOut method by Dr Wendy Sarkissian. Together with Wiwik's colleagues she successfully led and convened many key local community leaders to organize the Chinatown Honolulu SpeakOut called *Talk Any Kine* Festival in March 2006. Following the event, she completed her Master's thesis on the topic of integrating arts in a SpeakOut and received her Master's Degree in Urban and Regional Planning from the University of Hawai'i.

Growing up in fast-developing Third World cities in south-east Asia such as Kuala Lumpur and Jakarta, Wiwik has always been very keen on learning about ways to improve the lives of underserved communities. While studying at the Department of Urban and Regional Planning at the University of Hawai'i, Wiwik was involved in writing a study report, specifically on the chapter entitled 'Poverty: From Basic Needs to Entitlements in The Urban Transition in Vietnam' report (2002).

Wiwik continues to explore meaningful ways for the marginalized voices to be heard as part of processes in their communities. She is also engaged in efforts to integrate arts and culture in the area of community engagement and revitalization. Wiwik maintains her involvement in various community collaborations in Hawai'i through her consulting practice that focuses on community engagement.

Andrea Cook, MPIA

Andrea is a strategic urban/community planner with 19 years' experience in the public, private and tertiary sectors in Australia and on overseas development projects. Since 2004, Andrea has managed her own small consultancy firm, Red Road Consulting, which specializes in planning ethics, community-based strategic planning, participatory planning, creative consultation practice, capacity building, social research and policy development. Andrea's work has received 17 professional awards for excellence in planning and she writes and speaks about planning practice and theory regularly, in Australia and overseas.

Kelvin Walsh

Kelvin Walsh, BAppSc (Planning) BArch (Hons) [RMIT] M Metropolis [UPC], is an Urban Designer recognized for his innovative development work where new approaches and models have been required in response to the complexities of local environments and cultures. At the time of writing, Kelvin was an Associate Director with STRATA (RMJM HK Ltd) based in Hong Kong, working across Asia and the Middle East. He has held senior positions in Australia in the public and private sectors with a focus on cross-agency coordination; strategic design policy, plans and guidelines; targeted project-based advice to the private sector, development corporations and local and state governments; mixed-use development facilitation; transit oriented development; and urban renewal. He has received seven professional awards for excellence and played a significant role in projects that have received an additional 14 state, national and international awards. Kelvin combines practice with academic research where possible.

Steph Vajda

Until 2007, Steph had worked for five years as a social planner with one of Australia's leading social planning firms, Sarkissian Associates Planners, working predominantly on projects associated with understanding and facilitating positive social outcomes in urban development contexts. In 2007, Steph joined Plan C, a Brisbane-based cultural consultancy working in the public space realm. This work involved facilitating community involvement in developing social capital, creating and practising decision-making and governance structures, and designing and activating public spaces for children, young people and adults.

Steph has been closely involved in planning and community engagement projects that have received seven professional awards through the Planning Institute of Australia and the International Association for Public Participation (IAP2).

Prior to working in the planning sector, Steph focused on social justice and environmental advocacy campaigning. He is passionate about social change and working with communities to develop their ability to articulate and actualize their needs and preferences within a clear understanding of the principles of sustainability and community participation. Steph is interested in the power dynamics of participation and the ways in which young and marginalized people can be meaningfully involved in their communities. He approaches this work with a focus on empowerment and on facilitating outcomes that accurately represent needs and can be effectively implemented with a focus on developing community partnerships and definitions of community that are locally relevant, realistic and future-focused. He is a co-author of *Kitchen Table Sustainability* (Earthscan, 2008).

Index

Other books in the **Tools for Community Planning** series

Kitchen Table Sustainability

Practical Recipes for Community Engagement with Sustainability

Wendy Sarkissian with Nancy Hofer, Yollana Shore, Steph Vajda and Cathy Wilkinson

'Wendy Sarkissian and colleagues come through again, giving us fresh ideas and **perspectives.'** *John Forester, Cornell University*

This practical guide distils decades of wisdom from community planning, engagement and sustainability practice internationally into a user-friendly and engaging book that is both inspirational and packed with hands-on tools. The core of the book is a bottom-up approach to participatory community engagement and development, referred to as EATING, that consists of six components: Education, Action, Trust, Inclusion, Nourishment and Governance.

www.kitchentablesustainability.com

Paperback £19.99 • 400 pages • 978-1-84407-614-7 • 2008

The Community Planning Event Manual

How to use Collaborative Planning and Urban Design Events to Improve your Environment

Nick Wates with Foreword by HRH The Prince of Wales and Introduction by John Thompson

'Some books help you to learn – this one helps you to deliver! An invaluable tool.' *Professor Brian Evans, deputy chair, Architecture+Design Scotland and Partner, Gillespies LLP*

This book explains why and how to organize community planning events. It includes a step-by-step guide, detailed checklists and other tools for event organisers. The method is user-friendly, flexible and easy to employ in any context from small neighbourhood improvements to major infrastructure and construction projects anywhere in the world.

www.communityplanning.net

Paperback £16.99 • 128 pages • 978-1-84407-492-1 • 2008

The Community Planning Handbook

How People Can Shape Their Cities, Towns and Villages in Any Part of the World

Nick Wates

'An excellent book that will have a host of valuable applications ... It is an important and timely contribution.' *Jules Pretty, University of Essex*

Community planning is a rapidly developing field. Growing numbers of professionals and local residents are getting involved and there is a powerful menu of tools available, from design workshops to electronic maps. This handbook provides a practical guide to community planning with tips, checklists and sample documents to help the reader get started quickly.

www.communityplanning.net

Paperback £18.99 • 236 pages • 978-1-85383-654-1 • 1999

www.earthscan.co.uk